GOD'S ANSWER FOR AMERICA

DARREL & CINDY DeVILLE

CREATION
HOUSE

D0107779

GOD'S ANSWER FOR AMERICA: HOW TO SAVE AND CHANGE A NATION
by Darrel and Cindy deVille
Published by Creation House
A Charisma Media Company
600 Rinehart Road
Lake Mary, Florida 32746
www.charismamedia.com

Design Director: Justin Evans
Cover design by Justin Evans

Visit the author's website: shekinahtoday.org.

Library of Congress Cataloging-in-Publication Data: 2015934806
International Standard Book Number: 978-1-62998-429-2
E-book International Standard Book Number: 978-1-62998-430-8

While the author has made every effort to provide accurate telephone numbers and Internet addresses at the time of publication, neither the publisher nor the author assumes any responsibility for errors or for changes that occur after publication.

First edition

15 16 17 18 19—987654321
Printed in Canada

TABLE OF CONTENTS

Preface and Prayer vii
Acknowledgments viii
Prologue: Important to Know ix

PART I
THE SITUATION

SECTION 1: AN URGENT MESSAGE
1   God's Urgent Message to America 1
2   "America, America!" God's Cry to Awaken a Nation! 3
3   The Course of a Nation 9

SECTION 2: HOW FAR WE HAVE FALLEN AND WHY
4   Where We Began: America's Godly Foundations 16
5   America—A Prodigal Nation 25
6   The State of the American Church 40
7   The Gatekeepers 56

SECTION 3: HOW GOD GETS A NATION'S ATTENTION
8   How God Deals with a Nation 63
9   The Biblical Pattern: Three Ways 67

SECTION 4: WHAT IS GOD SAYING TO AMERICA AND THE NATIONS?
10   A Revealing Prophetic Sequence 77
11   What's Coming Next, If...? 82

      What's Next 1: Wealth and Economy | *83*
      What's Next 2: Natural Disasters | *85*
      What's Next 3: Enemy Attacks and War | *88*

12   America Has a Decision to Make! 98

PART II
THE SOLUTION

SECTION 1: PREPARING FOR CHANGE
13   Going to the Root of the Problem 108
14   Prepare for Radical Change! 113
15   God's Letter to His Pastors and Leaders 118

SECTION 2: GOD'S ANSWER
16   Mission Critical 125
17   The Pulpits Hold the Keys 128

18   Key 1: Opening the Door for Change........................136
19   Key 2: The Power to Change Everything....................143
20   Key 3: No Limits 158
21   Reviewing God's Answer..................................164

Section 3: The Call to Action

22   Step 1: The Pulpit Level 169
23   Step 2: The Local Church Level..........................178
24   Step 3: The National Level..............................186
25   The Results: Then We Will See...........................195
26   A Call to America's Leaders 201
27   A Final Word...210
     Epilogue: Entering a New Day: The Glorious Church 214
     Special Note to the Prodigal, Backslidden, or Those Who
     Have Never Accepted Christ 216
     Appendix A: Top 5 Prayer Guide 217
     Appendix B: A Classic Example from Early America 219
     Appendix C: Does God Still Bring Judgment Today?.........222
     Appendix D: Do True Prophets Still Exist Today?............224
     Appendix E: America Embracing a Lie 226
     Appendix F: Related Prophetic Words....................230
     Notes..231
     About the Authors 239
     Contact the Authors..................................240

PREFACE AND PRAYER

PLEASE KNOW THE prayer and cry of our hearts throughout this book has been:

O God, in Your mercy, because we know Your mercy is great, in Your mercy will You come—descend upon our land with the convicting power of Your Holy Spirit. Open up the blind eyes, set the captives free, bring our nation to its knees. We cry out to You, O God, please.

So many are lost and so many prodigals have left home, and still they roam. So many are hurting and deceived, held captive by the enemy.

Will You come and turn our hearts back to You. Not because America deserves You, but because we are in desperate need of You

For unless You come and turn our churches and our nation back to You and to Your truth, we have no hope and no future. Please hear our cry; do not let us die in our deception and our sin, but stir our hearts— awaken and revive us once again.

When You sent Your Son, You held nothing back but gave it all. And now we call upon You and ask You to do whatever You must do to turn our nation back to You!

—DARREL AND CINDY deVILLE

ACKNOWLEDGMENTS

ABOVE ALL WE'D like to honor and give thanks to our Lord and Savior Jesus Christ, who is our greatest love, the light of our world, and *always* faithful and true to His Word!

We'd also like to honor and thank our parents and close family members who have prayed for us, supported us, and helped make this book possible.

And to our son and daughter in law, Josh and Rachel deVille, whose love, faithfulness, and continual prayer and moral support have meant so much to us. We are so very blessed and thankful for your heart and passion for God!

To our daughter, Destiny Joy, whom we love dearly and pray for everyday as you walk through your teenage years. You are so very special to us and God. God has a great destiny for your life!

To our grandson Jeremiah, whose favorite song to sing to grandma was "You're an Overcomer." At such a young age God used you many times, Jeremiah, with a song to encourage all of us!

To our grandson Isaiah, who has also been a great encouragement, always lighting up the room with his smile. He is a true bundle of joy!

To our dear friend and assistant, Colleen Aitken, who has been like an angel to our ministry and family. You are always so gracious and helpful, always giving of yourself and so generous in serving. You most certainly were sent by God!

We would also like to sincerely thank Steve Strang and the team at Creation House for opening the door and for all their efforts to help us get this nation-changing message out.

And finally, to our partners and to those who gave towards the publishing of this book (of which all royalties go into the ministry). You will never know how many lives you have touched or changed. You helped make this all possible. *May God bless you!*

IMPORTANT TO KNOW

WHEN AND HOW GOD'S ANSWER CAME

IT ALL BEGAN for us in 2005 as God brought us personally to our knees and through a time of great repentance, brokenness, cleansing, and purifying. It was during this time we surrendered everything and rededicated our lives fully to Christ and the call He originally had given us twenty years earlier in 1985.

We had been on staff of what some would consider a budding, hip, seeker-friendly church, as are many churches today. Everything looked great and successful on the outside, but we were dying spiritually on the inside. Our love for God had been replaced by the love of the world and the pride of life. We were in a backslidden, compromising, sinful state and completely unaware of our blind and sorrowful condition. Then one day God in His great mercy opened our eyes to see our dire spiritual condition, deception, and just how far we had fallen from our first love.

God transitioned us out of that church as the Holy Spirit began to do a powerful work and a deep cleansing in us. He drew us in very close to Him and into an extended season (over seven years) of prayer and fasting. It was during this span of time God gave us a tremendous burden for His church and our nation. It was there on our knees as we sought Him that He began to speak to us, and the message of this book was born.

At times we were overwhelmed by the serious nature of what was revealed and also brokenhearted as we began to see things through His eyes. Yet, in the midst of all this, He also gave us great hope and vision for His glorious church and for our nation. God made it clear that the deep work He was doing in us He was also preparing to do throughout His church and in our nation.

Seeking God's Answer

Throughout biblical history we see that often when God's people faced a crisis or battle, their leaders would inquire of the Lord and seek out His counsel. God always had the answer and gave them specific instructions that if carried out in obedience would always lead them to amazing and often miraculous victories. God has not changed His ways (Mal. 3:6)!

This is one of the key parts of 2 Chronicles 7:14 that seems to be often overlooked: "If My people [will] . . . *seek My face*" (emphasis added). As God's people and leaders humble themselves, repent, pray, and seek Him—inquire of Him—God will present a solution, an answer for the nation. We believe He has done this. For it was during an extended season of prayer and fasting, that God revealed His instructions of how to bring a Great Awakening and turn America back to Him and greatly change our churches and our nation on multiple levels.

We believe *the answer* both the church and America seek does not come from men but from God in heaven (see Genesis 41:25; Daniel 2:28). We are just the messengers. And it has been only through much prayer that God, in His great mercy, goodness, and sovereignty, has seen fit to give us this message to pass on to you, His church, and America.

Is God really speaking?

Throughout scripture we see whenever God was about to do something of great significance, He would begin to move upon His servants, the prophets. God would speak and reveal His plans to them in visions, in dreams, and through prophetic utterance (see Amos 3:6; Acts 2:17–18). (See appendix D, "Do True Prophets Still Exist Today?") God is doing the same today as the prophet Joel foretold (Joel 2:28–29). We believe this is a very significant time in history and God is uttering His voice through many of His servants. He wants His people to be prepared and know what He is about to do in and through His church and in the earth.

Biblically, God is still speaking through His written Word (Holy Bible) and His servants in the five-fold ministry (see Ephesians 4:11), which includes His prophets. We believe you will see it is also very evident in light of the recent news that God is in fact speaking today. The important question is, what is He saying? And are we listening?

The prophetic words in this book

God's written and prophetic words are very valuable and precious to us, and we feel a great weight of responsibility to share them with you exactly as they came. All the prophetic words were recorded in times of prayer and intercession and then carefully transcribed word for word as received, nothing is changed in order to rhyme or adjust the message.

We believe you will clearly see that God's prophetic words in this book are powerful, potent, and beyond our level of speaking or style of writing. We hope (for the sake of the message) it is obvious *God is speaking* and not us.

God's written Word has many messages that contain both warnings and promises. The prophetic words we share reflect Holy Scripture—some will be very serious and sobering, while others are glorious and cast great vision and hope. In this we see both the goodness and severity of God (Rom.11:22). All have come through a heart of intercession and brokenness for our nation, the church, the many lost souls, and prodigals that need to come home. We pray everyone will have ears to hear, hearts to receive and respond to God's words and instructions.

Important to Understand

We want to make a few things very clear:

1. This book is *not* a *political* message but rather a *biblical* message. Our goal is to be "biblically correct" not "politically correct." We will mention and address some important issues usually labeled as "political," but first and foremost they are moral, spiritual, and biblical issues that greatly affect our nation.

2. The message in this book would be the same no matter who was in the White House or in the Congress, for America's problems go far deeper than political leadership, economics, or even legislation. More about this later. Please know we endeavor to honor and pray for our nation's leaders and president according to 1 Timothy 2:1–2.

3. Even though this book includes some very serious and weighty content, it is *not* a message of "doom and gloom," but rather one of "truth and great hope," like many of God's messages throughout biblical history. Also, please know we dearly love America, and we are speaking the truth because of our love for God, His people, and our country.

4. As this message unfolds we believe you will see this goes deeper and beyond saving, changing, and reforming just America; it's also about how we can begin changing and reforming the American church. This is the time to cleanse, purify, and make ready the bride to rise up glorious in the earth—to shine bright in the darkest of times (see Isaiah 60:1–3). The greatest days of the church are before us, and you can be a key part of it!

5. We believe the answers revealed in this book can be embraced by any nation that wants to see the goodness and glory of God and a powerful transformation in their land. God has the answer for every nation!

A Great Awakening

There is no question that God wants to bring a true Great Awakening and turn America back to Him, for God desires all men to be saved and to come to the knowledge of the truth (1 Tim. 2:4). The question is, how will it come? We are very excited to share that we believe this book reveals God's specific instructions of how this Great Awakening will come and bring sweeping change.

Our definition of a Great Awakening

When we use the term "Great Awakening" in this book, it is to denote a great spiritual awakening and outpouring of God's Spirit in two levels. This includes:

1. An awakening to the seriousness of the situation and how to solve it—first in the church, then the nation.

2. Then a great outpouring of God's Spirit—first upon the church, then all across America; an outpouring of God's Spirit so powerful it begins shaking and changing everything. It changes the hearts and souls of our nation, turning multitudes to Christ and sets America up for a great righteous reformation of our nation.

Some like to speak of "revival," which in proper context is life-changing. But sadly the word *revival* has been so abused and cheapened over the years by the American church that we personally prefer to use "Great Awakening" or a great spiritual outpouring. But for those who are endeared to the word *revival*—imagine great revival happening not just in one place, but in churches and cities all over the nation, from coast to coast—this is what we mean by a Great Awakening. Again, we believe God's answer in this book reveals exactly how this powerful move of His Spirit will come.

Big Picture Context

We are entering a turning point in history, and it will be unlike anything seen before. The signs are evident in the world and in the heavens (such as the current 2014–2015 sequence of "four blood moons"). Everything is building and shifting into a new day and drawing ever closer to Christ's glorious return. How does this relate to America and affect the church? In every way, for everything will be changing and the church needs to be ready. Church as usual is coming to an end. The days ahead will require a new kind of church to arise, the glorious church (Eph. 5:27)! Therefore, you will find that God's answer in this book is not just about how to save, change, and reform America; but it is also the catalyst to change and reform our churches to prepare to rise up glorious and shine with the ultimate answer for the nations (Isa. 60:1–3)!

For Pastors and Churches

This book also reveals:

+ What is God saying to His pastors and leaders?
+ How can our churches go to a whole new level?
+ How can you and your church influence and impact in your churches, community, and cities greater than ever before?
+ How can you help bring forth the greatest move of God in our nation that will change everything?
+ How can you be ready for the intense days ahead?

The first half of this book awakens us to the severity and urgency of the situation, setting up the second half of the book, which offers tremendous vision and hope of the astounding change that will come if we will simply heed God's answer and cooperate with Him.

So, it is in humility and with a great weight of responsibility we bring what we believe is a vital message to you, the church, and America. We pray you will look beyond us and have ears to hear God's heart and message to you. For those of you who embrace and run with God's Answer, you will help make history—in your church, your community, your city, and our nation.

Together (with God) we can truly save and change our nation!

PART I

THE SITUATION

SECTION 1:

AN URGENT MESSAGE

1

God's Urgent Message to America

2

"America, America!" God's Cry to Awaken a Nation!

3

The Course of a Nation

1

GOD'S URGENT MESSAGE TO AMERICA

Jesus said,
"As many as I love, I rebuke and chasten [discipline].
Therefore be zealous and repent."
—REVELATION 3:19

THERE ARE TIMES in history when God moves through His leaders and His people in such a way that everything changes. We saw this in Moses' and Joshua's day, in the Book of Acts with the disciples and Paul, with Martin Luther and the Reformation, and with the Pilgrims and Puritans helping to establish the godly foundations of America. Right now we are in such a time as this—with the future of America hanging in the balance.

God's Answer Changes Everything!

We believe this book carries a nation-changing message that holds the *answer* and the *keys* to unlock the door to the greatest awakening we have ever seen and to dramatically change everything—the self-destructive course of our nation, avert the greater judgment of God, and bring great reformation. But it all begins with God's leaders and people embracing and running with His answer and the truths found in this book. God's answer changes everything!

We begin by sharing an urgent message God is bringing to us as a nation, for time is running out! The message of this book is critical to the future of America. For what we do right now will determine the course of our nation—destruction or restoration.

We must be clear

Our personal preference was to start this book by painting a picture of great hope with all the glorious things we believe God wants to do in His church and in America. However, God knows best and what is necessary, and we believe His instructions to us were:

> Do not water it down, speak plainly.
> They need to know what's coming if they do not heed My warnings.

God then made it abundantly clear that if genuine repentance does not come, and if America does turn back to Him in time, then He would lift His hand of protection and use great calamity and America's enemies to awaken and bring great judgment and chastisement upon our nation (as He did with Israel's enemies).

The Goodness of God

The good news is God in His goodness, great love, and mercy is sending America a strong, clear warning today in order to save her from great destruction; as with Jonah when God in His mercy and love sent a warning to save an entire city (Nineveh). We must understand, God's objective is life and restoration, not death and destruction (John 10:10; Ezek. 33:11). God's warnings and judgments come not to condemn but rather to awaken and turn America from her path of utter self-destruction.

Bringing America to Her Knees

We should understand that from the very foundations God has been greatly invested in this nation, and we should believe He will do whatever it takes to save and turn America back to Him. Like a loving father disciplining his child, chastisement often requires pain and discomfort in order to change ones self-destructive ways.

We believe God has a destiny for America and He has the power to bring our nation to its knees and back to Him. The important question is, will America be brought to her knees through a nation-shaking Great Awakening or will she have to go through calamity, chaos, and great loss? Or will it be both?

We all have a choice to make, which path we will take—self-destruction and great judgment, or a Great Awakening and restoration.

No Other Way

From God's house to the White House, to every house in America, we will all stand accountable before God as to what we do with the urgent and vital message of this book; especially those in the pulpits across America. We truly believe this is it; there is no other answer, there is no other way!

How quickly we (God's leaders and people) respond to God's answer is critical and will determine much. The future of America is at stake—our families, our children, our churches, and our cities! Everyone will be affected—everyone.

God is counting on His leaders and people to embrace His answer found in this book, to rise up and lead the way into a new day for our churches and our nation, for one way or another things are about to change!

Next we share more details of God's urgent and compassionate message to America.

2

"AMERICA, AMERICA!" GOD'S CRY TO AWAKEN A NATION!

Therefore consider the goodness and severity of God.
—ROMANS 11:22

S PECIAL NOTE: THIS chapter provides insight and understanding of what has been happening in America and why—from 9/11, Katrina, the 2008 stock market crash, multiple historic natural disasters, and more. It also provides of glimpse of what is still coming if America does not turn from her self-destructive ways and back to Him in time.

In His Great Mercy

God has been speaking and crying out to America. When God speaks to us, it is most often through His written Word (the Holy Bible). However, when we as people or a nation choose to cast His Word (His truth and ways) aside, God, in His great mercy, will then send His servants, the prophets, to speak and to warn in order to save us from our self-destructive ways.

Today God is doing the very same thing through a modern day prophecy called "America, America!" This prophecy is a sobering yet compassionate cry from the heart of God to America that came late 2007 and began unfolding in our news since early 2008. The serious nature of this prophecy brought us to our knees to seek God regarding the course of our nation. It was there the message of this book was birthed and the great hope of *God's Answer for America* was revealed.

Although this is a strong and severe word, even controversial, it contains a message of redemption and great hope (just as many prophecies in God's written Word). Our prayer is that you and our beloved nation will hear the deep and consistent Fatherly cry of God's heart for America to awaken, to turn back to Him and His ways, before self-destruction and great judgment comes.

Is There Judgment Today?

While this prophetic word speaks of God's goodness and mercy, it also speaks of the severity of His justice and judgment. We know some reject the belief God still brings judgment today, but Jesus made it clear that the Holy Spirit would come not only to teach and help us, but He also came to convict the world of sin and of righteousness and of the judgment of sin (John 16:8–9).

God's judgment of sin is still in operation today. For more on this subject see "Does God Still Bring Judgment Today?" in appendix C.

His purpose—for our good

It's important to understand that God's warnings and judgments are motivated out of His love, are always just and redemptive, lead to good, and are ultimately for the best. Said another way, God's warnings come because of His great love, then His judgments come to deal with evil and turn people to righteousness. As the prophet Isaiah declares:

> When your judgments are in the earth, The inhabitants of the world will learn righteousness.
>
> —ISAIAH 26:9

God's judgments are redemptive and come to bring justice and end rebellion and evil that will ultimately destroy lives and a nation. God's judgments come to awaken the nation and restore righteousness which exalts a nation (Prov. 14:34) and opens the floodgates of His goodness once again.

Whatever your theology may be regarding modern day prophecy, warnings, or judgment, we ask that you would take this very seriously, humbly and prayerfully read it, and allow the Holy Spirit to speak to you; then judge it for yourself.

Special Note: Because of the serious content of this prophecy, we felt a great responsibility to send it to our nation's leaders (the White House) shortly after it came in December of 2007 and again in 2009 when our current president took office.

Please remember, this is not a politically-based message but a biblically-based message!

"AMERICA! AMERICA!"

December 5, 2007, prophetic cry and warning through Cindy deVille

> This is the second time in the last three weeks God has given me something like this (see "A Revealing Prophetic Sequence," chapter 10). On the night of December 5, I was reading an excerpt from George Washington's prayer journal. I then went to bed and was extremely restless, and for several hours lay on my side weeping and groaning as though I were in pain. I kept seeing visions of the streets of America. I believe this was intercession, groaning of the Spirit of God for our nation (Rom. 8:26–27). Unable to sleep, I got up and walked into the living room and had what seemed to be a vision. For a moment it's as though I was standing in the middle of America and saw enemies all around trying to get in. They were pressing from every side to get in. Then this word of prophecy and warning came, and I wrote it down:

Many enemies, many, many trying to get in!
America, America! You are filled with sin.
Guilty, guilty you stand before Me!
You are weighed in the balance and greatly found wanting.

If you do not turn from your sin, My protection over you shall subside
And the enemies will come inside.
For I've cried out to you, but you would not hear Me,
For you no longer love, honor, or fear Me.

Judgment, judgment, judgment is standing at your door.
It's standing at your door.
Yet, will you sin more and more?
You go on as if nothing is wrong!

Enemies, enemies, enemies, they all want in!
America, America! You are filled with sin.
You have exchanged My glory and My truth for a lie.
You have cast My Word and every restraint aside.
Turn away from your sin, turn away; pray, pray!
Seek My face and I will turn your enemies away;
I will not let them in.
Free yourself, America; turn from your sin.
Turn from your perversions, your lusts and greed.
Humble yourself and cry out to Me.

Choose life and not death!
For the cries of the unborn are calling out to Me.
The blood you have shed is knee deep.
Turn, turn or you will see blood run in your streets.
Turn Roe vs Wade or for all these lives you will surely pay.
For as you have sown much death, so shall you reap.
Judgment is waiting, judgment is waiting,
While you keep on debating.

Turn, turn, turn or you will see your cities burn.
There shall be bloodshed and war in your streets.
For without My defense you will see defeat at the hands of your
    enemies!

The Towers were just a warning.
The Towers, New Orleans, New York City, the natural disasters, fires,
    floods, droughts;
These are just the beginning of sorrows,
Warnings I am giving you this hour.

Why do you not heed, why do you harden your heart,
Why do you not turn and cry out to Me?
Hear My cry—for I long to shed My grace on thee!
I want to show you My goodness and My mercy,
But what else can there be?
If you will not heed My warnings, My judgments must come.
They will run, they will be swift and sure indeed.
They shall be swift, they shall be sure; who can endure.

For I AM the God of all the earth.
The wind and the sea at My command, they all obey Me!
Natural disasters will be multiplied unto thee
Because I have seen your sin and unrepentant heart.

For you must turn and repent,
Or I shall take your glory and your wealth from you
And you shall no longer be great.
For in My hands America, I hold your fate.
For I can cause your markets to fall in a day.
All that you trust in will dissipate.

I cry out to you this last time;
Turn, turn, turn, repent, repent, repent!
You must turn from your sin;
Then I can begin to heal and restore you.

I long to show you My mercy,
But you have turned Me away again and again—
Away from your schools, away from your children.
You have turned Me away from rule, from your government.
You have rejected Me, and you have given place to other gods.

So now, if you do not repent, I will leave as you have asked.
My protection shall leave you,
My goodness and mercy shall leave,
And My glory shall leave you.
You shall be left to your own ways.
The enemies will come in
And the devastation and destruction will begin.

America, America, America, I am your defense!
Only you must turn from your sin!
Turn back to Me and I will heal you, and I will help you,
And I will cover you, and show you My glory.

Humble yourself under My mighty hand
As you did when you were young.

Put no other gods before Me.
Then I will come and heal your land.
This is My final cry to you.
America, what, what will you do?

For the sake of your children, turn back to Me
Or all this devastation they shall see.
I cry out to you, turn back to Me!

God in His great love and mercy is sending a strong and clear message to America to save our nation from self-destruction and severe judgment.

This prophetic message drove us to our knees, for God does not delight in the death of the wicked or the destruction of sinful nations:

> Says the Lord God, "I have no pleasure in the death of the wicked, but that the wicked turn from his way and live. Turn, turn from your evil ways! For why should you die…?"
>
> —Ezekiel 33:11

The goodness and severity of God

From Genesis to Revelation there are two consistent themes—the goodness (love) and severity (judgment) of God (Rom. 11:22; Jer. 9:24). In this "America, America!" prophecy, we also see clearly both the goodness and severity of God. We hear so much of God's love and goodness today we are usually left with a one-sided, shallow view of God. The truth is we cannot truly know and appreciate how great God's love, mercy, and goodness are without understanding how great His justice, severity, and wrath against sin and it's destructive effects (Rom. 1:18). The truth is both the goodness and severity (wrath and judgment) of God are divine and based on His love and holiness. "It is a fearful thing to fall into the hands of the living God" (Heb. 10:31). Thus, we should stand in reverence and awe of His justice and His mercy, His severity and His goodness.

Note: Warnings of Judgment; Are They Negative or Positive?

There are also those in the American church who do not agree with modern day prophecy that speaks of "warnings" or "judgment." They view warnings of judgment as "negative"; but this is based on human reasoning not Scripture. One clear example of this was Jesus' last recorded message in Revelation (Rev. 2–3). He gave what some would consider "negative" warnings, but they were redemptive warnings to awaken those churches and to avert coming judgment.

Warnings are a good thing and meant to bring positive change! Warnings are like danger signs—they are for our good! If you are driving along and you see a warning sign, "Bridge out. Take detour," but you ignore it and stay on your current path, then you will suffer the consequences. All God's warnings and judgments are for the good. Warnings demonstrate the goodness, love, and mercy of God (Rom. 2:4).

It is worth repeating

We believe God (our nation's Founder) has a destiny for America, and He will do whatever it takes to turn America back to Him. Just as a loving father would do whatever it takes to awaken and turn their child from a path of self-destruction, God will allow great pain and discomfort if necessary for the ultimate good.

You probably have many questions; we believe this book provides many answers, including the prime answer of how to save and dramatically change our nation.

3

THE COURSE OF A NATION

I have set before you life and death, blessings and curses.
Now choose life, so that you and your children may live.
—DEUTERONOMY 30:19, NIV

I T IS EVIDENT that America, like a prodigal, is raging down a path of great sin and self-destruction. As a nation it seems we are in the midst of the greatest moral and spiritual crisis we have ever witnessed. At almost every level it seems America is in a state of emergency with many alarmed and deeply concerned with not only the moral and spiritual state, but the political, economic, educational, social, and cultural direction of our nation. In addition to this, we are seeing an ever increasing contention that threatens to rip our nation a part at the seams. Like ancient Rome, we are witnessing all the historical warning signs of an empire on the verge of implosion.

WHAT IN THE WORLD IS HAPPENING TO AMERICA?

Economic Stress

In 2008 America experienced a market crash reminiscent of the great depression, which left our nation reeling. The stress and uncertainty, along with a staggering runaway national debt of over 17 trillion dollars (at the time of this writing), has taken its toll. Currently we have record numbers struggling and on food stamps, while the federal government continues to spend more and prop up the economy by creating money out of thin air (printing trillions). Although some say there are signs of recovery, these signs are only masking the reality of an economy on the brink of collapse under the weight of great debt, greed, and corruption.

Is this all just a coincidence or are we seeing the beginning of the very thing God forewarned of in the "America, America!" prophecy:

> For you must turn and repent,
> Or I shall take your glory and your wealth from you
> And you shall no longer be great....
> For I can cause your markets to fall in a day.
> All that you trust in will dissipate.

Although today (at the time of this writing) our stock market is at record highs, all this can change in a day.

Civic Unrest and Terror

In the streets of America we hear increasing reports of killing sprees, public shootings, stabbings, and civil unrest (such as racial tensions in Ferguson and New York). We have witnessed the horror of children murdered in our schools (remember Sandy Hook Elementary), and terror in our streets with the Boston Marathon Terrorist bombings shocking the nation, putting the city on lockdown for days.

Historic Natural Disasters

On top of all this, since early 2008 we have witnessed a dramatic increase in unprecedented and historic natural disasters—deadly storms, massive droughts, wildfires, floods, snowstorms, and extreme weather across our nation, which are also negatively impacting our economy. Again, is this all just a coincidence or are we seeing the very thing God warned of in the 2007 "America, America!" prophecy:

> Natural disasters will be multiplied unto thee
> Because I have seen your sin and unrepentant heart.

Why?

It seems America is being hit from every side and at every level. Our nation's problems and issues seem only to grow more complex and volatile with each day. All this is causing many to wonder—what in the world is happening to America, and why?

Some would simply explain these all away as climate change (or global warning), financial cycles, and the need for better political leaders and legislation. Others would say these are just the signs of end-time events or part of the fallen world we live in. Although these may be part of the equation, we believe these historic happenings in America are primarily symptoms of much deeper issues in our nation (as we will see in chapter 5, "America—a Prodigal Nation," and chapter 6, "The State of the American Church").

Questions we must ask ourselves

In light of the "America, America!" prophecy, could it be we are actually reaping the fruit of our own ways as we have progressively and defiantly rejected, and even mocked, God and His righteous ways? Are we also experiencing the progressive warnings and judgments of God upon our land to get our attention, wake us up, and turn us from our self-destructive ways and back to Him?

If God is truly speaking and warning us as a nation, what then can we do to change our course? The truth is there is great hope—a historic opportunity stands before us to change everything! We provide details of how in the second half of this book. But first we must understand clearly the two paths set before us as a nation.

THE TWO PATHS

The path of the righteous is like the morning sun, shining ever brighter....But the way of the wicked is like deep darkness; they do not know what makes them stumble.

—PROVERBS 4:18–19, NIV

Choices have consequences

From the very beginning in the Garden of Eden, God set before mankind two paths—one that leads to life, blessing, and freedom; and the other path which leads to a curse, bondage, and death. In Matthew 7:13–14, Jesus referred to these as the narrow way (leads to life) and the broad way (leads to destruction).

The truth is our decisions and choices will always have consequences. A loving and wise parent will teach their children this truth because they know wrong decisions and choices in their child's life can destroy them and their future. This is why God gave man specific instructions and truths to live by in His Word (the Holy Bible). God's Word is full of proverbial examples (see Psalms and Proverbs) and historical accounts demonstrating the two paths set before mankind. In these we see the promises and rewards, the warnings and judgments.

Some examples:

+ Path of the righteous vs the wicked (see Psalm 1)
+ Path of the wise vs foolish (see Proverbs 10)
+ Results of good kings vs bad kings (biblical accounts)

The path of righteousness leads to life; the path of evil leads to death (Prov. 11:19).

Natural and spiritual laws

These two paths are framed with both natural and spiritual laws and principles. From creation, God set up laws in the natural realm for us all to operate in, such as the laws of physics and gravity. Just as natural laws have a cause and effect, God also set up spiritual and moral laws that have a cause and effect.

It is very important to understand God's spiritual laws and principles are in place, along with moral laws and boundaries, for our good and out of His love and desire to protect us. However, when we rebel against God and His ways, stepping outside His boundaries, we then separate ourselves from His protection, goodness, life, light, and blessing—then we become open prey for the kingdom of darkness and suffer the destructive effects of sin. It is simple cause and effect. This is also reflected in the "America, America!" prophecy (chapter 2) as well as the numerous examples of this truth throughout both biblical and world history.

One of the universal laws (natural and spiritual) God has put in place is the law of sowing and reaping (for good or bad).

> Do not be deceived, God is not mocked; for whatever a man sows, that he will also reap.
>
> —GALATIANS 6:7

God's Word is true whether we chose to believe it or not. Choices always have consequences, as America is finding out.

America's Path and Its Consequences

Jesus did not come to condemn the world but to save it (John 3:17). He has extended His love, forgiveness, and salvation to all of us. But when we as individuals or as a nation choose to reject Him and His ways, we are left to the fruit of our own ways, which lead to destruction.

> They will eat the fruit of their ways and be filled with the fruit of their schemes. For the waywardness of the simple will kill them, and the complacency of fools will destroy them.
>
> —PROVERBS 1:31–32, NIV

Decades of wrong choices (such as progressively rejecting and removing God from our nation) have been leading America down a path of self-destruction. Path 1 below shows the very real consequences we could face as a nation if we continue down our current path and don't turn back. We are already experiencing some of these to a degree. If it were not for faithful saints fasting, praying, and standing in the gap, we believe things would be much worse.

Path 1: Leads to Self-Destruction (America's Current Path)

It is evident God has already *begun to* lift His hand of blessing and protection from America. The question is—how bad could it get? Will this path include the following?

+ Economic collapse
+ Greater natural disasters and storms
+ Greater civil unrest, riots, and blood in the streets
+ Greater enemy attacks and war in America
+ Greater Christian persecution
+ Increasing loss of liberties
+ The demise of our nation

Are these really part of America's fate? We will show in the next series of chapters why America is on this path of self-destruction, and to what degree America has violated God's spiritual or moral laws that have opened the door for all these things to come upon our nation. We will also show how deadly serious it can get in chapter 11, "What's Coming Next, If...?"

Understandably, there are some who believe the fall and destruction of our nation is imminent; no matter what we do, that America is too far gone.

However, we believe there is great hope, there is still time to change our course; but we must act now for time is running out!

The Path of Life

In John 10:10, Jesus said, "I have come that [you] may have life, and have it to the full" (niv). He is the way and the truth and the life (John 14:6). And when we as individuals and as a nation choose to embrace and walk in God's ways, they will lead to healing, restoration, and fullness of life.

Path 2: Leads to Life and Restoration (God's Path)

If God's people—those in the pulpits and pews of the American church—will follow God's Answer and instructions (revealed in the second half of this book), we believe it will result in:

- The greatest awakening America has ever seen
- Multitudes coming to Christ and prodigals coming home
- America on her knees turning back to God
- A great cleansing in the land
- God's healing, protection, and blessing upon America again
- Our economy fully restored
- The opportunity for a great reformation
- The restoration of our godly foundations

While this may sound very optimistic, we believe by the end of this book you will see how this is all very possible. For "with God all things are possible" (Matt. 19:26)!

A GLIMPSE OF THE GREAT AWAKENING

This is not the first time America has been in desperate need of a Great Awakening. In America's first two Great Awakenings, we hear of entire cities being transformed by the power of God. The First Great Awakening also united a divided people and prepared them to fight for independence and birth a new nation. The Second Great Awakening shook the nation and changed society. It triggered the many social reforms, including the antislavery movement. The coming Third Awakening will be even greater. Next we pull back the veil of the future and take a peek at the greatest awakening yet to come.

The following is just a glimpse of the Great Awakening that we believe will be the result of God's Answer we reveal in this book. We pray it will give you great hope and a sense of the magnitude of what God wants to do all across America. In the midst of very dark and dire conditions in our nation, God is setting before us a vision of great hope and restoration.

The Vision: A Great Awakening Sweeps across America!

It was May, 2009, when Cindy had an open vision following a time of prayer for America:

> I saw a map of America. I first saw youth gathering at schools around flag poles, then I saw the same thing happening at universities and colleges. I began to see prayer sweeping across the nation from coast-to-coast. I saw people praying outside of government buildings, in businesses, financial districts, on Wall Street, and in Hollywood. As I saw this vision, I kept hearing what seemed like a loud cry from heaven, "Pray, America! Pray!"
>
> Then, I saw the Spirit of God descend upon the nation, and I saw people begin running into the streets, crying out in repentance and for salvation, as they fell under the convicting power of the Holy Spirit. What I saw swept over every sector of society in America. It was a nation-shaking move of the Holy Spirit that began changing everything.

Can you imagine this happening all across America? Rejoice, for this is just a sample of what God wants to do in our nation!

How Do We Get There?

Now we must ask ourselves: If God wants to bring this Great Awakening, and His people want it, then what is holding it back? The truth is we are not waiting on God; He is waiting on us (His church)! He is waiting on His leaders and people to cooperate with Him and do things *His* way! We believe the second half of this book reveals exactly what *His* way is (God's Answer).

We have a choice

As we stated in the opening chapter of this book, we do have a choice. For God will bring America to her knees either through

+ Path 1: Calamity, chaos, great judgment, and loss
+ Path 2: The greatest awakening ever seen

A truly historic opportunity stands before the American church to dramatically change the course of our nation before greater judgment comes. But God's leaders and people must respond to God's answer in this book and implement it quickly!

Now, before we reveal what we believe God's answer is, it is very important we first understand the seriousness of the situation and the problem: why America is on a path of self-destruction and great judgment and the sobriety of what is coming if we do not change course in time.

Let us then start at the beginning.

SECTION 2:

HOW FAR WE HAVE FALLEN AND WHY

4

Where We Began: America's Godly Foundations

5

America—A Prodigal Nation

6

The State of the American Church

7

The Gatekeepers

4

WHERE WE BEGAN: AMERICA'S GODLY FOUNDATIONS

Righteousness exalts a nation, But sin is a reproach to any people.
—PROVERBS 14:34

MERICA'S RISE TO prominence was quicker than any other nation, it stunned the world. Many wonder, how did this happen? Upon investigation of the historical records and writings, beginning with the early years, it is clear to see God's mighty hand at work in the birthing and formation of our nation. This is why our Founding Fathers acknowledged "Divine Providence" was guiding them in the birthing and destiny of America. In fact, the evidence is such that in 1892, the U.S Supreme court declared:

> From the discovery of this continent to the present hour, there is a single voice making this affirmation [citing dozens of precedents]...We find everywhere a clear recognition of this same truth...These, and many other matters which might be noticed, add a volume of unofficial declarations to the mass of organic utterances that this is a Christian nation.[1]

Their conclusion was based on a mountain of evidence they had reviewed, making it very clear that America had indeed a rich Christian heritage. In spite of secularists trying to rewrite American history—it is indisputable that the Christian faith, devotion to God, Jesus Christ, and biblical principles had been heavily weaved throughout the fabric of our nation's history.

It is in fact an incredible journey to review the rich Christian heritage of America, from the early settlements to the birthing of our nation, and beyond. There are many great books documenting the Christian faith and Holy Bible's influence upon the early settlers, our Founding Fathers, the Constitution, our education, the founding of prominent universities (like Harvard and Yale), and our culture, as well as the first two Great Awakenings coming at key times in our nation.

This chapter highlights just some of these, along with some insights that relate to our message, and also shows God's fingerprints upon America from the beginning. Understanding America's foundations also helps us better understand just how far we have fallen away from those foundations today, and why.

THE EARLY YEARS

First Settlements—Two Ways

In the previous chapter we briefly talked about the two paths that are set before America today. Our nation's first settlements had this same choice to make in their day—man's way or God's way, dependence upon man or dependence upon God.

Man's—Jamestown (1607)

The first settlers from England arrived in Jamestown in 1607. And upon landing on America's shores at Cape Henry, Reverend Robert Hunt prophetically proclaimed:

> From these very shores the Gospel shall go forth to not only this New World, but the entire world.[2]

However, these settlers seemed to have mixed agendas and some soon gave way to greed, human reasoning, and selfish motives and actions, leading them to even mistreat the native Indians. They often faced hard times with despair and the mindset became "every man for himself!" Eventually other settlers came to Jamestown helping bring stability. However, that first few decades they depended heavily on supplies from England to sustain them.

God's way—Plymouth (1620)

History shows the Pilgrims had a different paradigm and motivation. Their prayers for divine guidance led them to America. Inspired by the Holy Scriptures, they believed God was directing them to build a "New Jerusalem" (not a replacement) in a new "promised land"—a place where people could live in covenant with God and each other, unhindered. With great faith, they set out for this new land and finally settled in Plymouth, Massachusetts.

The Mayflower Compact—A cornerstone

Before the Pilgrims went ashore to settle, they knew they would need to have a governing agreement to keep civil order. Through prayer and dedication they drafted a compact based upon biblical principles, with equality and covenant, to form a new civil government. This Mayflower Compact would become a cornerstone of our American constitution and republic. Their intentions were clearly seen in this foundational agreement which included (original was written in Old English):

> Having undertaken, for the Glory of God, and advancements of the Christian faith.[3]

First years and God's provision

The Pilgrim's first year was very hard. It tested their resolve and dedication. Unlike those in Jamestown, the Pilgrims responded to their hardships by drawing closer to God and each other. The harder things got, the harder they prayed and the more they put their trust in God.

In answer to the Pilgrims prayers, God soon brought them a miracle in the form of an Indian called Squanto, who "just happened" to speak English. He had actually lived in this same area years before. He had been taken to England for a few years where he learned English, was exposed to the Christian faith by monks, and then returned to his native land.

Squanto's showed the Pilgrims how to cultivate and prosper off the land, and also helped them live peacefully with nearby Indian tribes. It was God's amazing hand of providence. The Pilgrims' faithfulness was richly rewarded by God with a bountiful harvest and more food than they could have imagined, leading to the first Thanksgiving where they honored God for all He had provided.

What a contrast between the Pilgrims "dependence upon Almighty God," versus those in Jamestown who had depended mostly on England for provision. The results speak for themselves.

The Puritans

Then in 1628 the Puritans began coming in droves to New England. The Puritans, more than any other, were responsible for establishing the deep Christian roots in our nation. The Puritans were humble, deeply devoted to Christ, in covenant with each other, and grounded in sound doctrine. They believed they could release God's kingdom into the earth and bring lasting change to society with proven Christian principles. Many of them believed there was a divine purpose in their coming to America at this specific time in history.

The first Puritan colony in Massachusetts became the model for all others, with their governmental system based upon strong biblical principles that honored God and His ways. They would even have a holiday before elections so people could fast and pray to seek God's guidance on who should lead them.

God at the Center

God and the Bible were the centerpiece of the Pilgrims' and Puritans' lives.

Because of this, their new settlements started by building the church first, making it the centerpiece of the community, and then everything else was built around it. This is a biblical pattern demonstrated by Moses. The tabernacle of Moses, with the ark of the covenant representing God's presence, was always the centerpiece of the camp. God should always be the center of everything we do as churches and a nation.

City on a Hill

The Puritan, John Winthrop (who became the first governor of Massachusetts), envisioned them as "a city on a hill" and an example to the world and the other colonies being established. In his message called "A Model of Christian Charity," he proclaimed this, and yet also warned:

For we must consider that we shall be as a city upon a hill. The eyes of all people are upon us. So that if we shall deal falsely with our God in this work we have undertaken, and so cause Him to withdraw His present help from us, we shall be made a story and a by-word through the world.[4]

Let John's Winthrop's words resonate, for they apply to what America is experiencing today.

The First Great Awakening

As America began to experience decades of peace and prosperity, sadly the people became complacent in comfort, apathy, and sin, much like the pattern we see throughout history and with ancient Israel. By the early 1700s this was widespread throughout all the colonies. America had gotten off course. God responded by raising up leaders like Jonathan Edwards and George Whitefield who called the people back to God and ushered in the Great Awakening that began in the 1730s and lasted until around 1770.

This Great Awakening not only revived the thirteen colonies spiritually, but it also brought great unity in heart and mind. In essence, it prepared the thirteen colonies to answer the call for independence from tyranny and also brought a deep resolve to endure the hardest times. God was preparing them to birth a new nation.

Not all good

As we look at the early years, we see that America was founded on godly principles. However, as we have seen, there were some that had ungodly motives driven by greed and selfish ambition; and so not all was good. Although there were many God-honoring, God-fearing men and women committed to biblical principles, there were also mistakes made and some dark times in American history (such as unfair treatment of the Indians and slavery). We should also keep in mind that there was (and still is) a spiritual battle going on for our nation; Satan was and is working hard to derail the great work God began in America.

LIBERTY AND DEPENDENCE ON GOD

First prayer and independence

Years later, in response to British pressure to control the colonies, the Continental Congress convened for the first time on September 7, 1774. At the initial gathering, Psalm 35 was read, which calls upon God to fight for them against their enemies. This gathering also became a time of prayer to seek God for wisdom and direction on how to proceed. Then, July 4, 1776, the Declaration of Independence was signed.

During the Revolutionary War "An Appeal to Heaven" flag was flown declaring their hope and trust in God against incredible odds. And numerous historical accounts show time and time again the amazing intervention and hand of God as our nation fought to gain her independence and officially birthed a new nation, the United States of America.

Unless God builds the house...

After America won her historic independence, leaders attended the Constitutional Convention of 1787 and began the creation of a constitution to provide political and economic stability for a new nation.

Weeks had passed with much debate, and sometimes tempers flared with some sticking points threatening to derail everything. Unity was unraveling. Then again divine intervention came, this time from a man most historians consider as one of the "least religious" of the Founding Fathers, Benjamin Franklin.

The account was that during this time of great contention, this elder statesman stood up to address the assembly. He reminded them that at the beginning of the contest with Great Britain they had depended heavily upon Almighty God in daily prayer for His guidance and divine intervention, and that their prayers were heard and graciously answered. Yet it seemed peace and comfort had dulled their memory and they had seemed to have forgotten that powerful Friend. Then Benjamin Franklin said:

> The longer I live, the more convincing proofs I see of this truth—that God governs in the affairs of men. And if a sparrow cannot fall to the ground without his notice, is it probable that an empire can rise without his aid?[5]

He continued,

> We have been assured, Sir, in the sacred writings, that "except the Lord build the House they labour in vain that build it." I firmly believe this; and I also believe that without his concurring aid we shall succeed in this political building no better than the Builders of Babel: We shall be divided by our little partial local interests; our projects will be confounded, and we ourselves shall become a reproach and bye word down to future ages.[6]

He then called for them to reinstitute daily prayer before proceeding with their duties. They did so promptly. Soon afterwards our Constitution of the United States was completed, and is considered to be the most brilliant governing document ever written. Once again, honoring God and acknowledging our "dependence upon Him" had proven its worth.

Covenant with God

In 1789, when our new nation's government was officially formed, President George Washington and our nation's leaders committed America to God in prayer at St. Paul's Church, in New York, which happens to be right at Ground Zero where 9/11 took place. This is well documented in the best-selling book, *The Harbinger,* by Jonathan Cahn.

In this it is said, America's first President and leaders (on behalf of the nation), made a covenant with God and He honored that covenant by making America the greatest nation on earth. But America has now broken that covenant, not only turning away from God but becoming even antagonistic towards Him and His ways.[7]

HOLY BIBLE'S INFLUENCE ON AMERICA

The Bible's influence on world history, nations, laws, literature, art, and all areas of life is unparalleled. Early American writings also reveal how the Bible was very influential for our most important foundations, including our unprecedented constitution, our form of government, our laws, our education, the free enterprise system, and traditional family values that helped make this nation so unique and great. Early America and our Founding Fathers understood that:

1. "Righteousness exalts a nation" (Prov. 14:34).
2. "Blessed is the nation whose God is the Lord" (Ps. 33:12).

We wholeheartedly encourage you to do your own research from reliable sources that reference original writing and documents. For more in-depth study, we recommend resources such as *The Influence of the Bible on America* by David Barton, *America's God and Country Encyclopedia of Quotations* by William Federer, *America's Godly Heritage* by David Barton, and *The Light and the Glory* by Peter Marshal and David Manuel.

One example is that our republic includes three branches of government, for checks and balances are modeled in God's Word in Isaiah 33:22:

> For the Lord is our judge [judicial],
> The Lord is our lawgiver [legislative],
> The Lord is our King [executive];
> He will save us.

Education

In Europe injustice prevailed through corrupt civil and religious leaders and led to widespread illiteracy. The Pilgrims and Puritans would not allow this again. They wanted to have biblically literate people, so they started schools in America teaching literacy and the Bible. They knew that the fear and reverence of God was the beginning of wisdom and knowledge (Prov. 1:7; 9:10), so they started a school in each community, with much of their curriculum based on the Bible, such as learning their ABC's with scripture verses.

> "The Bible...should be read in our schools in preference to all other books from its containing the greatest portion of that kind of knowledge which is calculated to produce private and public...happiness."
> Benjamin Rush, Signer of the Declaration of Independence.[8]

Universities were raised up with the intent to develop godly leaders to lead the nation in every sphere of life. America's first university, Harvard, was founded in 1636 as a Puritan college with its main purpose to train new ministers. Yale was founded in 1701, also to train ministers and Christian leaders. The Puritans believed their leaders should be well educated to help lead their colonies and nation and also able to speak to the culture and times from a biblical perspective.

During the early years of America's universities they clearly proclaimed their devotion to God and the Bible, such as Harvard and Yale.

Harvard's University Rules and Precepts from 1646 included:

> Let every Student be plainly instructed, and earnestly pressed to consider well, the main end of his life and studies is, to know God and Jesus Christ…the only foundation of all sound knowledge and Learning. And seeing the Lord only giveth wisdom, Let every one seriously set himself by prayer in secret to seek it of him.[9]

Also, Harvard's early motto was "Truth for Christ and the Church." Since then it has been shortened to simply "Truth."[10]

Yale University requirements for students in 1745 included:

> All Scholars Shall Live Religious, Godly and Blameless Lives according to the Rules of God's Word, diligently Reading the Holy Scriptures the Fountain of Light and Truth.[11]

How do these compare to our universities today where we see God mocked and the Bible ridiculed by many professors? How could such God-centered and honoring universities now be so far from their godly roots? Knowledge is a powerful thing, but can also puff up and lead to great pride if not tempered with humility of heart. This can happen when we seek knowledge more than we seek God and His truth.

Noah Webster, called the father of American scholarship and education, produced the *American Dictionary of the English Language 1828*. Webster believed God's Word was the foundation for all truth and that "education is useless without the Bible."[12] And because of the Bibles proven principles and virtues Webster also said:

> In my view, the Christian religion is the most important and one of the first things in which all children, under a free government, ought to be instructed…No truth is more evident to my mind than that the Christian religion must be the basis of any government intended to secure the rights and privileges of a free people.[13]

Most in early America believed this, and it stands in stark contrast to America today.

Webster's promise and warning to future America

Daniel Webster, a famous attorney and a leading political figure of the United States house and senate, served as secretary of state for three presidents. He is also considered one of the greatest orators in American history. He issued a promise and warning regarding an attempt to separate teachings of the Bible from the education of youth.[14] Webster's warning rings just as true and relevant to America today:

> If we abide by the principles taught in the Bible, our country will go on prospering and to prosper...If we, and our [future generations], shall be true to the Christian religion, if we and they shall live always in the fear of God, and shall respect His Commandments....we may have the highest hopes of the future fortunes of our country.....But if we and our [future generations] reject religious instruction and authority; violate the rules of eternal justice, trifle with the injunctions of morality, and recklessly destroy the political constitution which holds us together, no man can tell how sudden a catastrophe may overwhelm us and bury all our glory in profound obscurity.[15]

We wish all of America and our nation's leaders could hear those words, especially in light of what God said in the "America, America!" prophecy, and the urgent message of this book!

Indeed, honoring God and His ways propelled America to become the most powerful and most prosperous nation in history, and in record time. We believe God has had a plan for America throughout time—to be that shining "city on a hill," and also a friend and protector of Israel. But, something has gone terribly wrong! America has forgotten her "powerful Friend" again, turned away from the very Source of her greatness and blessings, and drifted further than ever from her godly foundations. The adverse effects of this are clearly seen in the state of America today.

IMPORTANT STATE OF AMERICA AND THE CHURCH

THE ESSENTIALS

AS WE WERE finishing this book, we came across an article by Larry Tomczak. He said, "Christian researcher George Otis Jr. has traveled to more than 100 countries in the past twenty years documenting more than 800 communities that saw radical transformation by a genuine visitation of the presence of God. His meticulous research identifies three essentials that must be in place before a city can experience supernatural transformation by the power of God:[1]

1. An understanding of the gravity of the situation. People need a real sense of urgency before they will alter their priorities and relationships to seek God in a desperate way.[2]

2. A recognition that time is running out. Individuals must know that time is of the essence and that they must move out of their comfort zone to align with God.[3]

3. An opportunity presented by the living God. In other words, God extends a lifeline so the people can see a turnaround.[4]

This is exactly what this book is doing. This first half shows the gravity of the situation and that time is running out. The second half shows God's Answer to turn it all around.

How serious and how urgent?

These next couple chapters are hard to share but are necessary. We cannot stick our heads in the sand. Scripture also tells us to expose the darkness (Eph. 5:11). We need to know what is happening and from a biblical perspective why God is saying:

> America, America, you are filled with sin....
> You are weighed in the balance and greatly found wanting.
> —"AMERICA, AMERICA!" DECEMBER 5, 2007

This should deeply concern all of us.

The following chapters show the gravity of the situation—to awaken the church to action and show our nation the profound need to turn back to God, without delay! Also keep in mind, there is great hope: God has the answer to change it all! So hang in there with us, for great change is on the horizon if we will do what He says!

5

AMERICA—A PRODIGAL NATION

The State of America

But if our hearts shall turn away so that we will not obey, but shall be seduced and worship other gods our pleasures, and profits, and serve them . . . we shall surely perish out of the good Land whether we pass over this vast Sea to possess it. Therefore let us choose life, that we and our seed may live, by obeying His voice and cleaving to Him, for He is our life and our prosperity.[1]
—JOHN WINTHROP,
FIRST GOVERNOR OF MASSACHUSETTS, 1630

WITH SUCH A rich Christian heritage, it's hard to believe the dramatic shift we have witnessed in our nation over the past fifty-plus years. It is becoming more difficult with each day to even recognize this United States we grew up in. As a nation we have become like the Prodigal Son and have wandered far, far from home.

Today, there are many voices sounding the alarm regarding the severe moral and spiritual condition of America. One great voice to our nation is well-known evangelist Billy Graham. In a 2012 open prayer letter called "My Heart Aches for America," he expressed some of his deep concerns:

> Self-centered indulgence, pride, and a lack of shame over sin are now emblems of the American lifestyle. Yet the farther we get from God, the more the world spirals out of control.[2]

Another great voice is Jonathan Cahn, author of *The Harbinger* and *The Mystery of the Shemitah*, who at the 2013 Inaugural Prayer Breakfast gave a painfully accurate assessment of American's serious state:

> American . . . a civilization at war against the very foundation on which it has been established. And those, who simply remain true to what had always been known as true, are now vilified, marginalized, mocked, labeled 'intolerant,' and increasingly banned from the public square, and, ultimately, persecuted. . . . It is a new America in which one can be banned from the public square simply for believing the Bible, where profanity is treated as holy and the holy as profane, a new America where the Bible is treated as contraband and nativity scenes are seen as dangerous . . .

It wasn't that long ago that American television closed its broadcasting days with sermons. Now our televisions and computers screens are filled with words and images once unimaginable and God and Jesus have now become objects of comedy and mockery. It's as if a spiritual amnesia has overtaken the land.[3]

It's evident that many in America have deep concern for the state of our nation and the depths to which we have fallen.

HOW FAR HAVE WE FALLEN?

We are in a time in America—in a dangerous and deceptive time—when evil is called good and good is called evil. And unless these things change, America's days are numbered. The true depths of America's fall and great sin is too vast and some too reprehensible to detail. What follows is a broader brush view highlighting some of the key areas destroying our nation. However, we will expound on some critical moral and biblical issues that have also become more political in our day.

When we take a close look at the State of America, it will become clear why God in the "America, America!" prophecy said:

America, America! You are *filled with sin*.
You have *exchanged* My glory and My *truth for a lie*.
You have cast *My Word* and every restraint aside....
Free yourself, America; turn from your sin.
Turn from your *perversions*, your *lusts* and greed
Humble yourself and cry out to Me.

Choose *life* and not death!
For the *cries of the unborn* are calling out to Me.
The *blood* you have shed is knee deep.

The following are four specific biblical issues God addresses in this prophetic message. These show why America is weighed in the balances and greatly found wanting (Dan. 5:27).

Please Note: It is out of a heart of deep concern and brokenness that we share these things with you. We are not here to condemn America, but we hope to clearly communicate the dire state and condition of our nation so eyes will be opened to see how far we have fallen and why God is passionately calling out to America to return to Him before we reap the bitter harvest of our self-destructive ways.

1. REJECTION OF GOD AND HIS WAYS

There was a time when it seemed most Americans loved, reverenced, and honored God and His ways. They attended church and understood the value of prayer and righteous living. Sadly, it seems all that has changed.

While there are some who still love, honor, and respect God and cherish America's godly foundations, there are a growing number who are bent on pushing God and His righteous ways out of our nation. Yet, when convenient, many (including national leaders) will invoke God's name at an official event or during the time of crisis—to ask for His blessing, help, or comfort; but these words ring hollow when our hearts are far from God or our actions reject His ways (Isa. 29:13).

The truth is, through our actions, our words, and our legislation, America has rejected God on multiple levels just as He described in the "America, America!" prophecy:

+ You no longer love, honor, or fear Me...

+ You have *exchanged* My glory and *My truth for a lie.*

+ You have *cast My Word* and *every restraint aside*...

+ You have turned Me away again and again.

+ You have turned Me away from your schools.

+ You have turned Me away from your children.

+ You have turned Me away from rule.

+ You have turned Me away from your government.

+ You have rejected Me and you have *given place to other gods.*

This did not happen overnight, but there was a defining time that appeared to set much of this in motion.

A Defining Time

It's evident that for decades now, America has progressively abandoned our godly foundations and the God who made our nation great. The most significant evidence of this began in 1962 and 1963 when daily prayer and Bible reading were banned from our schools. What a sad time this was for America, for our children could no longer honor God with this simple prayer:

> Almighty God, we acknowledge our dependence upon Thee, and we
> beg Thy blessings upon us, our parents, our teachers, and our Country.[4]

A Progressive Stripping Away and Aggressive Attack

The removal of prayer and Bible reading from our public schools was the sign of a critical turning point in our nation, and it was just the beginning of a progressive attack that began to strip away the godly foundations that had made and kept America great and strong for so long. For, a mere decade later (1973), the fundamental "right to life" was stripped away from children in the womb. Then came the removal of the Ten Commandments in our schools and courts, even though God's laws are supreme over ours! And today the name of Jesus

Christ is considered taboo at public school graduations and the use of His name discouraged at government events.

As never before, we are also seeing an aggressive attack against fundamental Christianity and biblical truths. Those who hold to the truth of God's Word were once honored in our society, but now they are painted as extremists and hateful bigots. In fact, a recent study reported that anti-Christian faith sentiment is growing at breakneck speed.[5]

We have also seen a seismic shift in our schools to a humanistic worldview that denies the need for God, exalts man as the answer, and teaches there are no moral absolutes. We are also seeing aggressive attempts by atheists (less than 3 percent of America) to intimidate the majority of the country through letters or lawsuits stating they are "offended" by anything or anyone honoring God in public.

On top of this we have even seen recent efforts to raise public monuments to Satan (with children) and even attempts to conduct a wicked and blasphemous satanic ritual called "Black Mass" as a public event.[6]

Mocking God and Fundamentally Changing America

Imagine if Presidents George Washington and Abraham Lincoln were alive today to witness what has become of our nation? If they could see many of our nation's leaders mocking God's Word, calling biblical values "old-fashioned" and no longer "relevant," while at the same time celebrating and championing anti-biblical values in the name of "tolerance" and "political correctness," they would no doubt stand stunned in utter disbelief! And, if they could see today's political leaders (including our current president) attempting to "fundamentally transform the United States of America," they would surely be outraged![7]

The Fruit of Rejecting God and His Ways

Righteousness exalts a nation, but rejection of God and His righteous ways has the opposite effect, as we are clearly seeing in America. The truth is as a nation we have progressively slapped the hand of God and His goodness off of every part of our society—then we wonder why God is lifting His hand of blessing from our nation. We wonder why our troubles and problems continue to multiply and escalate.

We are reaping the fruit of all this in every sector of our society. We see our government overbearing and plagued with scandal, corruption, increasing contention, and even lawlessness. We see our national debt escalating and our economy on the brink. Public education is in decline. We see media and entertainment defiling and polluting our culture and the souls of America as never before. It seems the floodgates of sin and darkness have been opened up!

In the wake of all this, it's heartbreaking to see all the effects this has had on the people across our nation. We see multitudes of broken lives and broken families; the hurting, deceived, and bound trying to numb and escape the pain and fill the void with addictions of every kind. In addition to this, America's children are growing up confused, not knowing what to believe, longing for the stability of some absolutes. It's heartbreaking! The land has been slowly ravaged by darkness because we have progressively rejected God and the light of His truth (Ps. 119:105).

Rejection of God = Evil Allowed to Invade

We must understand God will not force Himself or His goodness upon us. The truth is, when we continue to reject Him and His righteous ways, then He slowly and reluctantly lifts His hand and withdraws His goodness. Just as the removal of light allows darkness, the removal of God and His ways allows darkness to pervade our nation. The more God is removed, the more dark demonic influence and evil forces rush in bringing deception, destruction, calamity, chaos, and death across our nation. Is it really then any wonder why we are seeing violence and many other negative effects in our schools and in our streets across nation? The more we reject God and His ways, the darker and more deprived and lawless our nation becomes and the greater the evil will increase and bring greater destruction.

Loss of freedoms

In addition to all this, we are witnessing our freedoms and sovereignty of the United States of America "progressively" stripped away. And, if not stopped, this will also affect the church and will cause greater Christian persecution. And our iconic Liberty Bell displayed in Philadelphia to proclaim liberty throughout the land (Lev. 25:10) would become meaningless.

Example: Our fundamental right to free speech was attacked when in October 2014 the mayor of Houston tried to subpoena pastors' messages and silence them standing up for truth and righteousness in our land.[8] Also the mayor of Atlanta declared war on religious freedom when he fired the fire chief, Kevin Cochran, for his Christian views on homosexuality.[9] Such attacks on religious freedom and speech appear to be increasing at an alarming rate.

The truth is, the more the nation moves into sin, the more it loses its true liberties. It becomes a slave held captive by sin. True freedom and liberty come from God alone, for "where the Spirit of the Lord is, there is liberty" (2 Cor. 3:17). Satan and his deceptive ways always promise pleasure, freedom, and gain; but they will instead always lead to misery, bondage, and pain.

> The way of the Lord is strength to the upright: but destruction shall be to the workers of iniquity.
>
> —Proverbs 10:29, KJV

The progressive rejection of God and His ways has opened the door to great sin and self-destruction in our nation.

2. THE FLOOD OF SIN AND PERVERSITY UNDERMINING THE FOUNDATIONS

There was a time in America when media and TV shows had high standards and moral guidelines. An example would be the following:

Once upon a time, Hollywood's production code of 1930

It's interesting to note, that after the great market crash of 1929, Hollywood (with the approval and commitment of the major studios) set in place a "code." They recognized entertainment and art were important influences in the life of a nation; therefore, one of their core "general principles" included:

> No picture shall be produced that will lower the moral standards of those who see it. Hence the sympathy of the audience should never be thrown to the side of crime, wrongdoing, evil or sin.[10]

Some of the reasons they cited for this "code" included:

+ High moral standard in motion pictures "can become the most powerful force for the improvement of mankind." [11]

+ Correct entertainment raises the whole standard of a nation...Wrong entertainment lowers the whole living conditions and moral ideals of a race.[12]

These are stunning statements compared to today's standards. America needs to return to this "code" for the betterment of the nation.

Now to the nation's detriment, it seems most "every restraint" has been "cast aside" as we are seeing unprecedented levels of sin and perversion flooding our land. Our new code now seems to be *almost anything goes!*

Seductive and polluted media and entertainment

In all forms of media (movies, TV shows, internet, games, music, and books), we are seeing the celebration of perversion, violence, occultism, and moral decay at levels today that decades ago would have appalled and shocked us! These things are not only polluting and defiling the hearts and minds of those in our culture but also the airwaves and atmosphere of our nation.

Some current examples of popular media revealing the true heart condition of many and the depths to which our nation has fallen include: *American Horror Story, True Blood, Game of Thrones, Orange Is the New Black, The Wolf of Wall Street,* and *50 Shades of Grey,* just to name a few. These often include vile and unspeakable wickedness, seduction, explicit sex and perversion, nudity, profanity, graphic violence, blood lust, or occultism masquerading as entertainment. In addition we are seeing an obsession with the dark side, such as zombies, vampires, demons, and witchcraft, often mixed with seduction and sexual perversion. It is little wonder we are seeing our culture sinking lower in the pit of moral decay and debauchery.

The music industry has also cast off almost every restraint. Now even mainstream songs and music videos are laced with profanity and seduction. Also, both sad and shocking are entertainers such as Miley Cyrus and Katie Perry, who now use their God-given gifts to exalt sin, perversion, and the occult.

Sexual sin flooding our nation

There was a time in America when sexual purity before marriage was considered virtuous and honorable and committing adultery was taboo. But, today sex outside of traditional marriage is considered normal.

Today every form of sexual sin is running rampant in our nation, including the increase of sex trafficking (even of children). Because we have "cast aside" the truth of God's Word, it seems America has lost all sense of what is morally right or wrong. It seems we have cast aside all restraint and self-control. As a result, we have become a perverse, unruly, and undisciplined nation. Fornication, sexual promiscuity, adultery, divorce, and even homosexuality have become so acceptable in our culture that it seems most no longer consider these a sin issue. Is it any wonder then why sexually transmitted diseases are at epidemic proportions? Yet, many are deceived into thinking they can go on sinning without consequences.

God's boundaries are for our good

It is important to remember, as a loving Father, God sets boundaries in His Word for our protection. When we step outside of His boundaries, it will always lead to destructive consequences; sooner or later we will reap the bitter fruit of sin. Jesus confirmed that the boundaries God set in the beginning for sex and marriage were to be between a man and a woman (Matt. 19:4–5; Mark 10:6–7). God designed marriage this way for a reason. For all sex outside of traditional marriage—sexual perversion, lust, pornography (sexual fantasy), fornication, adultery, and homosexuality—undermines, corrupts, and rips at the very fabric of marriage, family, and ultimately a nation.

Biblical View: Sexual Sin and Perversion Defiles the Land

All sin is destructive (Rom. 6:23), but Scripture points out the fact that sexual sin is more damaging and destructive because it is a sin against our own bodies, as Paul warns believers:

> Flee from sexual immorality. All other sins a man commits are outside his body, but he who sins sexually sins against his own body.
> —1 Corinthians 6:18, NIV

God gave a specific list of sins that defile a nation and also defile the land; these sins included adultery, incest, bestiality, and homosexuality (see Leviticus 18, especially vv. 24–25). Note that the context shows these were universal sins for *all* nations and *all* time (not just for Israel or ancient times).

While all sexual sin is in the "greater sin" category, the worst sexual sins are those which go against nature, and these bring even greater consequences, as described in Romans 1.

> Therefore God also gave them up to uncleanness, in the lusts of their hearts, to dishonor their bodies among themselves, who *exchanged the truth of God for the lie*...God gave them up to vile passions. For even their women exchanged the natural use for what is against nature. Likewise also the men, leaving the natural use of the woman, burned in their lust for one another, men with men committing what is shameful, and receiving in themselves the penalty of their error which was due.
> —ROMANS 1:24–27, EMPHASIS ADDED

It is very important we see these things as God does and not according to the trends of our culture.

Homosexuality = Sexual Perversion and Destructive

One reason homosexuality has such extreme consequences and is so destructive is because it is a perversion. To "pervert" something is to twist it or distort it, to change it from its original use or intention. When this happens it throws everything into chaos and confusion, including the body, mind, emotions, and even society. This is why we see such high rate of depression, mental illness, drug abuse, disease, death, and suicide rates among those practicing homosexual sin, even in nations that fully accept the gay lifestyle. Those are stats you probably won't see on the mainstream news. Here are just a few:

+ Reports show the life expectancy for homosexuals average twenty-four years less than heterosexuals. (This is due to a much higher rate of sexual disease, substance abuse, depression, and suicide).[13]

+ One study reports that of homosexuals questioned 43 percent admit to 500 or more partners in a lifetime, 28 percent admit to 1000 or more in a lifetime, and of these people, 79 percent say that half of those partners are total strangers. This is a lifestyle driven by lust and perversion, which always demands more. This is why we see 78 percent of homosexuals are affected by STDs.[14]

+ An even more troubling report show homosexuals molest children at least ten times the rate of heterosexuals. While homosexuals make up less than 3 percent of the population, homosexual pedophiles are responsible for 33 percent of all child sex offenses.[15]

In light of these and many other statistics, we find it outrageous that our political leaders or corporations promote and celebrate such a destructive lifestyle in the name of "love" or "equality." If they truly cared about the well-being of our youth and America, they would instead discourage such a lifestyle.

Special Note: For more details of how the homosexual agenda is negatively affecting our nation, along with a related prophetic perspective, please see appendix E, "America Embracing a Lie: A Special Biblical Issue and Prophetic Perspective."

Destructive results of sexual sin

If homosexuality and other sexual sins are allowed to spread through society, it will defile our nation and wreck havoc on God's divine order of marriage, family, and a healthy growing nation. As demonstrated throughout history, a society that embraces sexual sin, especially homosexual sin, eventually leads to some form of destruction, such as Sodom and Gomorrah and Pompeii.

Historical example: Pompeii

Pompeii was considered the richest and most luxurious city of ancient Roman times. It also had become inundated with great perversion—public and private sexual idols and sexually explicit imagery including homosexual acts of men with boys. Pompeii had brothel houses everywhere, to suit every taste.

Then suddenly in AD 79, it was destroyed in one day when a nearby volcano erupted and buried it all under many feet of ash. It became Rome's Sodom and Gomorrah.

The flood of sin and sexual perversion is destroying America's foundations from the inside out!

3. GREAT GREED

There was a time in America when it seemed most corporations and businesses were run by men of integrity and high moral character. They respected God and honored His ways. But today greed and selfish ambition (even fear of loss) drive many. Sadly, many are willing to lie, cheat, steal, and manipulate to get what they want.

It is true that "the *love of* money is the root of all evil" (1 Tim. 6:10, NIV, emphasis added). Money itself is a tool, a resource to be used for good or evil. The *love* of it, including greed, lust for wealth, and power (control), leads to all kinds of sin including corruption and injustice.

Greed has been a driving force behind many damaging things in America such as the polluting media and entertainment we highlighted earlier. An example would be one of the most popular video games called "Grand Theft Auto," a game celebrating lawlessness, including violence and sex. The latest version (at the time of this writing) of it sold over $800 million worldwide in the *first day!* [16] That of course is a strong motivatation for more games like this to be made.

When greed is the driving force, our decisions are no longer based on what's right or wrong, but rather on, "What's going to get me the most of what I want?" We see this in:

+ The entertainment industry with "what will get us higher rat-ings or make us the most money?"

Example: One recent study showed that frontal nudity increased over 6,000 percent over the previous year.[17] Lust and greed have driven many of the net-works to keep pushing the envelope and pressure the FCC to lower their stan-dards in order to improve their ratings which brings them more money.

+ It appears many in the legal profession have lost sight of doing the "right thing" or seeing justice be done. Rather, it seems to be about "winning at all cost."

+ Power-hungry politicians are compromising and corrupting themselves (and our nation) in order to stay in power. Many are willing to do whatever is necessary to advance their agenda, thinking the end justifies the means.

+ Lust for money, power, and control also drives gambling, drugs, and organized crime, including corruption in both business and government.

The list goes on and on. The result often includes others (especially the weak and poor) being taken advantage of or injustice done.

God takes all this very seriously. We should understand, God judged and wiped out Sodom and Gomorrah not just for great perversion, rampant homo-sexuality, and wickedness, but also because of great pride, greed, and injustice (Ezek. 16:49–50).

Greed was also one of King Belshazzar sins (Dan. 5). He led the people into worshiping the gods of gold, silver, bronze and iron, and wood and stone, which is idolatry. That is exactly what many in America do today through the lust for material things that dominate their lives and desires.

Example: The day after Thanksgiving, known as Black Friday, is often filled with reports of some trampled underfoot when the doors open and fights as people scramble and claw to get the "deal of the year."

Great greed is destroying America!

Now, we look at one of the most serious things that has opened the door to terrible judgment and destruction upon our nation.

4. THE FLOOD OF BLOOD

There was a time when America valued life and the unborn. Obviously this changed in 1973 when it became legal in America to kill innocent children in the womb and call it "choice." Over forty years later, the barbaric practice of abortion has resulted in the slaughter of over fifty-five million innocent and defenseless babies![18]

While abortion is a highly politicized issue, from God's perspective, abortion is a very serious moral and injustice issue—murder. This is not about a woman's right to choose; this is about taking life and the shedding of innocent blood (more about why this is so serious in a moment)!

Women have "rights"

Many say abortion is about women's rights, and the fact is women do have rights! They have a right to take contraceptives. They have a right to abstain from sex outside of marriage. They have a right to put their child up for adoption. But no woman and no doctor should have the right to take the life of an innocent and defenseless child! Abortion is killing our own flesh and blood. Scientifically (DNA), biologically (blood and heart beat), and biblically (see Jeremiah 1:5; Leviticus 17:11) it is undeniable—abortion ends life. How can we as a people and nation justify the right to kill our own children?

The horror of abortion

To help you see what is really taking place we challenge you (everyone) to go online today (even right now) and watch just the first 15 minutes of a documentary rightly called "Eclipse of Reason" and see a baby being aborted.[19] It will horrify and enrage you! Brace yourself. During abortion the babies are usually killed by being ripped from the womb limb by limb, including their head being crushed and brains spilling out. Sorry to be so graphic, but it is a reality we cannot ignore. Unbelievably, some are even partially born then decapitated or left to die. Abortion is happening in your city and thousands of times nationwide, daily! It must stop! We are greatly deceived if we think God is simply ignoring all this and just turning His head the other way.

SPECIAL BIBLICAL ISSUE AND PROPHETIC PERSPECTIVE

It is critical America understand why this is so very serious and why this issue alone will bring devastating judgment upon our nation if not repented of and stopped—quickly.

The Biblical View

God hears the babies' blood crying out!

Did you know blood has a cry that can be heard by God? After Cain killed Able, God said, "The voice of your *brother's blood* cries unto Me from the ground" (Gen. 4:10, emphasis added). Now imagine this—God hears the blood of over fifty-five million babies crying out and thousands more every day! This is why God said in the "America, America!" prophecy:

> For the cries of the unborn are calling out to Me.

The shedding of innocent blood pollutes the land!

The "shedding of innocent blood" results in what is known as "blood guilt" that must be accounted for (Deut. 19:10, AMP). The shedding of innocent blood also defiles and pollutes the land (Num. 35:33).

> They shed innocent blood, the blood of their sons and daughters. By sacrificing them to the idols of Canaan, they polluted the land with murder. They defiled themselves by their evil deeds, and their love of idols was adultery in the LORD's sight.
>
> —PSALM 106:38–39, NLT

Psalm 106 describes people sacrificing their children to idols. Abortion is really like a child being sacrificed to the gods of choice, self, and convenience. In biblical times "child sacrifice" was often to the god Molech for the promise of financial blessing and gain. Greed and the daily murder of thousands of babies in the womb have likewise brought great financial gain to those involved, with industry estimates of over a billion dollars annually (again, greed raises its ugly head). But abortion in America is also bringing something else—a day of reckoning!

A day of reckoning!

The word *reckoning* means a settlement of accounts, retribution for one's actions, an appraisal or judgment, or an accounting as for things done. And God's Word clearly says there must be an "accounting" for the shedding of innocent blood.

> Surely for your lifeblood I will demand a reckoning...Whoever sheds man's blood, By man his blood shall be shed; For in the image of God He made man.
>
> —GENESIS 9:5–6

God takes this very seriously!

America's Greatest Debt

Right now, America's greatest debt is *not* an economic or financial accounting; America's greatest debt is the accounting for the *flood of innocent blood* shed—over fifty-five million human lives aborted! God requires there be an accounting, a day of reckoning (avenging), for the murder of each and every innocent unborn child. This is why God said:

> Choose life and not death!
> For the cries of the unborn are calling out to Me.
> The blood you have shed is knee deep.
> Turn, turn or you will see blood run in your streets.
> Turn Roe vs Wade or *for all these lives* you will surely *pay*.
> For as you have *sown* much death, so shall you *reap*.

Judgment is waiting, judgment is waiting,
While you keep on debating.

— "AMERICA, AMERICA!" PROPHECY, 2007, EMPHASIS ADDED

Over forty years and fifty-five million aborted babies have symbolically brought a "flood of blood" knee deep polluting our land! God in His *incredible* mercy and patience is warning America what is to come if this not repented of and stopped. In the upcoming chapter, "What's Coming Next, If...?" we will reveal just how severe this "day of reckoning" will be if America continues on her current path of great sin and destruction.

God does not want to bring great judgment, but His justice can only be delayed so long. Regarding this, Thomas Jefferson once said:

> Indeed I tremble for my country when I reflect that God is just, that his justice cannot sleep forever.[20]

An American leader who understood God's justice

President Abraham Lincoln knew the Bible and understood very well the effect of nation's sins. He believed the brutal Civil War was the judgment of God for over 200 years of bloodshed because of the injustice of slavery in America. He proclaimed this in his Second Inaugural Address, March 4, 1865, (emphasis added):

> If God wills that [the Civil War] continue...*until every drop of blood drawn with the lash, shall be paid by another drawn with the sword*, as was said three thousand years ago, so still it must be said "the judgments of the Lord, are true and righteous altogether."[21]

Think about this: it's estimated 750,000 died in the civil war; what do you think will happen as a result of the slaughter of over fifty-five million innocent babies? Let the sobriety and severity of that statement sink in.

Facts to ponder

1. In 2001, approximately 3,000 Americans died during the 9/11 attack on the Twin Towers of the World Trade Center. Every single day, more than 3,000 American defenseless babies are killed by abortion. Is the similarity of numbers related or a coincidence or a sign of things of come?

2. The Two Towers were opened the same year abortion was legalized in America, 1973.

Judgment is standing at America's door, and only by America turning to God in genuine repentance and stopping abortions can she hope to be set free from the "flood of blood" and its deadly consequences—a day of reckoning!

Special biblical issue focus

So we see rejection of God and His ways and the flood of sin, sexual perversion, great greed, and blood are destroying our nation. Critics will point out that Christians focus too much on the sin of homosexuality and abortion; but as we have shown, there is good reason for this—if unchanged, they will be our undoing!

Why America Is "Greatly Found Wanting!"

When we see the state of America today it is easy to see why the "America, America!" prophecy began with:

> Many enemies, many, many trying to get in!
> America, America! You are filled with sin.
> Guilty, guilty you stand before Me!
> You are weighed in the balance and greatly found wanting.

God is the judge of all the earth; He is the Creator and He sets the standards, not us. He has looked at America, and is making a judgment, just as He did with king Belshazzar of Babylon (Dan. 5), who was weighed in the balance and is greatly found wanting and then invaded and overthrown by his enemies. The writing is on the wall for America, and this should strike the fear of God in hearts and drive us to our knees in national repentance and prayer.

The Scales: Positives vs the Negatives

America's once positive effects have become outweighed by far greater negative effects upon the nations.

Example: For decades America has been number one in sending forth missionaries throughout the world, but now America is also number one in pumping out pornography throughout the world. Dr. Bill Bright, founder of Campus Crusade for Christ, says,

> We are not only destroying ourselves but are playing a major role in helping to destroy the moral and spiritual values of the rest of the world as well.[22]

Some presumably say God would not bring judgment upon America because of all the righteous people in our nation. But biblical history shows that God protects His people in the midst of judgment, as He did with Noah and his family and His people dwelling in Goshen within Egypt in Moses' day. Read more about this in "Answering Objections to God's Judgment Today," in appendix C.

Our Founding Fathers warned us

When we compare the godly foundations of America to where we are today, we believe one can plainly see how far our nation has fallen. We must return to and embrace God and His ways—to love, honor, and fear (reverence) Him once again, as we did when America was young.

Our Founding Fathers knew if America were to abandon God and His biblical truths and principals, then everything would fall apart. This is why we have been witnessing a nation unraveling before our eyes. These Founding Fathers understood the importance of adhering to "two pillars"—both biblical morals and "religion" (which their writing made clear this "religion" was the Christian faith).

President George Washington in his farewell address said these two pillars, "religion" (Christian faith) and morality, are "indispensable supports" for the nation. He continued by declaring one could not truly claim to be a patriot if they "labor to subvert these great pillars of human happiness, these firmest props of the duties of men and citizens. The mere politician, equally with the pious man, ought to respect and to cherish them."[23]

President Washington continued by proclaiming there are so many connections between these "two pillars"—morality and religion (Christian faith)—with public and private well being, that a volume of writings could not adequately trace them all.

When we see the strong biblical perspective most our Founding Fathers had compared to what we see in our nation today, it begs the question, "What has happened and why?"

How did we get like this?

Overall, we believe there are five main things that have been very influential in shaping the direction and current state our nation. These include the power of communications through media, education, and the pulpits of America. The other two reasons America is such a desperate state we address in the next two chapters, "The State of the American Church" and "The Gatekeepers."

6

THE STATE OF THE AMERICAN CHURCH

Are we living in Laodicea?

Awake, you who sleep, Arise . . . And Christ will give you light.
See then that you walk circumspectly, not as fools but as
wise, redeeming the time, because the days are evil.
—EPHESIANS 5:14–16

WE HAVE LOOKED at the state of America; now it's time to look at the state of the American church, the one called to influence the nation.

Christ died so that He might present to Himself a glorious church, a church saved by His blood and sanctified and matured by His Word (Eph. 5:25–26); a church called to be the salt of the earth, preserving the good, and the light of the world, pushing back darkness in spirit and truth and glorifying God (Matt. 5:13–16; John 4:24); a victorious church that the gates of hell cannot prevail against or stop (Matt. 16:18); a victorious glorious church rising up and shining bright with the answer of Jesus Christ, and advancing the kingdom of God (Isa. 60:1–3; Matt. 6:10); a glorious bride making herself ready for Christ's glorious return (Rev. 19:7); for,

> You are a chosen generation, a royal priesthood, a holy nation, His own special people, that you may proclaim the praises of Him who called you out of darkness into His marvelous light.
>
> —1 PETER 2:9

When our nation was young, God's people had great vision and tremendous influence in establishing the godly foundations of America. From the pulpits of our nation they led the way and raised a standard of righteousness throughout the land. With the understanding that righteousness exalts a nation, most were willing to make sacrifices to do what was just and right (Prov. 14:34). With a God-given dream and destiny stirring in their hearts, they lit the path and helped pave the way for a history-making nation. With few resources to communicate the truths of God's Word, they influenced and impacted most everything; with many leading the way in our government, our laws, and our education. They truly were salt and light.

Today's American church

In comparison, the American church today has more Christian TV, radio, books, music, media, schools, tools, teaching, and communication resources than ever in our history, with more exposure than ever due to the internet; yet the state of America is worse than ever. How can this be? Today we have more mega churches, along with the latest and greatest in marketing, mega screens, music and light shows, and lots of seeker friendly, candy coated messages (things we are told we should have); yet the spiritual and moral condition, both inside and outside the church, continues to spiral downward and out of control. We believe this chapter helps reveal why and offers some solutions along the way, with the primary solution revealed in the second half of this book.

For decades much of the American church has been like a sleeping giant that has fallen into a lukewarm and disrepute state. Instead of taking her place as salt and light, she has instead given way allowing the kingdom of darkness to invade, to sow, and take root all across our nation. "While men slept, [the] enemy came and sowed tares" (Matt. 13:25). As a result we have allowed the progressive stripping away of our godly foundations in our churches and nation. There is a universal law (natural and spiritual): the greater the light, the less the darkness. Darkness can only prevail if there is little or no light. Thus, the darkness prevailing in our nation is a brazen statement of the condition of the American church.

Satan knows his time is short

Before we look closely at the state of the American church, we believe it's important to recognize the church does have an enemy who is forever bent on our destruction. This does not give an excuse; but it does explain one reason why we are seeing so many casualties in our churches.

Right now it's like a war zone and the casualties are everywhere! We are seeing broken, confused, backslidden pastors; lives, marriages, and families with broken hearts, broken homes, and broken dreams. So many have gone astray, they no longer know who or what to believe and many have become prey to the lies of the enemy.

Satan knows his time is short and knows he must stop the church if he is to advance. So, with a violence and a vengeance he has unleashed diabolical forces to seduce, deceive, oppress, intimidate, silence, and lull the church to sleep.

The truth is, Satan absolutely fears the church of Jesus Christ that is fully devoted to Him, awake and alive, pure, holy, and is uncompromised. He knows nothing can stop or prevail against her (Matt. 16:18). If he can succeed at deceiving, oppressing, silencing, and stopping the church in America, he will succeed in destroying the nation; and multitudes of souls will be lost eternally. This is why the battle is so fierce and victory so critical for the church in this hour! Cindy had the following vision:

A Vision of the Bride—the Church

Years ago I had a vision of a bride, which I knew represented the church. This bride was lying on the ground in the mud, with her face turned sideways. She had been seduced, badly beaten, and left for dead. Her once beautiful white gown was all muddied and torn in several places. She lay there hopeless and in pain, too weak and numb to move. I also saw Satan walking around her, kicking, mocking, and taunting her, laughing as he said "Can't you get up? She must be asleep or dead!"

Although this vision was heartbreaking to see, we believe it was somewhat prophetic picture of where much of the church in America is today.

Like Sampson with Delilah

Like the bride in the vision, and like Sampson with Delilah, we (the American church) have allowed ourselves to be lured away, seduced, and deceived. In playing with the world, we have fallen into Satan's well laid trap. We have been stripped of our strength, our vision, and our voice. We have given place to the devil, have become his prey and appear to be left for dead.

The American church today is in desperate need of a great visitation and awakening by the Spirit of God. The church—the bride—needs the breath of life to awaken her so she can arise and be cleansed, purified, healed, and restored. As you continue to read this chapter, we believe it will become exceedingly evident that we must have radical change! (See Hebrews 12:26–29; Malachi 3:1–3.)

THE STATE OF THE AMERICAN CHURCH

We are reminded of John's vision of our Lord Jesus Christ in the Book of Revelation and His instructions to write to the seven churches (Rev. 2-3). "These things says He who holds the seven stars in His right hand, who walks in the midst of the seven golden lampstands [the churches] ... who has eyes like a flame of fire" (Rev. 2:1, 18).

In each letter Christ first identifies Himself and then He says, "I know your works." (We must remember that God alone sees and knows everything.) He commends them for their good works, and then He lets five of the seven churches know specifically what He holds against them.

I have a few things against you…

—Revelation 2:14, 20

Then Christ, who is the Head of the church, boldly calls them to repentance, making it very clear what will take place if they do not turn and repent. He then closes the letters by casting great vision, hope, and promise before each church. He lets them know what awaits them if they overcome. It is interesting to note that overcoming is a choice for these churches, as it is for all of us today. We are not *victims*, but are called and equipped to be *victors* in Christ (Rom. 8:37)!

Jesus still walks among us

Jesus still walks among His church and His people today (Rev. 2:1). He sees everything, and He is searching the thoughts and the intentions of our hearts.

He knows our works and every hidden thing. In this chapter you will see many are the same sin and compromise issues that Jesus confronted with the churches in the Book of Revelation. We realize not all these issues exist in every church; but overall the American church is affected, for we are one body.

Our approach, like Daniel: "We have..."

Please understand we are not here to bash the church but to give an honest assessment as we look closely at the state of the American church overall. It is with a heavy heart we share these things, yet with hope we know that God will come to our rescue as we turn to Him with all our hearts in repentance and in obedience.

Like Daniel and other prophets of old who cried out in brokenness over the sins of God's people, they included themselves as part of the whole, "*We have sinned...*"

> O Lord, great and awesome God...we have sinned and committed iniquity, we have done wickedly and rebelled, even by departing from Your [ways].
>
> —Daniel 9:4–5

In the American church today there are some good (even great) things happening, but overall the church is in a weakened and compromised state, allowing our nation to continue in its downward spiral.

Life, Love, and Light?

The good

There is a godly *remnant*, a core of godly ministers fully devoted to Christ, seeking first His kingdom and righteousness who are fighting the good fight. They are uncompromising, undefiled, and filled with love and light! Some are already well-known, others God has been grooming behind the scenes to bring to the forefront for such a time as this. But there are many others in the American church where some things need to be addressed and change.

1. Sin and Compromise Abounds in the Pulpits and Pews

We have greatly compromised on most every level. In both the pulpits and pews, we are seeing unbelievable statistics of adultery, divorce, drunkenness, homosexuality, abortions, and over 68 percent of men in church and over 50 percent of pastors regularly viewing pornography![1]

Many in the five-fold ministry living in hidden sin

For centuries those in our pulpits were duly honored and respected as holy men of God. But now, before all of America, Christian leaders, one after another, are being exposed for drunkenness and drugs, financial greed and embezzlement, adultery, prostitution, sex scandals, and homosexuality. And, divorce has become so acceptable in our churches that it seems it's no longer considered an issue. We recall several years ago reading an article of another scandal titled "Another One Bites the Dust!" What a sad day for the church in America.

We are also seeing the unthinkable as mainline denominations abandon the truth of God's Word and cave to pressures and deceptions of the day by even ordaining homosexuals and transgenders into the pulpits of America. Recent news of a transgender pastor preaching at the historic Washington National Cathedral in DC is a statement on the alarming moral condition of our churches and nation.

Note: Regarding the five-fold ministry, God has given us a tremendous burden for those in the pulpits of America. We are seeing so many pastors and leaders overwhelmed, burned out, and leaving the ministry in record numbers. Many do not have the strength or power to stand against the spiritual forces raging across our land. In the second half of this book, we address this issue and God's desire to help and strengthen and prepare His leaders for the days ahead.

2. MANY OTHER LOVERS

Christ is returning for a fully devoted bride with oil in her lamp and a heart burning for Him. But, like the church in Ephesus (Rev. 2:1–7), we have forgotten our first love. In place of our one true love (Jesus Christ), we have been lured away and seduced by many other lovers, therefore giving place to idolatry. We are exhorted to "flee from idolatry" (1 Cor. 10:14). Yet it seems everything else has stolen our hearts and taken His place—the love of money, success, fame, and the distraction of excess media and entertainment, along with many other "things."

We have forgotten the greatest commandment of all is to love the Lord our God with all our heart and life (Mark 12:28–30). Paul warned us in 2 Timothy 3:1–2, 4: "In the last days…men will be lovers of themselves…lovers of pleasure rather than lovers of God." This is exactly what we are seeing today. In both the pulpits and pews, it seems we have focused more on temporal things like pursuing the "America dream" instead of pursing the "kingdom of God" and His destiny for our lives, while keeping an eternal perspective (Matt. 6:33; Phil. 3:14).

3. SEDUCED AND DEFILED BY THE UNHOLY AND UNCLEAN

God's Word clearly instructs us to "abstain from all appearance of evil" (1 Thess. 5:22, kjv). "For what fellowship has righteousness with [wickedness]? And what communion has light with darkness?" (2 Cor. 6:14). Yet instead of coming out from among them and being holy, many are playing and dancing in the dark with the world (v. 17). Instead of confronting sin and calling to repentance, we have blended in, making sin and compromise our familiar friend (Eph. 5:11).

Polluted by the world's entertainment

Like Samson and the church in Pergamos (Rev. 2:12–17), we have allowed ourselves to be seduced, influenced, and defiled by the world. The sad truth is we appear no different than the world in almost every aspect of life. Romans 12:9 instructs us to love what is good and hate what is evil, yet many professing Christians today are bowing down and drinking from the same polluted wells as the world. They take in the same shows, movies, books, and games filled with perversion, cursing, sex, and violence; while others embrace the occult and demonic in shows that glorify the dark side. Satan, in his cunning craftiness, is seducing, deceiving, and defiling God's people; and most don't even realize it.

All this must grieve the heart of God, as His people are being entertained by the very evil we are supposed to oppose and the very things Christ came and died to set us free from! And sadly, when anyone does address these important issues, often they are labeled "legalistic" or "judgmental."

We simply cannot continue to walk in these things, trample on the grace and goodness of God, and expect no consequences. Jesus made it clear to five of the seven churches that sin and compromise have serious consequences. Those professing Christians that think they can dabble in sin and be unaffected by its consequences are fooling themselves; for it's the little foxes that spoil the vine (Song of Sol. 2:15).

The sad truth is that many professing Christians spend hours partaking of the world's polluted media, yet spend little to no time in God's Word or communion with Him (prayer). Is it any wonder why so many think, act, and look just like the world with the same bondages and sins holding them captive?

Note: Guard the gates! There is a reason God's Word warns us to guard our hearts with all diligence, to give no place to the devil (Prov. 4:23, Eph. 4:27) and to "have no fellowship with the unfruitful works of darkness" (Eph. 5:11). This is also why God's Word urges us not to be conformed to this world, but instead be transformed by the renewing of our mind (to His Word) for His will and purposes (Rom. 12:2).

> So you must live as God's obedient children. Don't slip back into your old ways of living to satisfy your own desires. You didn't know any better then. But now you must be holy in everything you do, just as God who chose you is holy. For the Scriptures say, "You must be holy because I am holy."
>
> —1 Peter 1:14–16, nlt

As children of God we should hate sin and evil, and cling to what is good (Rom. 12:9). Paul also writes twice to young Timothy to flee evil desires and pursue righteousness (1 Tim. 6:11; 2 Tim. 2:22). Pursuing righteousness is a choice.

Holiness vs Legalism

Scripture is clear regarding the call to "be holy" (1 Pet. 1:15–16), yet so many in our churches today consider "holy" to be a negative "four-letter word" and relate it to "legalism." This is a gross misconception. Legalism is rules without relationship. Living a holy life is *not* legalism! Living holy is *love* in its purest form and *life* at its highest level. Jesus says, "If you love Me, you will keep My commandments" (John 14:15, nas). True holiness and obedience are a natural extension of our love relationship with God and walking close to Him. Many have set our standards according to the culture or their own desires rather than the balanced truth in God's Word.

4. Living in Laodicea

Just like the church in Laodicea (Rev. 3:14–22) we have allowed ourselves to be lulled to sleep by the enemy, wallowing in comfort, complacency, and compromise. We have become spiritually blind to our lukewarm and backslidden state. The Laodicean church was also deceived, thinking she was rich and had need of nothing; but in God's eyes she was wretched, pitiful, and poor (Rev. 3:17). When the church is lukewarm and asleep, she is greatly compromised and easily deceived. Instead of living with a kingdom of God mindset, many have settled for a worldly mindset which is self-centered and self-indulging. We have settled for crumbs from the table of all God has for us to walk in. Salvation (the cross) is just the entry way into a whole new dimension of living for God's glory and purposes (Matt. 16:24–25).

Called to be soldiers of light

We have forgotten the many warnings in Scripture instructing us to put on the full armor of God, to be sober, vigilant, and alert because our enemy walks around seeking whom he may devour (Eph. 6:11; 1 Pet. 5:8). We have forgotten that we are called to wage a good warfare and fight the good fight (1 Tim. 6:12). Also a "distorted grace" teaching has caused many to disarm and throw down their weapons, thinking the fight is over. This has caused many to become open prey to the enemy. It's time for the church to wake up!

Because of this Satan has taken much ground in our churches and our nation, and continues to advance and ravage our land. God wants a church that is wide awake; filled with life, love, and light; dressed for service; and ready for battle to advance the kingdom of God in the earth!

Note: Some encouragement

Although what we are sharing may seem overwhelming or even depressing at times, please stay with us—there is great hope ahead! We are taking the time to go over some details so we can all see a biblical perspective and why things must change.

Next, we enter into the major issues of *why* we are seeing the American church in such a weakened and defiled state. These must be addressed.

BUILDING, EQUIPPING, AND ADVANCING?

The good

Thankfully, there is a *remnant* of pastors and churches building God's way. Prayer paves their way and powers everything they do. They rejoice in the full, balanced, and uncompromising Word of God. They are feeding and equipping the troops to know God, know who they are, know why they are here, and know what they believe and why (Eph. 4:11–13). They are positively impacting the community, city, and nation as rich salt and a bright light for the glory of God. They will help save cities and disciple nations.

But there are many other churches in cities all across America where things need to change.

1. BUILDING GOD'S WAY OR OUR WAY

Why does it seem that the gates of hell *are* prevailing against the church? We believe the answer to this can be found in Jesus' words, *"I will build My* church, and the gates of Hades shall *not* prevail against it" (Matt. 16:18). The secret to victory and prevailing is building God's house *His* way instead of *our* way. Satan's kingdom cannot prevail against the house that God builds. But, it's a different story if built man's way. When we build through the arm of the flesh, we are setting ourselves up for shallow results and national ineffectiveness.

New revealing Barna Group research (2014) provided more insight how *man's ways* seems to be dominating our churches. A two-year study revealed the vast majority of pastors measured their church's "success" by:

- Attendance
- Giving
- Number of programs
- Number of staff
- Square footage (of facilities)[2]

Good attendance can be a great thing if lives are being truly saved, transformed, and discipled. But the majority of this list is wood, hay, and stubble (see 1 Corinthians 3:12–15). When we stand before Christ's throne, He's not going to ask how big our church was, how many programs we had, and the square footage of all our facilities. He will be judging by *His* standards, *not* ours.

The sad truth is, many pastors are doing things God has never instructed them to do. And because most pastors are busy doing many "good" things, they have little to no time to do what is the "most important" thing, which is to build their relationship with God and build His house His way.

2. EVERYTHING BUT A HOUSE OF...

Jesus made it clear that His Father's house should be a "house of prayer" (Matt. 21:13; Luke 19:46; Mark 11:17). In fact He was so zealous and passionate about this He overturned the tables and drove out those who had their own selfish agendas instead of Gods plans (Matt. 21:12; Luke 19:45; Mark 11:15–16).

"A house of prayer" is God's mandate for His house, and it is *not* optional (Isa. 56:7; Mark 11:17). However, many of our churches today appear to be everything but a house of prayer. They have all the bells and whistles to attract man, but are sadly lacking Jesus' foundational blueprint every church must incorporate. Prayer should be at the core of our churches and a part of everything we do. Scripturally, if a church is not a house of prayer then does not qualify to be God's house. In relation to this E.M. Bounds wrote in his book *The Necessity of Prayer:*

> Prayer is always in place in the house of God. When prayer is a stranger there, then it ceases to be God's house at all.[3]

God declared His house to be a house of prayer, not a house of programs and activities to please everyone. The church is *not* called to be a religious social club to entertain or fulfill a religious duty. There is nothing wrong with having God-ordained programs, family and social activities at a church; but it is a matter of priorities. It seems most churches have the cart before the horse.

Polls vs Prayer

In today's church culture, we are concerned that many pastors are leaning on and following the latest polls, fads, trends, and marketing schemes to guide and direct them. It is good to get understanding, yet this should never take the place of seeking the heart, ways and wisdom of God as we build His church. Sadly, statistics show that many pastors have almost no prayer life. Regarding this, Leonard Ravenhill once said:

> No man is greater than his prayer life. The pastor who is not praying is playing; the people who are not praying are straying....Failing here, we fail everywhere.[3]

The prayerless church is a powerless church. Because of this lack of prayer in our churches, strong spirits of deception and seduction have infiltrated our churches and spread like a heavy blanket upon the land. And because the power of prayer has not been high priority, many pastors and churches are fighting spiritual battles in the arm of the flesh and they cannot stand against the forces in the land. Therefore, so many are falling prey, led astray, and becoming casualties. This has to change!

Note: There is nothing wrong with getting understanding of the culture, what the trends are, and being "relevant," to a point. However, many are using these to build their church rather than building on the foundation of God's

Word and prayer, seeking the wisdom and direction of God. James 1:5 instructs us, "If any of you lacks wisdom, let him ask of God," (not the polls or trends).

3. COMPROMISING THE TRUTH OF GOD'S WORD

When we look at the condition of our churches and our nation, we have to ask, "What in the world is being preached from the pulpits of America?" The sad truth is the American church is steeped in compromise because the teaching of God's Word has been compromised.

Intended or not, many in our pulpits today have compromised the truth in order to serve and please man rather than God. In our efforts to make God and His Word more marketable, unoffending, acceptable, relevant, feel-good, and seeker-friendly, we have watered it down and avoid life-changing words like *repentance, surrender, sacrifice,* and also the word *sin.* We have replaced the fear of God with the fear of man; and in doing so we have made the "narrow way" broad and paved with compromise (Matt. 7:14). Then we scratch our heads and wonder why America has lost her moral compass and why sin is running rampant, even in our churches. While this soft, sugar coated, seeker-friendly approach may be gaining attendees in our seats, we are losing a nation!

Man's Word vs "Preach the Word"

The church in Thyatira (Rev. 2:18–29) was guilty of *tolerating* Jezebel, who called herself a prophet, yet misled God's servants by her false teachings. In the same way many, even in our pulpits, are casting aside the full truth and counsel of God's Word to embrace the popular trends and humanistic mindset of the culture, like scraps from a carnal table.

We must remember that the Word of God "is living and powerful, and sharper than any two-edged sword" (Heb. 4:12). It alone has the power to set men free (John 8:32). The Word of God must be the foundation and center of everything. This is why Paul instructed Timothy "Preach the word" and to "correct, rebuke, and encourage" (2 Tim. 4:2, NIV). We hear and see lots and lots of encouraging but very little correcting and rebuking. And too often we ignore or reject anything that challenges, demands, or asks anything of us, such as laying down our lives as a living sacrifice holy and acceptable until the Lord, which is the least thing we should do (Rom. 12:1). This must change!

We must return to the cornerstone—the teachings of Christ. His teaching in the Gospels, the Sermon on the Mount, and the Book of Revelation should be foundational for every believer to live by.

Revealing Research: American pastors' view on addressing "today's issues"

The same 2014 Barna Group research we mentioned previously revealed one major reason why the American church is so unprepared and ineffectual as salt and light in our nation.

When American pastors were asked if the Bible addressed "key [social/moral] issues" of the day, 90 percent affirmed yes. But when asked how many of them teach what the Bible says about these "key issues," the number dropped to a dismal 10 percent. It seemed most pastors avoid "controversial" subjects because it might keep people from giving or attending.[5]

Could you imagine what Jesus' or the apostle Paul's response would have been to all this? Something is seriously wrong in the pulpits of America! Jesus told us to let our light shine before men; this includes countering and exposing" the darkness with the light of truth (Matt. 5:16; Eph. 5:11).

Equipping or entertaining?

We (the American church) have promoted a culture of entertainment more than the pursuit of God and His kingdom. It appears for many our worship services are more like rock concerts and many in our pulpits feel the pressure to be more like rock stars instead of servants of God. It seems churches are spending more time and money entertaining the troops and our youth than they are equipping them with the fullness and richness of God's Word. Thus, our sermons and messages are filled with lots of cotton candy and sweets, but little meat. As a result, much of the body (American church) is weak and frail, open prey for the lies of the enemy. This is why so many have become casualties, because they are not equipped to stand and fight in the days we live. This is why so many are falling away, giving in to the pressures and deceptions of the day. If the American church is going to survive and thrive in the days ahead, she must be equipped and ready for battle!

God has not called the five-fold ministry to entertain the troops, but rather to equip the saints and to build up of the body of Christ, until we come into full maturity in Christ (Eph. 4:11–13). Compromising God's Word and embracing man's ways have hindered this so far. One of the most serious results of all this is how it is affecting our youth.

We Are Losing Our Youth!

It's evident that Satan is out to destroy the seed of the righteous. At an alarming rate we are seeing our young people being sucked into the vortex of today's polluted and delusional culture. It seems most don't know what to believe anymore.

It appears most our youth groups in churches across America are more like party places. We have pizza night, movie night, game night, and concert night; and if there is any teaching it's a few crumbs from the table, mostly sweets and very little milk and meat. Yet all week our youth are bombarded with lies from the media and ungodly, humanistic ideals in our schools, such as having two daddies or two mommies is normal and that gay is the way, that there are no absolutes, everything is gray, there are many ways to God, or there is *no* God. Is it then really any wonder why record numbers (two-thirds) of young people are leaving our churches and abandoning the faith?[6]

Our youth don't need us to babysit or entertain them. Our youth in America need something more, something to live and to die for. They want something to be radical and passionate about! What they need is to be equipped and ready for the battle of the ages they will be thrust into. It's time for both the parents and our churches to start equipping these young people for the days we live in. If we don't, few of them will survive the days ahead.

4. Extremes, Unbalanced, and Distorted Doctrine

When we see abuse or extremes in the church, many times our first response is to turn and run all out in the opposite direction. We all have probably been guilty of this at some point in our lives. But we must be careful not to "throw the baby out with the bath water." We must not abandon the pure truths of God's Word because someone mixed them with error or excess or manipulated His Word for their own personal gain.

When the Word of God is compromised, it often leads to extremes and throws the church and lives out of balance and into a danger zone. Scripture tells us: "Watch your life and doctrine closely. Persevere in them, because if you do, you will save both yourself and your hearers" (1 Tim. 4:16, niv). We must all be careful, lest we be deceived, become confused, and blown around by every wind of doctrine (Eph. 4:14).

Assaulting the Character of God

To know and embrace God as both a loving Father (His goodness) and all-consuming fire (His severity) is an amazing reality (1 John 3:1; Heb. 12:29; Rom. 11:22). Yet, as we mentioned in chapter 2, many in our pulpits are guilty of presenting a false and shallow view of who God really is. In an attempt to make God Himself "seeker-friendly" and an easy sell, many have stripped away many facets of His character that might challenge us or make us feel uncomfortable.

What America and the church desperately needs is the true and living God and not a stripped-down version of who "we think" the world might like. Everyone needs to understand *both* "the goodness and severity of God" (Rom. 11:22). God has not changed (Mal. 3:6). The world needs to see God in His glory and fullness—the One who is an all consuming fire; the One whose eyes are life flames of fire and out of His mouth comes a two-edged sword; the One who judges and makes war; the One who has conquered death, hell, and the grave; the One who came to give life and set the captives free; the One who is both the Lion and the Lamb! We need to bow in fear (reverence) and stand in awe of Him, His beauty, His power, and His majesty (see Hebrews 12:28–29, Exodus 24, Psalm 29, 104, Daniel 7, Isaiah 6, Ezekiel 1, Revelation 4)!

Indeed, we cannot truly understand and know the depths of God's love, goodness, mercy, and grace apart from understanding and knowing His holiness, justice, judgment, and divine wrath.

Distorted Grace Message

A major reason we are seeing rampant sin in the church (pulpits and pews) is because there is little acknowledgement of the consequences of sin. This is largely due to an extreme and distorted grace teaching, often called "hyper-grace."

The true message of grace is life-changing (and not limited to salvation alone). Yet some popular teachers today greatly distort the message of grace—teaching Christians they will no longer reap what they sow, even though God's Word makes it clear to not be deceived for we will reap what we sow to the flesh (corruption) or to the Spirit (life) (Gal. 6:7–8). Some even teach asking God for forgiveness or repentance is no longer necessary, even though Jesus' last message to the church included the command to "repent" over and over again (Rev. 2 and 3). Although not intended, this distorted grace teaching has caused many to adopt a casual view of sin within the delusion that "under grace" they can live any way they want without consequences. This dangerous deception must stop!

The results of "distorted grace"

Now we see things such as worship leaders having drinking parties and using profanity and believers partying at nightclubs Saturday night and attending church Sunday morning as if nothing is wrong. Or a pastor divorcing his wife to marry a younger one and justifying it with "God wants me to be happy."

One more example of this dangerous "distorted grace" mindset is an account told by well-known minister who said:

> When talking to a young group of leaders that are well-known in the nation. And one of them said, "I don't have to worry about sin. I could literally have an adulterous affair and be back in the ministry in two months." And this attitude is beginning to permeate…and that's very concerning to me. They see righteousness or holiness as legalism because that's what they told me.[7]

This mindset is absolutely unbiblical and contradicts numerous scriptures throughout the New Testament, such as:

> For the grace of God that brings salvation has appeared to all men, teaching us that, denying ungodliness and worldly lusts, we should live soberly, righteously, and godly in the present age.
>
> —TITUS 2:11–12

As we have already shown, it seems many in the church have become sin friendly, taking it lightly and feeling no need for repentance. Yes, Jesus was merciful to those like the woman caught in the sin of adultery; but then He said "go and sin no more" (John 8:11). And He said to the healed man at the pool of

Bethesda, "Sin no more, lest a worse thing come upon you" (5:14). There is little fear for the consequences of sin in our churches or nation.

An Important Note: The New Testament Greek word translated "grace" does not just mean "unmerited favor"; that is only half the truth (depending on context). God's "grace" is just as much His divine power to empower and transform us. We are empowered with God's divine nature to overcome all sin and walk as He does (2 Pet. 1:2–4).

We have much more we could say about this "distorted grace" subject, but instead we point you to a more detailed resource that will be out by the time you read this: *Hyper-Grace: Exposing the Dangers of the Modern Grace Message* by Michael L. Brown.

OTHER EXTREMES

The following are a few other key issues we believe have weakened the church and opened the door for deception. Although there are other extremes we could address, we believe these are some of the most glaring.

The Gifts vs the Fruit

On the charismatic side, many have promoted and exalted the *gifts* of the Spirit far more than the *fruit* of the Spirit. We have exalted the anointing above character. This has and will continue to lead to major problems, including deception. While the gifts are important; in the end, *who we are* (the fruit) is more important than *what we can do* (the gifts).

Chasing after Signs and Wonders

We believe God will be moving in powerful ways in these last days with glorious signs and wonders. However, it is very important that God's people do not merely seek or follow after signs and wonders and supernatural experiences but rather pursue God Himself. Jesus clearly warned that false prophets will deceive many with signs and wonders (Matt. 24:24). We must keep our eyes fixed on Christ and live by His Word, not by signs and wonders (Heb. 12:2).

Shutting Out the Holy Spirit

While we have charismatic extremes such as the grievous "toking the Ghost," we also have extremes on the other side. Some are great Bible teachers, yet reject and even attack with broad brush any form of the outpouring of the Holy Spirit and the gifts. It seems we (the American church) have a lot of growing up to do.

The Prosperity and Poverty Message

When we walk in the full counsel of God's Word it will always keep us strong and in balance. Some have embraced extreme doctrines regarding prosperity and poverty. There are those who believe to be truly humble means you should have almost nothing, while others latch on to certain scriptures to teach that as children of the King we should all be very wealthy (and if you're not then you need to give more or you don't have enough faith). There must be balance, and it really comes down to the motives of the heart. It is disturbing to hear of extreme messages taught with wrong motives and being used to fleece the sheep.

Because of extremes we also see divisiveness across the American church. Instead of praying for each other, we get into heated debates and thrust each other with our words, blogs, forums, and social media, usually born out of pride. There is a place for healthy, mature, and prayerful discussion, but it all has to begin with humility. Humility, speaking the truth in the spirit of love, and truly praying for each other is the starting place, along with being humble and teachable before the Lord; for none of us have perfect theology on everything.

OVERALL

While there are some good and even great things, overall the American church is in a serious state. The vast majority of the American church is living far below our calling and our capacity as the "glorious church" Jesus said He is coming back for (Eph. 5:27). She has forgotten her God, her identity, her mission, and her destiny. Great sin, compromise, other lovers, little prayer, building man's way, unbalanced doctrines, and extremes have cost the church and our nation dearly. This has to change!

Is there any wonder why?

It's been said that the state of the nation is a reflection of the state of the church. How true! When we look at the desperate state of the American church today, is it really any wonder why our nation is also in a desperate state? Is it really any wonder why the church has been largely ineffective? Is it really any wonder why our nation doesn't take the American church seriously and sees her as weak, hypocritical, and shallow?

Is it then really any wonder why in our nation a growing number of those under thirty (the future leaders of America) have no religious affiliation (the "nones")· (one in three)?[8] In addition to those considered "the nones," there are those now called "the dones." They are a growing number of Christians who say they are "done with church." We have met many ourselves who are very sincere and yet frustrated. They have *not* abandoned God or denied Christ, and they believe in the Bible; but they feel they can no longer find a church that is not compromising (in the ways this chapter has highlighted). They often end up gathering in homes with other people who are starving for the "real thing."

Looking at all of this, is it really any wonder why our society has become darker in a landslide of moral and spiritual decay and on the path to destruction?

Note: Pray for our pastors! It has been hard for us to share many of these things regarding the church today, especially what many in the pulpits of America have allowed or neglected. But we encourage everyone to take what you have read in this chapter and turn it into a prayer of repentance and intercession for our churches, and especially for those in our pulpits of America.

Trodden underfoot

Jesus said when salt loses it savor it is "good for nothing…cast out, and…trodden under foot of men (Matt. 5:13, KJV). And, this is what we see in America today regarding the church. We have seen our beliefs and voice for good trampled on because much of the American church has defiled herself, lost her saltiness, and diminished her light by compromising the truth.

Christ did not die a horrific death and rise again so that He could present to Himself a half-hearted, sin-filled, compromising, defeated church. He died that He might present us to Himself as a glorious, victorious church (Eph. 5:27)! And to the world, she will rise as a great light to dispel the darkness and lead the way to Christ before His return (Isa. 60)!

The good news

There is good news! God has the answer (a rescue plan) to turn this all around. God wants to awaken the church out of her lukewarm, defiled, and weakened state. He is coming to visit and dramatically cleanse, purify, revive, and restore His church for the days ahead. However, this process will include a time of separation; and you will need to decide where you will stand—on the Rock or on the sand (Matt. 7:24–27). There will be more about all this later in the book.

We have covered what *we* see when we look at the state of America and the American church; but what does God see? Also, what or who is He saying has opened the door to the destruction of our nation?

7

THE GATEKEEPERS

When the righteous are in authority, the people rejoice;
But when a wicked man rules, the people groan.
—PROVERBS 29:2

THIS IS THE final chapter regarding what has led our nation down the path of destruction. In the previous two chapters, we showed some of the primary reasons we believe America has fallen into such a dire state in both our nation and churches. There is one more thing that has opened the door to all we have seen and described—the gatekeepers.

THE GATEKEEPERS: AMERICA'S NATIONAL AND SPIRITUAL LEADERS

The "gatekeepers" of our land start at the top—America's civil and spiritual leaders. They are entrusted with power and authority to lead our churches and nation. And what they allow or disallow affects the nation. They do this through their words and actions that either honor or dishonor God and His ways. Both honoring and dishonoring God has consequences.

> Those who honor Me I will honor, but those who despise Me will be disdained.
>
> —1 SAMUEL 2:30, NIV

The Biblical Perspective

There was an obvious pattern throughout biblical history. When the leaders or kings honored God and His ways, rooted out evil, and acted righteously, then God gave them favor, caused them to prosper, delivered them from trouble, and gave them peace. The whole nation was positively affected because righteousness exalts a nation (Prov. 14:34). However, when a nation's kings or leaders dishonored God, were bad or wicked, the whole nation was negatively affected (Prov. 29:2).

National Leaders Note: It's interesting to see in biblical history how God would even judge Israel by putting weak or poor leadership over them (Isa. 3:4). God rules over the kingdoms of men and puts them in place as He wills (Dan. 4:17). God often gives a nation the leaders they deserve.

Next, we share biblical examples how national and spiritual leaders' sins in words, actions, and what they permit, not only negatively affect a nation but can also open the door to judgment and destruction.

Example 1: The King

A clear example showing how the sin of leadership affects a family and a nation was during King David's reign when he sinned with Bathsheba. Yes, God forgave him; but the consequences were severe and rippled throughout his family and once great dynasty.

Example 2: The Priests

Aaron, a key leader and priest for God's people, affected the whole nation by compromising and giving in to the pressure of the people, what they wanted—to make their version of God, a golden calf. His weak leadership allowed an open the door for great sin as he watched on. The result was great judgment and even the death of thousands (Exod. 32).

Example 3: The Leaders and Priests

In Ezekiel 8 and 9 God gives the prophet a vision which reveals the great sin and abominations being done in secret by the leaders and the priests.

God showed Ezekiel that leaders of the nation were meeting in secret chambers with idols they worshipped and practicing occult ceremonies (see Ezekiel 8:6–12). Some even believe this also goes on today in relation to demonic plans regarding America and a "New World Order."

Then God showed Ezekiel many leaders and priests turning their *backs on the temple of the Lord and* their faces toward the east, to worship the sun god (v. 16).

> And He said to me, "Have you seen this, O son of man? Is it a trivial thing to the house of Judah to commit the abominations which they commit here? *For they have filled the land with violence; then they have returned to provoke Me to anger."*
>
> —EZEKIEL 8:17, EMPHASIS ADDED

Then Ezekiel 9:9 God says, "*The iniquity of the house of Israel and Judah is exceedingly great, and the land is full of bloodshed, and the city full of perversity; for they say, 'The LORD has forsaken the land, and the Lord does not see!'"* (emphasis added).

These leaders assumed that because God did not respond quickly to judge their actions and sin they were getting away with it. Many seem to think the same way today. But what they didn't know is their great sin was setting up their nation for judgment and destruction. (See the rest of Ezekiel 9.)

As we highlighted previously, there are also many of God's leaders (five-fold ministry) in hidden sin today. They may think God is OK with their sin because their anointing or gift is still working. This is a great deception. At the same time they are leading America down the same path and result as Israel and Judah—opening the door to national judgment and destruction!

OPENING THE DOOR TO DESTRUCTION

In 2010 during prayer, God began speaking to us about what He was seeing in our nation and regarding America's gatekeepers, especially in the church.

As you read this, please keep in mind that there are godly pastors and leaders in our nation who are faithfully devoted to God and His ways. But, as God says in this word, there are "many" in His church "in gross sin." Note, He is saying "many," *not* "most." Keep in mind God sees it all, we do not. This is part of a prophecy from June 07, 2010, through Cindy deVille.

> The sin in your land is great, it is great.
> The sin in My church, it is great.
> Even many of those that lead, those that feed My sheep,
> Many are in gross sin.
> They've opened the door, they've let it in.
>
> Just as you see, as the political leaders of your land,
> Much adultery, much sin, much perversion, much greed.
> So these are in the lives of those who lead My sheep.
> Many are trying to cover them up.
> But I will come by My Spirit and expose...[1]

God still opposes and takes sin very seriously, even more so for those who lead because they have tremendous influence and can impact multitudes, even a whole nation, either positively or negatively (James 3:1).

Indeed, the pulpits of America have played a key role in what we are seeing in our nation. The following prophetic word provides more insight regarding this.

The Pulpits: Allowing Great Sin and Destruction

In June 8, 2008, in a word God gave Cindy, He was speaking of how great sin in many pulpits of America was severely affecting both His people and our nation:

> You say mercy, mercy, grace, grace
> And you think that will erase the hidden sin you continue to live and
>   revel in!
>
> Your words are nothing to Me,
> It is your actions that I see!
> You have trampled on My grace,
> And made a mockery of My mercy,
> And you have taught My people the same,
> And now My name is shamed!
>
> Now My people think that I am OK with sin.
> You have opened the door and let it into My sanctuary,
> Into My Holy place,

You have made My house one of disgrace.
You have defiled My house and defiled My people!
The sin is destroying My people, destroying My church,
And destroying your nation!

(You can access the full word "Judgment is Coming to the Pulpits of
America" in appendix F.)

Pastors, you are the gatekeeper of your church. What you allow or disallow in as a shepherd and steward over God's house and people you will stand accountable for before the Lord. This is very serious!

The biblical examples we shared earlier of how spiritual leaders affect a nation was also clearly addressed by a prominent leader of America's Second Great Awakening.

The pulpits are held accountable for the nation

It is said that Charles G. Finney's life and writings influenced more people toward revival and reformation than any other preacher of the 1800s. He recognized the important role the church, especially the pulpits—the five-fold ministry, plays in the shaping of our culture and nation. A portion of his classic sermon "Decay of Conscience" says it very well.

Our preaching will bear its legitimate fruits. If immorality prevails in the land, the fault is ours [the pulpits] in a great degree.[2]

Note: This goes back to the compromise of God's Word and unbalanced doctrine we previously covered. Note that Finney says to "a great degree," because when truth is spoken, the people must then respond and live it out. But it all starts with the pulpits. Finney continues:

If there is a decay of conscience,
the pulpit is responsible for it....
If the church is degenerate and worldly,
the pulpit is responsible for it.
If the world loses its interest in [God],
the pulpit is responsible for it.
If Satan rules in our halls of legislation,
the pulpit is responsible for it.
If our politics become so corrupt that the very foundations of our
government are ready to fall away,
the pulpit is responsible for it.[3]

We believe the case could be made that biblically speaking, the highest place of ultimate authority for our nation lies not in Washington, DC, but rather in the pulpits of America; for the spiritual affects everything in the natural (Eph. 6:12). God's leaders hold the greatest spiritual authority as ambassadors representing the kingdom of God and Christ, the King of kings (Matt. 28:18–20; Rev. 19:16). What the church allows or stops can affect the whole nation (Matt. 18:18).

In relation to all this, Martin Luther King Jr. prophetically wrote in 1963:

> The church must be reminded that it is not the master or the servant of the state, but rather the conscience of the state. It must be the guide and the critic of the state, and never its tool. If the church does not recapture its prophetic zeal, it will become an irrelevant social club without moral or spiritual authority.[4]

The pulpits of America (five-fold ministry) have played a major role in the condition of our churches and nation and they will also play a major role in turning it all around with God's Answer (in the second half of this book).

While the pulpits of America are the spiritual gatekeepers, our nation's governmental leaders are also very accountable for their key role.

TO AMERICA'S LEADERS

America's president, Congress, judges, governors, and mayors, biblically you are considered public servants of God (see Romans 13:3–7). The foundation of God's throne is righteousness and justice (Ps. 89:14). Therefore, you as leaders are accountable before Him to govern and judge righteously according to His standards and not according to your own. The unbiblical legislation and judicial decisions we are seeing in America are opening the door to severe judgment upon our land.

King Belshazzar's example

King Belshazzar, in his pride, led the people in defiling and taking lightly the things of God (see Daniel 5). The king and the people also worshipped the gods of gold, silver, bronze, and iron, wood, and stone. This brought judgment on the whole nation in the form of an enemy invasion and overthrow of the kingdom.

In essence, many of America's leaders have done the same kind of thing. Many have taken God Himself and the things of God lightly. Then driven by great greed, the desire to stay in power, and an ungodly agenda, many have become corrupt and have opened the door to destruction and judgment upon our land.

A coming shift

Thankfully, there are some great and godly leaders in America standing up to fight for what is right, to honor God, and to restore the godly foundations; but there seem to be so few. However, as God's people rise up and run with God's Answer in this book, a shift will take place, a great house cleaning to help change the course of our nation; and God will put righteous leaders and judges in place to help restore and reform the nation. You can read more about this in the second half of this book.

Will America end up in the pig pen?

When we look at the godly foundations America was established upon and how far our nation has fallen, this seems parallel to the parable of the Prodigal Son. He grew up blessed in his father's house, but his own ways lead him far, far away from home and finally to a pig pen, until one day he came to his senses.

God wants to get America's attention, bring her to her senses, and turn her back to Him before she ends up in the pig pen! The question is—how does God get a nation's attention?

SECTION 3:

HOW GOD GETS A NATION'S ATTENTION

A BIBLICAL VIEW

8

How God Deals with a Nation

9

The Biblical Pattern: Three Ways

8

HOW GOD DEALS WITH A NATION

I am the LORD, I do not change
—MALACHI 3:6

HROUGHOUT BIBLICAL HISTORY we see multiple examples and patterns of how God warns and deals with cities and nations in great sin. In the next two chapters we believe you will see how the "America, America!" prophecy of 2007 aligns with the biblical pattern of how God gets a nation's attention.

Old Testament vs New Testament examples

Many seem to forget, the Old Testament covers about 4,000 years of human history, while the New Testament covers less than 100 years. So naturally the Old Testament holds many more examples of God's dealing with nations than the New Testament.

Although over two-thirds of the Bible is the Old Testament, many incorrectly assume it's not that relevant today, which is a both a great shame and gross misunderstanding. The Old Testament is as relevant to the New Testament as the first floor is to a two-story building. The second floor cannot stand or be relevant without the first. We should understand that the apostle Paul wrote the following verse when the New Testament had not yet been completed or complied:

> All scripture [only the Old Testament at that time] is given by inspiration of God, and is profitable for doctrine, for reproof, for correction, for instruction in righteousness.
>
> —2 TIMOTHY 3:16

Biblical patterns and examples

The truth is that from Genesis to Revelation there are two consistent themes—both the goodness (love) and severity (judgment) of God (Rom. 11:22; Jer. 9:24). The judgment and wrath of God are fundamental truths seen throughout biblical history and writings, Old and New Testaments. (For more on this subject see "Answering Objections to God's Judgment Today" in the appendix C.)

There are many levels and forms of judgment—from God lifting His hand of blessings and protection, the effects of sin itself, to His wrath being poured out (Rom. 1:18). Here are some Old and New Testament examples:

Some Old Testament examples of judgment (over 4,000 years)

+ Worldwide flood in Noah's day
+ Sodom and Gomorrah (brimstone and fire)

- Judgment on the priests (Aaron's sons and Eli's sons)
- Plagues upon Philistines when ark of covenant came near
- Rebellious Korah, priests, and followers swallowed up by earth
- Canaanites (natural disasters and war)
- National disasters, enemy attacks, and invasion numerous times throughout Israel and Jerusalem's history
- Judgment on many other nations (see Isaiah, Jeremiah, Ezekiel, and Amos)

New Testament record of God's judgment *after* the Cross (less than 100 years)

- Ananias and Sapphira dropped dead for lying to the Holy Spirit (Acts 5)
- King Herod struck and consumed by judgment (Acts 12)
- The destruction of Jerusalem (AD 70) (Jesus prophesied this in Mark 13:1–2.)
- Jesus spoke judgment on several towns because they wouldn't repent, and these towns no longer exist (Matt. 11:20–24).
- The Book of Revelation's future trumpets and the bowls of wrath

It is still revealed

Jesus dying on the cross did not change the nature of God. Malachi 3:6 declares, "I am the LORD, I do not change." Also John 3 says, "Whoever believes in the Son has eternal life, but whoever rejects the Son will not see life, for God's wrath *remains* on him" (John 3:36, NIV, emphasis added). Note that "God's wrath remains" is *present* tense. This also reflects what Paul wrote in Romans 1:18: "For the wrath of God *is revealed* from heaven against all ungodliness and unrighteousness of men" (emphasis added). Notice Paul says the "wrath of God is revealed"—also *present* tense. God's wrath and judgment still *remains* and *is revealed* against sin today.

The apostle Peter, while warning the prophets, the teachers, and people of coming destruction because of their sinful ways, reminded them of God's past judgment of sin (John 16:8–9). Peter then cited how judgment upon the angels of Genesis 6, the great worldwide flood in Noah's day, and the destruction of Sodom and Gomorrah were *examples* of *how* God will deal in the future with the ungodly, which includes today (2 Pet. 2:4–6).

God's example to Jeremiah

God gave two clear examples of how He deals with nations to the prophet Jeremiah, which he records in Jeremiah 18:7–11:

Example 1: "If I announce that a certain nation or kingdom is to be *uprooted, torn down, and destroyed,* but then that nation *renounces its evil ways,* I will not destroy it as I had planned" (vv. 7–8, NLT, emphasis added).

Example 2: "And if I announce that I will *plant and build up* a certain nation or kingdom, but then that nation *turns to evil and refuses to obey Me,* I will not bless it as I said I would" (vv. 9–10, NLT, emphasis added).

Then God told Jeremiah to go and warn all Judah and Jerusalem. Say to them, "Thus says the LORD: *'Behold, I am planning disaster and devising a plan against you.* Return now every one from his evil way and make your ways and your doings good'" (v. 11, emphasis added).

We see this pattern throughout biblical and world history, and we are also seeing it again today in America. We see this reflected in the "America, America!" prophecy in chapter 2. This is how God operates.

Now let's look at how God would work to get a nation's attention before judgment and destruction came.

GETTING A NATION'S ATTENTION

Ask yourself these two questions: When God has something to say, how does He do it? How does God get a nation's attention?

Word Warnings: Written and verbal

The typical biblical pattern was that in a time of spiritual and moral crisis, God, in His goodness and mercy, would send a message through His servants the prophets to the people or nation. They would warn of God's coming judgment of sin (John 16:8–9), calling them to turn away from (repent) of their sin. These warnings usually included a word of hope and redemption if they responded in obedience to His words.

Today, just like a parent, Father God will instruct, guide, and correct us through His Word first and by His Spirit who leads and guides us into all truth (John 16:13). This is the preferred way to bring correction when needed. If we will simply abide by His ways already written, then God's favor, protection, and blessing shines—as it once did upon America.

But, as we saw in Jeremiah 18:7–11, if a nation ignores His Word and continues in its rebellious and arrogant ways, then God in His mercy will send warnings (written or verbal warnings) through His prophets or other servants to be sure we are getting the message clearly.

> Surely the Lord GOD does nothing, Unless He reveals His secret to His servants the prophets.
>
> —AMOS 3:7

In ancient Israel's day God went to great measures to warn them because He did not want to see their destruction. Consistently He sent prophets to warn the leaders, kings, entire cities, and nations. God's love would not easily let go, sometimes warning them for years of the consequences of their sin if they did not turn back to Him. And when the people sincerely repented, then God relented from bringing judgment.

One classic example is the prophet Jonah's warning to the wicked city of Nineveh recorded in the Book of Jonah. They heard the simple warning, responded, and repented; then God relented and they were spared. However, about 150 years later, the prophet Nahum had to also warn them again of destruction because they had returned to their wicked ways, and this time they were destroyed (see the Book of Nahum).

We should also note that God often speaks and warns of things to come through dreams and visions which are shared through verbal or written words. We see this throughout both the Old and New Testaments.

It is God's perfect will that we respond in obedience to His written and spoken words of warning. However, if we continue to ignore and reject His warnings, He will then use greater measures as warnings to get our attention in effort to save us from greater judgment and destruction resulting from the consequences of sin.

Before we proceed, we offer an understanding of God's warnings in relation to His judgments.

Warnings vs Judgment

It is important to understand there is a difference between God's "warnings" and His "judgments." Warnings come to get our attention before judgment comes. Judgment is often considered more severe and final. However, it is also important to note, lesser judgments can also serve as warnings (even progressive warnings) of a greater and more severe judgment coming—the ten plagues upon Egypt is a clear example of this (Exod. 8–11).

After 400 years of slavery, God sent Moses to warn Pharaoh. He brought progressively worse warnings in the form of judgments, resulting in great destruction and suffering all over Egypt. Then came even greater judgment with of all of Egypt's firstborn killed (Exod. 11). It was God's justice for eighty years earlier when Egypt's ruler declared the killing all the male babies of Israel. The other greater judgment was Egypt's army being drowned in the Red Sea (Exod. 14). All these judgments were a collective part of God's great judgment upon Egypt (and all it represented).

Now, if God's verbal or written warnings are ignored, biblical history shows how He would go to greater measures (three main ways) to get a nation's attention.

9

THE BIBLICAL PATTERN: THREE WAYS

I seek You early; For when Your judgments are in the earth,
The inhabitants of the world will learn righteousness.
—ISAIAH 26:9

WHEN GOD'S VERBAL or written warnings are not heeded, then He will speak to us through our circumstances. Biblical history demonstrates ways God would continue to warn, even through progressive levels of judgment. He will use both natural and supernatural ways:

- Natural elements, such as fire, floods, wind, waves, earthquakes, lightning, and drought
- Animal kingdom, such as locusts, insects, frogs, and wild beasts
- The microscopic world, such as plagues and disease
- Mankind, such as enemy attacks, invasion, and captivity

Also in the supernatural realm, angels were used to both bring judgment and protect God's people (Isa. 37:36; Ps. 91:11).

Now we will examine three of the primary ways God deals with nations when they have ignored His initial warnings. As we move through these you will begin to see a biblical pattern unfold, a pattern that one could easily say America has been experiencing.

Note: all three of these are seen in the "America, America!" prophecy because this is how God gets a nation's attention. This chapter also sets a biblical precedent for what's coming next (revealed in upcoming chapter 11).

1. WEALTH AND ECONOMY AFFECTED

With Israel when God's warnings were ignored, He would negatively impact their economy by affecting their crops, water, and food supply, such as withholding rain—leading to drought and sometimes even famine, as in Elijah's day. God would also use other natural means, such as locusts, to destroy crops and more, on which their economy depended.

> Example 1: In Joel 1–2 the nation was in great crisis as never before. God had sent an army of locusts and fires, leaving the land stripped bare and in economic woe. Their crops were ruined, fruit was withered, vineyards were dried up, and water was scarce.

Example 2: Solomon was forewarned of this kind of disaster by God: "When I shut up heaven and there is no rain, or command the locusts to devour the land, or send pestilence...if My people who are called by My name will humble themselves, and pray and seek My face, and turn [repent] from their wicked ways, then I will hear from heaven, and will forgive their sin and heal their land" (2 Chron. 7:13–14).

These plainly show ways God can affect a nation's produce and economy, by using such things as great pestilence, droughts, and fires. Is it a coincidence that America has had record droughts and historic wildfires these past several years, along with economic stress? This has included rising food prices, along with water supply shortages across the nation.

2. NATURAL DISASTERS

There are biblical accounts from Genesis to Revelation of God consistently using floods, fires, storms, hail, earthquakes, drought, famine, plagues, and more. God can control all these natural things for His purposes as both warnings and judgments. Again, the ten plagues upon Egypt are a classic example of the progressive warnings and judgments of God through natural means.

God's control and uses of natural elements and weather

There are numerous scriptures showing God controls the weather and natural elements and uses them for His divine purposes. Here is one quoted scripture followed by other scripture references:

Take heed to yourselves, lest your heart be deceived, and you turn aside and serve other gods and worship them, lest the LORD's anger be aroused against you, and He shut up the heavens so that there be no rain, and the land yield no produce, and you perish quickly from the good land which the LORD is giving you.

—DEUTERONOMY 11:16–17

Biblical accounts show God controls and uses:

- Lightning, hail, snow, wind, and clouds (Ps. 148:8)
- Stormy winds, sea, and waves (Jer. 10:13, Jon. 1:4)
- Whirlwinds and tornadoes (Nah. 1:3)
- Earthquakes and fires (Isa. 29:6)
- Rain, flooding, and great hailstones (Ezek. 13:9–13)
- Withhold and directing rain to certain cities (Amos 4:7–8)
- Drought and famine (Deut. 11:17)
- Plagues as judgment (Num. 16:46; 2 Sam. 24:15)

Note: Does Satan cause bad weather?

Some believe that only Satan causes destructive weather, often citing Job 1 and the storm Jesus rebuked; however, only those two accounts point to that possibility. On the other hand, there are numerous biblical accounts that both good or destructive weather (or natural disasters) came by God's hand, not Satan.

Now, if it so happens that the kingdom of darkness does have the ability to influence weather, it is limited to when allowed by God. "For the earth is the LORD's, and all its fullness" (Ps. 24:1). He controls it all. Also, keep in mind Jesus Christ (not Satan) holds all of creation and nature together (Col. 1:16–17).

God uses weather as both blessing and punishment

Does God really use weather as a form of reward and punishment? Yes. The blessing of rain for crops and water supply and the punishments of the worldwide flood in Noah's day, great hail upon Egypt in Moses' day, great hail in Revelation 16:21, and drought are examples of judgment or punishment. One other very specific scripture that reveals how God uses weather is in the book Job.

> He loads the clouds with moisture;
>> he scatters his lightning through them.
> At his direction they swirl around
>> over the face of the whole earth
>> to do whatever he commands them.
> He brings them *to punish men,*
>> or to water his earth and *show his love.*
>> —JOB 37:11–13, NIV, EMPHASIS ADDED

One more example:

> You have polluted the land with your harlotries and your wickedness. Therefore the showers have been withheld, And there has been no latter rain.
>> —JEREMIAH 3:2–3

It is clear that sin negatively affects the land while righteousness opens up the door to bring both the favor and blessings of God (Prov. 14:34; Ps. 112).

ANSWERING A KEY QUESTION ABOUT NATURAL DISASTERS: ARE ALL NATURAL DISASTERS JUDGMENT OF GOD?

Before we move forward we believe it is important to answer this question. It is very clear throughout Holy Scripture that God controls and uses natural elements for His divine purposes. However, as Christians we need to be careful not to pronounce every natural disaster as the judgment of God. Understanding the reasons for natural disasters today helps explains why.

REASONS FOR NATURAL DISASTERS

We believe there are three main reasons natural disasters come. In fact there could be a combination of the following working together depending on the situation.

1. Natural Cycles in a Fallen World

Since the fall of man we have been living in a world affected by sin, a world God originally created as "very good" (Gen. 1:31). So there may be times when some natural disasters are part of the natural process of things shifting.

2. The Birth Pains (*Not* Global Warming or Climate Change)

Shortly after the "America, America!" prophecy from 2007 came, Cindy was reading news of an earthquake taking place at the United Nations Summit where they were talking about fears of "global warming" impact. Then God spoke to her and said:

> They call it global *warming*,
> But know, these are My global *warnings*.

At the time of this prophecy, "global warming" was the term used most; now we mostly hear of "climate change." No matter what they call it, these things are all part of the birthing pains and natural disasters that will increase as Jesus prophesied (Matt. 24:7; Mark 13:8; Luke 21:11, 25–26). These are not "global *warming*" (or "climate change") but they are part of God's "global *warnings*" as signs for these last days. These will continue to increase and shift as the return of Christ gets closer to birth a new age, His millennial reign. We also believe things will be happening and shifting in the days ahead that will cause scientists to be baffled.

Politicians claim we all need to work together to "battle climate change," but there is nothing they can do to stop it. Like a woman in labor, the contractions will become more frequent and more intense the closer the new birth gets. So this is not about "climate change," but the earth is instead preparing for a "kingdom change"—the coming glorious kingdom and reign of Christ on earth (Rev. 11:15).

3. God's Prophetic Warnings or Judgments

When God in His mercy sends His prophets with a warning and redemptive message, it typically includes a call for repentance. This message may sometimes include warnings of natural disasters coming if not obeyed. These natural disasters can serve as a warning, a wakeup call, or a form of judgment, like Moses saw upon Egypt.

These kinds of natural disasters are often unusual or extraordinary in some way, including in size and impact. This often reveals its supernatural connection, if a prophetic warning has been spoken (as we will show later with Superstorm Sandy). This is exactly the case for America today.

God's warning about multiplied natural disasters

In the 2007 "America, America!" prophecy, God said New Orleans (Hurricane Katrina in 2005) was a warning. He also said:

> For I AM the God of all the earth.
> The wind and the sea at My command, they all obey Me!
> Natural disasters will be multiplied unto thee
> Because I have seen your sin and unrepentant heart.

We will show later how days after this prophecy there began a dramatic increase in multiple and historic natural disasters in America, coming as warnings to get America's attention, just as God said.

America's response so far

America's response to God's warnings so far has been unrepentant and defiant (or seemingly oblivious). One example is in the 2013 State of the Union speech. The president of the United States tried to explain away the increase in frequency and intensity of the droughts, wildfires, floods, and historic storms as the "overwhelming judgment of science"[1] (e.g., climate change), rejecting any thought that God has anything to do with it.

The fact is that throughout most of human history when cites and nations experienced catastrophic disasters, they were usually considered the judgment of God (or perceived by pagans as one of their gods). This is one reason many refer to large-scale disasters as "of biblical proportions."

Now, what if both economic woes and natural disasters sent as warning are ignored by a nation? How would God deal with a city or nation that continues to rebel against or ignore Him? As with Israel, God would often allow even more severe things to come, such as enemy attacks and war.

3. ENEMY ATTACKS AND WAR

God often used Israel's enemies (more sinful than themselves) to attack and bring judgment (or punishment), such as the Philistines, Assyrians, and Babylonians. When God's hand of protection was lifted from a city or nation, the enemies were allowed to attack or invade and bring destruction. Psalm 127:1 declares, "Unless the LORD guards the city, The watchman stays awake in vain."

Biblical Example:

The following scripture shows a clear example of a nation (Israel) that persists in ignoring God's warnings and mocking His messengers:

> Moreover all the leaders of the priests and the people transgressed more and more, according to all the abominations of the nations, and defiled the house of the LORD which He had consecrated in Jerusalem. And the LORD God of their fathers sent warnings to them by His messengers, rising up early and sending them, because He had compassion

on His people and on His dwelling place. But they mocked the messengers of God, despised His words, and scoffed at His prophets, until the wrath of the LORD arose against His people, till there was no remedy.

—2 CHRONICLES 36:14–16

This then led to the invasion by Babylon, and eventually seventy years in exile. God was not playing games!

Note how in the above scripture those in the position as spiritual leaders and priests (the gatekeepers) opened the door to great sin by defiling and destroying His house, which brought judgment upon the whole nation.

There are many biblical examples of enemy attacks being a part of God's judgment upon nations. For America, many have wondered if 9/11 was the judgment of God.

Was 9/11 the judgment of God?

The attack on 9/11 was obviously a very shocking and heartbreaking time. Surely, we all remember where we were when we heard the news, especially when the second plane hit or when we watched the towers fall.

Soon after this a couple of prominent Christian leaders caused a great uproar when they implied the 9/11 attacks were the judgment of God. Yet in Bible days, even decades ago, such a significant disaster would be considered as the judgment of God (Amos 3:6).

Some say 9/11 was an inside job, as part of a plan to lessen our freedoms in the name of protection and progressively shift control of our nation towards a New World Order, etc. Regardless of how 9/11 came to be (terrorist attacks, conspiracy, or both), it was a wakeup call—a warning that something bad is happening to America because of her great sin.

In the "America, America!" prophecy, God said: "The Towers were just a warning." God's hand of protection was temporarily lifted (Ps. 127:1) and enemies were allowed to strike suddenly to awaken our nation. It was a warning, a sample of something much greater coming if America does not turn back to God in time. We share exactly what that *greater judgment* is in chapter 11, "What's Coming Next, If…?" It is very important we understand the gravity of what America faces if she does not change course.

Question: "How could a loving God allow deadly disasters?" We answer this in "Does God Still Bring Judgment Today?" in appendix C.

America's response to 9/11

After the shock and devastation of 9/11, the country responded by uniting in patriotic song and encouraging words. People filled our churches searching for answers, comfort, and help. We even saw members of Congress from both parties standing together on the capitol steps in a heartfelt song of "God Bless America."

All this was very moving to see and hear; but one thing was missing—there was no genuine repentance. The many patriotic songs and speeches invoking the name of God rang hollow because: "These people honor me with their lips, but their hearts are far from me" (Matt. 15:8, niv).

There was no national public acknowledgement that this horrific event could possibly be a wakeup call from God after decades of great sin and progressively removing Him from our society. To some it was unthinkable, because how could such a loving God allow this to happen? It comes back to the fact that most in the church have painted a shallow view of God. The pulpits of America have not adequately communicated the fullness and justice of God—both the goodness and severity of God or the devastating effects of sin.

So sadly, after 9/11 there was no genuine repentance or turning back to God and His ways. And before long churches where back to pre 9/11 levels and most everyone was back to business as usual. But America would never be the same again.

Generally, enemy attacks and war are a last resort God uses to warn or bring judgment because they can be very terrifying and devastating. But sometimes God will allow a limited enemy attack first as a wakeup call, as 9/11 was for America.

Again, we must remember, God does not delight in the death of the wicked or the destruction of sinful nations but wants them to turn from their sin and evil ways and back to Him (Ezek. 33:11). This is one reason why God in His great mercy often brings His warnings and judgments progressively to allow time for repentance before greater judgment comes (Rom. 2:4–5). For God delights in mercy; He wants to bring life and not death, blessing and not a curse. But we must choose *His* path, which leads to life.

GOD'S MERCY: PROGRESSIVE WARNINGS AND JUDGMENTS

It is actually because of God' great mercy that His warnings and judgments often happen over a span of years. Mistakenly, many in our hi-tech, instant-minded society completely disregard these warnings and even mock them if they don't see them carried out within a short period of time.

Henry Wadsworth Longfellow said, "Though the mills of God grind slowly, yet they grind exceeding fine."[2] God may seem slow in responding to great sin and injustice; but when He does, you can be sure His judgment is thorough and complete.

Biblical Example: All "three ways" in operation to get a nation's attention

In the prophets Amos and Hosea's time, Northern Israel had become prosperous but also very corrupt and filled with injustice, pride, perversion, and drunkenness and very idolatrous. They worshipped the sun god and fertility god, which included mass temple prostitution as a form of worship.

Amos 4:6–12 demonstrates how God brought progressive warnings and judgments with a call to turn them back to Him every step of the way.

1. Food shortage with hunger in all their cities

   "'Yet you have not returned to Me,' Says the LORD"
   (v. 6).

2. Fresh water shortage by withholding rain on certain cities

   "'Yet you have not returned to Me,' Says the LORD"
   (vv. 7–8).

3. Blight, mildew, and locusts destroyed crops

   "'Yet you have not returned to Me,' Says the LORD"
   (v. 9).

4. Plagues of Egypt upon the people

   "'Yet you have not returned to Me,' Says the LORD"
   (v. 10).

5. Enemy attacks and war

   "'Yet you have not returned to Me,' Says the LORD"
   (v. 10).

6. Fires destroying cities like Sodom and Gomorrah

   "'Yet you have not returned to Me,' Says the LORD"
   (v. 11).

7. Then came a massive earthquake (Amos 1:1)

8. Then eventually came enemy invasion and exile (Amos 5:27;
   Hosea 8–10)

In this we see the biblical pattern in operation—God using all three ways progressively to get the nation's attention: economy affected (crops destroyed, plus lack of food and water), natural disasters (drought, fires, plagues, earthquake), and the enemy attacks and war, then invasion and exile. America is on the very same path today.

Genuine repentance will lead to mercy

During the Civil War, President Abraham Lincoln, in his National Day of Prayer Proclamation, declared: "Genuine repentance will lead to mercy."[3] This is really important to understand, because crying out for mercy alone does not deal with the sin or the effects of sin, rather it delays and heaps up a greater judgment for later. Jonathan Edwards, who helped begin the First Great Awakening, said it this way:

The wrath of God is like great waters that are dammed for the present.
They increase more and more, and rise higher and higher, till an outlet

is given, and the longer the stream is stopped, the more rapid and mighty its course, when once it is let loose.[4]

This is what America is facing, and only genuine repentance will bring forgiveness of sin and turn away God's great wrath and judgment.

> Rend your heart and not your garments. Return to the LORD your God, for he is gracious and compassionate, slow to anger and abounding in love, and he relents from sending calamity.
>
> —JOEL 2:13, NIV

What would you do if you were God?

Now, we ask you to really think about this. Put yourself in God's place for just a moment. What would *you* do if a people or a nation you loved were progressing into great sin that you knew was going to end up destroying them both now and into eternity. If you foresaw the destructive effects of sin spreading like a disease causing much pain and suffering to families, children, and the nation; what would you do? How would you speak to them and warn them?

Likewise, what else could God do to get a nation's attention, short of splitting the sky and speaking with an audible voice?

IN REVIEW

We shared the way God deals with nations and a biblical pattern of how God works to get a nation's attention. He will first use written or verbal warnings; but if these are ignored, then He will progressively use natural means we can see and hear which usually include:

1. Affecting the wealth and economy
2. Natural disasters (usually extraordinary ones)
3. Enemy attacks and war.

Note: You can also see how this has played out before in American history; see appendix B, "A Classic Example from Early America."

Again, we want to remind everyone that the economic woes, great natural disasters, and enemy attacks and war are not God's perfect will. God desires that we first heed His written Word (the Holy Bible) and His prophets who come to warn us motivated out of love. God's Word instructs us to "believe His prophets, and you shall prosper" (2 Chron. 20:20).

We pray this chapter has been insightful and helped answer some important questions many have had. This section is also important because it provides the biblical basis and pattern we are seeing unfold in relation to what God is saying to America and the nations, and what's coming next.

SECTION 4:

WHAT IS GOD SAYING TO AMERICA AND THE NATIONS?

10

A Revealing Prophetic Sequence

11

What's Coming Next, If...?

10

A REVEALING PROPHETIC SEQUENCE

Surely the Lord GOD does nothing Unless He reveals His
secret counsel To His servants the prophets.
—AMOS 3:7, NAS

THIS SHORT CHAPTER provides global context to what God has been speaking to America. It also reveals some prophetic understanding to what has been happening globally since 2008. Right now God is working in all the nations to bring about His plans and purposes.

GOD SPEAKS TO AMERICA AND THE NATIONS

This prophetic sequence began in 2007 during a time of prayer with the following vision and prophetic word. Although these may be very serious in nature, as with many biblical prophecies of warning, they also carry with them a ray of hope.

1. Vision: "Judgment Is Running"
Late November 2007 through Cindy deVille

It all began a couple days after thanksgiving in 2007. During prayer with Darrel late one night, I sensed a great weight of God's presence. Then I had a very intense vision that left me stunned and speechless for some time. The following is what I saw and heard.

> I saw four horses running, and they seemed to be overtaken by a great zeal and fury. I did not see the color of the horses; they may have been white, but I am uncertain. They were pulling a chariot and someone was driving it but I could not see who it was.
>
> These four horses were running all out as if in a fervent race to get to America and the nations of the earth. It was terrifying as I could feel a fierce wrath and judgment coming as I saw them. I could literally hear the hoof beats and all the sound effects as if in high definition; they were very, very close, almost here. As I saw and heard this, a dread and fear came over my spirit like nothing that can be explained or described. It took my breath away.

As I witnessed this I could hear the Spirit of God and I spoke as if a great weight was on me:

Judgment is coming, judgment is running.
Judgment is coming, judgment is running.
It shall be swift, it shall be sure.

I could feel it; I could hear it; I could see it. Then I looked down, and God showed me *there would be bloodshed and war in the streets. Blood would run in the streets of America.*

I was overwhelmed by what I experienced and could not speak for some time. Since this vision we have been praying and crying out to God for our nation and know we must share what God has been speaking and showing.

Scriptural Note: In relation to this chariot vision of white horses, it's interesting to note that Zechariah 6:1–8 speaks of chariots coming out from God's presence and running to the earth. The prophet Zechariah describes the chariot with white horses as going west. And as we all know, American is part of what is called the "Western world."

Since then

We have witnessed the world shaking economically, and a significant increase in history making natural disasters and earthquakes and the increase of global calamity, uprisings, and wars. These will continue to escalate.

2. Vision and Word: "America, America!"
December 5, 2007

Then about two weeks after the "Judgment Is Running" vision came the powerful and compassionate cry from the heart of God we call "America! America!" (shared in full in chapter 2). As we have seen, God was warning America that she was in great sin and that if the nation did not repent from her destructive ways and turn back to Him, three things would begin to happen.

Since then

Two of the things God spoke of began to unfold in the news within months; the third is yet to come *if* America continues on her current path. We will reveal more specific things about these warnings in the next chapter.

A prophetic link

If you read closely in the "America, America!" prophecy, you will see a link to the previous "Judgment Is Running" vision.

Judgment is coming, judgment is running.
Judgment is coming, judgment is running.
It shall be swift, it shall be sure.

—"Judgment is Running" vision and prophecy

If you will not heed My warnings, My judgments must come.
They will run, they will be swift and sure indeed.
They shall be swift, they shall be sure; who can endure.

—"America, America!" prophecy

Both these prophetic messages were just a couple of weeks apart and linked.

3. Word: "Shifting Economies" (Global)
December 13, 2007, through Cindy deVille

Then eight days later, December 13, while in prayer came a word called "Shifting Economies." God spoke of coming global economic shiftings and storms, along with great market swings.

Economies, they will shift and they will turn,
One day, one way; another day, another way,
Shifting sands, shifting, shifting.

All that they have trusted in, it shall shift, it shall spin
Till no one knows the way.
To all the experts they will turn, and nothing will be learned.

For I will shift and I will turn [the economies].
Like a drunkard it will be unstable, unsettled, uncertain.
All things shall seem to come undone,
Till the whole world knows I AM the only One.

God then went on to say some very encouraging things He would do for and through His people (those close to Him) in the midst of the economic storm. Also He said that a shift was coming as He lifts His people up (You can see how to access the full the word "Shifting Economies" in appendix F.)

Since then
We saw this begin on September 29, 2008, with a record stock market drop followed by numerous wild market swings, as described in this prophecy.[1] This has all resulted in global economic shifting and shaking that continues today.

4. Days of Wonder and Days of Dread...Ahead

This final word provides more global context for the days ahead, including our nation, as we highlighted in the "Big Picture" section of the prologue of this book. We believe are entering a turning point in history and it will be unlike anything seen before. The signs are evident in the world and in the heavens (such as the current and significant sequence of the "four blood moons" on Jewish seasonal feast days in 2014–2015). Everything is building and shifting (including "Shifting Economies") into a new day and drawing ever closer to Christ's glorious return.

Days of Wonder and Days of Dread

October 2009 prophecy through Cindy deVille

Days of wonder and days of dread,
These are the days that lie ahead.
Great and grave things will be happening,
All at the same time—intertwined.

Great and grave things,
Great and mighty shakings,
Even Great Awakenings.
Great things in My church,
Grave things in the earth.
All in line, with the seasons and the time.

(Relating to the four blood moons?)

Great things in the church,
Grave things in the earth.

Earthquakes and floods, famines and wars;
So much more than you've seen before.
Famines, famines in the land.

Grave things in the earth.
But know that I'm preparing My church.
Preparing My bride, to rise up and be a light,
To rise up in great darkness and night.
She will arise, she will rise.

Great things, Grave things, will be happening,
All at the same time—intertwined.

Glory, judgment, and wrath.
Glory, judgment, and wrath.
Glory, judgment, and wrath.
For My Word shall come to pass.
It shall come to pass.
For we are in the last, in the very last.
In the very last times.

You'll see My plans unfold.
Then you'll see the doors close.
The end of time,
My church will shine!

Scriptural Note: This word reminds us of Isaiah 60.

Arise, shine; For your light has come! And the glory of the LORD is risen upon you. For behold, the darkness shall cover the earth, And deep darkness the people; But the LORD will arise over you, And His glory will be seen upon you. The Gentiles shall come to your light, And kings to the brightness of your rising.

—ISAIAH 60:1–3

Yes, there will be days of dread ahead in the world; but for those who are fully devoted to Christ, they will arise and shine brightly bringing life and hope to a dark world. As in the days of Moses, there will be a separation between those close to God and those who are not (see Exodus 8:23; Psalm 91). While we believe this means God's people can be protected in the midst of judgment, it does not means we will be excluded from persecution. On the contrary, we are promised persecution and trails (see Matthew 24, 1 Peter 1:7 and 4:12, and 2 Timothy 3:12). And we are already seeing great persecution in other countries. But rejoice! For we are reminded that "the sufferings of this present time are not worthy to be compared with the glory which shall be revealed in us" (Rom. 8:18)!

GOD HAS A GLORIOUS PLAN!

In the midst of all this is God's plan for His church to arise glorious in the earth (Isa. 60; Eph. 5:27). The days ahead will be the most exciting, glorious times, as well as the most intense times in history! We will see the truth of God's Word come into play; and even the greatest skeptics will know He is the living God.

The key to timing of all this will be related to Jerusalem. God is saying, "Watch Jerusalem." This may relate to a coming war against Israel and attacks upon Jerusalem or when nations try to divide Jerusalem, God's holy city; but they will pay for doing so.

Four blood moons note

There has been much talk of the four blood moons (2014–2015 on Jewish feast days), which are very significant. Genesis 1:14 tells God placed the lights in the sky for appointed times and seasons. Joel 2:30 also declared there would be signs in the heavens towards the end of time before Christ's return.

We believe these four blood moons are a sign to the whole world of a transition into great change—we are entering a new day. To be clear, we do not believe these four blood moons mean the Lord is coming back at this time but rather it is a sign of His near coming and the shift into a new end-time phase. Both intense and glorious days are ahead (Isa. 60:1–3).

In the midst of all this we believe God has a plan for America, which is why He is in the process of getting her attention and back on the right path. If America doesn't respond in time, things could get very, very difficult for our nation. How hard could it get? We share next what we believe God has said is coming if America does *not* change her self-destructive course quickly.

11
WHAT'S COMING NEXT, IF . . . ?

*If the watchman sees the sword coming and does not
blow the trumpet to warn the people and the sword comes
and takes someone's life . . . because of their sin . . . I will
hold the watchman accountable for their blood.*
—Ezekiel 33:6, niv

THIS IS THE most sobering chapter in the book. We reveal in this chapter
some details of the things we are accountable to make known. We shared in
chapter 1, that God instructed us:

Do not water it down, speak plainly.
They need to know what's coming if they do not heed My warnings.

We shared the state of America and the church to give clear understanding
why these things are coming. Then we shared *how* God deals with nations and
the biblical pattern (three main ways) God gets a nation's attention. These help
set up this very important three-part chapter.

Our goal in this chapter is to help everyone know and understand:

1. God Is Speaking to America!

Always keep in mind that God speaks first through His written Word and
then through His servants. But, if we harden our hearts in rebellion and refuse
to listen, He will then speak through our circumstances and most often progressively to get our attention.

We believe showing what God has said and then the specifics of what has
unfolded in our nation's news since then will give great credibility to the fact
that God really is speaking to America today. When God spoke through the
prophet Ezekiel, He said over fifty times: "So you will know I am the Lord."
God wants everyone to know He is the living God and is speaking to America
and the nations and His church.

Our hope, then, is that the church and America will heed God's warnings
and quickly respond so we can avert (or at least mitigate) terrible judgment and
destruction.

2. God Is Serious!

This cannot be overstated. In this chapter you will see why this is a very critical and even dangerous time for America. If the church and America do not
take this seriously and respond to God's warnings, what is coming is beyond
anything America has seen before. Again, God is well able to bring a nation to

its knees, just as He did with Egypt. The time will come when everyone will know God is getting our nation's full attention.

3. This Is Urgent!

We are sounding an alarm to help awaken both the church and the nation to change course before it's too late. These are not just empty words, this is very real—a nation is at stake, millions of lives and souls are at stake. And one way or another everyone will be affected—everyone. We pray it will stir you to hear God's Answer and act upon it quickly!

We hope everyone will understand the urgency of the hour, be motivated to listen carefully, and respond in obedience—following God's Answer and instructions in the second half of this book. For God's Answer can change everything for the good!

Important Note: Above all God desires to bring salvation and a Great Awakening to our nation, not judgment and destruction. As a ministry, we have spent much time in prayer for our nation. However, we need to make it clear that the things we are about to share will come if America does not change course. This is why we have poured our lives, sweat, tears, and resources into writing this book and getting this critical message out to you and the nation.

"Prophesy in Part" Note: As we share these prophecies, it's important for us to remember that scripture tells us that "we know in part and we prophesy in part" (1 Cor. 13:9). We are sharing with you what we believe God has revealed to us as we have prayed for our nation. We do not have the full picture and do not know all the details or exact timing; but we believe much can be averted, if God's people do as He instructs (God's Answer), and America turns back to God.

WHAT IS COMING NEXT, IF... IN THREE PARTS

The following is to alert you to what is on the horizon if our nation proceeds down the current path of great sin and destruction. We share these things with a heart of heaviness and brokenness as we continue to intercede for our nation.

WHAT'S NEXT 1: WEALTH AND ECONOMY

America, known as the financial capital of the world, has long been considered the wealthiest and most powerful nation in history. However, America is now feeling the effects of rejecting God and His ways, along with the weight of great greed, sin, and corruption. God who made her great is in the process of shaking America's financial foundations to the core in order to get her attention.

What God said:

December 5, 2007, in the "America, America!" prophecy (see chapter 2):

> For you must turn and repent,
> Or I shall take your glory and your wealth from you
> And you shall no longer be great.

For in My hands America, I hold your fate.
For I can cause your markets to fall in a day.
All that you trust in will dissipate.

What has happened since then:

Nine months later on September 29, 2008, the stock market dropped a record 777 points, the biggest single drop ever. It is an interesting number, 777; is that a coincidence?[1] With God there are no coincidences. News headlines declared that this was the biggest financial crisis since the Great Depression that began in 1929. Our economy is reaping the fruits of greed that have been sown. But also, on one level it was a warning to America while on another level it began the previous "Shifting Economies" prophecy—a global economic storm, shifting, and shaking for God's plans and purposes.

Related news

+ Decline Began December 2007: Official news reports declared the 2008 recession actually began in December 2007, the same month the "America! America!" prophecy came.[2]

+ Typical Household, Now Worth a Third Less: Decline of households' net worth also started in December 2007.[3]

+ Americans wealth plummet 40 percent since 2007.[4]

+ Record 20 Percent of Households on Food Stamps: A dramatic increase from 15 million households in 2009.[5]

+ If America continues down her current path and refuses to respond to God's compassionate cry and warnings (see "America, America!" chapter 2), then we will see those warnings carried out.

THE ECONOMY: WHAT IS COMING NEXT?

What is going to happen with the economy of America? The economy may have some positive signs here and there, with one of those being the stock market over 17,000—an all time high (at the time of the writing). But God has said it's all "smoke and mirrors" and that there have been many fluctuations, caused by man's manipulations, all to create a sense of peace and security because they don't want America to panic. It is all an illusion! In reality—America's economy is teetering on the edge of a financial cliff. (**Note:** you can access the "Smoke and Mirrors" word in appendix F)

As with 9/11, the record 777 market drop of September 2008 that shook everything up was in one sense a judgment, but it was also a warning of much greater judgment coming if we do not change course.

Economic Collapse

So far, God has been extremely merciful and He has held things back from totally unraveling—so far. We believe it is the prayers of the saints that have extended God's mercy to allow time for national repentance. But time is running out!

We believe God has said the economy will not truly recover until America turns back to Him. If America turns back to God, then we will see peace, prosperity, and security restored to our nation again. But if America refuses to hear God's cry, then, just as He said in the "America, America!" prophecy, we will see:

+ America's wealth taken away and no longer great

+ The markets fall in a day

+ All America trusts in (great wealth and power) will dissipate

We believe this means a very serious economic collapse, including the stock market falling significantly, possibly more than once. We should all be reminded everything can change in one day.

Again, will America have to lose everything and end up in the pig pen like the prodigal before she comes to her senses and returns to God (her Founder) and His ways? We hope it doesn't have to get to that point!

What's Next 2: Natural Disasters

There have been major natural disasters in America before 2008 but not to the extent and frequency we have seen since then. We believe it is clear why, for God said:

> For I AM the God of all the earth.
> The wind and the sea at My command, they all obey Me!
> Natural disasters will be multiplied unto thee
> Because I have seen your sin and unrepentant heart.
> —"America, America!" prophecy, December 5, 2007

What has happened since then:

Since the "America, America!" 2007 prophecy, the news headlines continue to use words such as *historic, unprecedented, extraordinary,* and *record breaking* weather and natural disasters. Even by June 30, 2008, America experienced the highest mid-year total of natural disasters ever for our nation at that time.[9]

Our intention is not to provide a complete list of all the natural disasters in America since early 2008, but instead to give you a sense of what has been happening so it is clear that God has done just as He said—to get our nation's attention.

Related news

The following are some related news samples just from 2008 after the God's prophetic warning and cry to America in December 2007.

2008 Headlines

Record Tornado Season

* January: "A rarity for January in the Midwest...over 70 torna-does were reported that day."[10]
* March: "Our Extraordinary Tornado Year: Early 2008 Has Set an Unprecedented Pace for Twisters."[11]
* October: "2008 tornado season could blow away records."[12]

Great Historic Flooding

* June: "Flooding Hits Historic 500-Year Levels in Iowa." "Historic" and "unprecedented" flooding in Iowa.[13]
* August: "Fay's 4th Florida Landfall One for the Record Books."[14] Great rain and flooding from Hurricane Fay hitting Florida repeatedly over seven days.

Unprecedented Lightning

* June: More than 840 wildfires sparked by an "unprecedented" lightning storm in California. "This is an unprecedented light-ning storm in California, that it lasted as long as it did, 5,000 to 6,000 lightning strikes."[15]

After a while it is so easy to go on with life and forget the magnitude and frequency of these things, so the following will help remind us all of what has been happening.

More related news headline from 2009–2015

The following are just *some* of the main ones from the last several years (not a complete list).

* 2009: California facing worst drought in modern history.[16]
* 2009: Unprecedented flooding forces evacuations, closes highways.[17]
* 2009: Kentucky ice storm called worst in history.[18]
* 2010: A 1000-year flood event in Tennessee.[19]
* 2011: Largest Tornado outbreak ever recorded.[20]
* 2011: Magnitude-5.8 earthquake shakes Washington, DC.[21]
* 2011: Hurricane Irene brought epic floods to 100 year levels.[22]
* 2011: "Obama Has Declared Record-Breaking 89 Disasters."[23]
* 2012: Half of the nation's counties considered disaster areas (due to the massive drought across much of America).[24]

+ 2012: Record breaking superstorm Hurricane Sandy hits New York.[25]

+ 2013: 100-year flood hits twice in three years.[26]

+ 2013: Monster EF5 tornado hits Moore, Oklahoma.[27]

+ 2014: "Historic" and "catastrophic" winter storm.[28]

+ 2014: "Storm of Historic Proportions' Dumps 13 Inches of Rain."[29]

+ 2015: "It's Historic . . . It's Biblical . . . I think we're in uncharted territory" series of storms hits New England.[30]

Do we see a pattern here? The fact is since early 2008 America has witnessed "multiple" record and historic natural disasters and extreme weather, just as God said in 2007.

Some will contend this is because of "climate change" (or global warming), but God has also spoken specifically about certain things coming to get our nation's attention (remember chapter 9). These include deadly storms and strong winds since 2011.

Deadly storms and strong winds

We do not take delight in sharing all these with you, but we are accountable to God to let these be known because God wants America to know that He is speaking. He is speaking through His Word, His servants, and also our natural circumstances (see chapters 8 and 9).

In June 2010 and March 2011, God spoke more about some specific kinds of natural warnings He would be *sending to get America's attention*. He said these would include:

+ Deadly storms hitting densely populated areas.

+ Greater storms and strong winds blowing across our land.

+ Strong winds coming from the sea—greater than ever before (such as great hurricanes)

Related news events confirmed these months later. Again we share these only so you know God is in the process of getting America's attention.

1. Deadly storms began to hit April and May of 2011. News reports were that what made these two historic storms systems so rare the "tornadoes took direct aim at populated areas."[31] Just as God had described.

2. Then in 2012 came the historic and record breaking superstorm Hurricane Sandy that came from the sea and took direct aim at the most populated area in the nation, New York City, just as God had been warning.[32]

3. Then in 2013 a monster EF5 tornado ripped through a highly populated part of Moore, Oklahoma.[33]

Important Timing Note: Over the past few years, the more severe natural disasters have been coming in waves, with some extended time (a lull) between each. Even the past two hurricane seasons have been fairly quiet. Again, we believe the prayers of many, along with great prayer events incorporating repentance, have been instrumental in extended God's mercy and grace to America, allowing time for repentance. But again, time is running out!

NATURAL DISASTERS: WHAT IS COMING NEXT?

If America stays on her current path of rebellion and great sin, natural disasters of all kinds will continue throughout the land—deadly storms, strong winds, floods, fires, and drought. This could include severe earthquakes, tsunamis, volcanoes, and even viruses, diseases, and more.

Again, although some may point to "climate change" (or global warming) as a cause for some disasters, we believe the time is coming when America will know it is the "hand of God" bringing these extraordinary natural disasters and weather as both warnings and judgment to get America's attention.

Also keep in mind, these increased natural disasters, including droughts, will continue to affect the economy, food supply and prices, and water supply, as previously described in Amos 4 (in "The Biblical Pattern: Three Ways," chapter 9).

God's perfect will

Please always remember God's heart. God's perfect will for America is *not* deadly storms, natural disasters, drought, calamity, economic collapse, and chaos. God wants to instead bring a Great Awakening and pour out His Spirit from shore to shore. But if God's people ignore *His answer* for America or America's leaders stiffen their necks and refuse to respond to God's cry, we will instead see these natural disasters continue to increase across our land.

So, we have looked at what God is saying about the economy and natural disasters, now we see exactly what God is saying about the most serious things coming if America stays on the current path of moral degradation leading to great judgment and destruction.

WHAT'S NEXT 3: ENEMY ATTACKS AND WAR

While an economic crash and catastrophic natural disasters could cripple America, the most serious and devastating would be what we share in this final part regarding God's warnings of coming enemy attacks and war if both the church and America do not heed His cry.

What God said December 5, 2007, in the "America, America!" prophecy

Enemies, enemies, enemies, *they all want in!*
America, America! You are filled with sin....

So now, if you do not repent, I will leave as you have asked.
My protection shall leave you,
My goodness and mercy shall leave...
You shall be left to your own ways.
The *enemies will come in*
And the devastation and destruction will begin.

Psalm 127:1 says, "Unless the LORD guards the city, The watchman stays awake in vain."

What has happened so far:

Since 9/11 multiple attempts have been exposed in time to avert them. But while writing this book news came of a new attack; this time it was 9/11/2012 and overseas upon our embassy in Benghazi, Libya. Of course, the fact this occurred on "9/11" was not a coincidence. Then months later came another attack, another warning.

The 2013 Boston terrorist bombing attack

On April 15, 2013, the horrific news flash of the Boston Marathon terrorist bombing with deaths, serious injuries, chaos and confusion in our streets, and an entire city being put in lockdown for several days.[34]

Now imagine a 9/11 or these kind of terrorist bombings occurring regularly at different cities all over the nation! The reality is this; like 9/11, the *Boston terrorist bombing* was just a sign, a warning, a taste of what is coming if America continues down her current path without God—rejecting God and His ways, which is also a rejection His goodness and His protection.

Update: Related news

August 20, 2014—ISIS plans to blow up major city
As we were finishing this book related news also came from ranking member of the Senate Armed Services Committee, Senator Inhofe, warning of a potential terrorist attacks on a U.S. city: "We're in the most dangerous position we've ever been in as a nation...They're rapidly developing a method of blowing up a major U.S. city and people just can't believe that's happening."[35]

This news is not only confirming the path of destruction America is on, but just as God warned, it's all leading to...

ENEMY ATTACKS AND WAR: WHAT IS COMING NEXT?

God warned America to turn away from her great sin otherwise...

America, America, you are filled with sin.
Turn, turn, turn or you will see your *cities burn.*
There shall be *bloodshed and war in your streets.*

Why war and blood in the streets?

Cities burning and bloodshed and war in the streets of America? Why so severe? Besides much sin, one of the major reasons God is warning of these is because God will not be mocked, "for whatever a man sows, that will he also reap" (Gal. 6:7). And in light of this, what is one the thing America has been sowing over 3,000 times day for over forty years now? It's the bloodshed of over fifty-five million innocent babies crying out for justice! This is why God said, and it is well worth repeating:

> For the cries of the unborn are calling out to Me.
> The *blood you have shed is knee deep.*
> Turn, turn or you will see *blood run in your streets.*
> Turn Roe vs Wade or *for all these lives you will surely pay.*
> For as you have *sown* much death, so shall you *reap.*
> Judgment is waiting, judgment is waiting,
> While you keep on debating.
>
> —"AMERICA, AMERICA!" PROPHECY, 2007

Update: Related news

August 18, 2014

Once again as we were working to finish this book, additional news broke related to why God is warning America about the "flood of blood" she has shed and what our nation will *reap* if things do not change. A recent threat came from terrorist group ISIS to America: "We will drown all of you in blood"[36]

The Pentagon does not see this as an empty or idle threat, and neither should we! Defense Secretary Chuck Hagel made this alarming statement about ISIS and their Islamic State: "They are beyond just a terrorist group. They marry ideology, a sophistication of…military prowess. They are tremendously well-funded. This is beyond anything we've seen."[37]

Could it be, as God said, He is *preparing* America's enemies to attack as He did with Israel's enemies? Just as the prophet Jeremiah warned:

> This is what the LORD says: Look! I am preparing a disaster for you and devising a plan against you. So turn from your evil ways, each one of you, and reform your ways and your actions.
>
> —JEREMIAH 18:11, NIV, EMPHASIS ADDED

Related prophetic update

Coming New York Attack

August 19, 2014, during prayer, God gave us another serious word regarding bombs in certain locations going off in New York City and buildings crashing down.

Often as God has shared these types of things with us, He says, "Tell them they must turn back to Me or these are the things they will see." He continues to tell us to warn the nation and to tell them. This is not an easy thing for us to do, as most people mock these types of warnings. Nevertheless, we must be faithful to speak when He says to speak as they must be clearly warned.

If necessary, God will allow another significant enemy attack upon a major city like New York to send shockwaves to the rest of the nation so they will listen to His cry. Interestingly the news report we shared earlier about ISIS planning to blow up a major American city actually came out August 20, 2014—the day *after* this "New York" prophecy. Is that a coincidence?

We must wake up and take this very seriously! There is a day of reckoning, and if America does not change her course we will see devastating consequences. How serious could it get? The following is a glimpse:

THREE PICTURES OF WHAT'S COMING, IF...

Now we enter the most severe and sobering part of the book.

Please Note: Before we share these we want you to understand that we do not take these lightly. It is with a great weight of responsibility, concern, and knowing we stand accountable before God to share what we believe He has revealed to us and what's coming (Ezek. 33:1–11). We realize some may reject and even mock what is being said. We earnestly pray America will never have to see these things.

The following is prophetic insight into what the greater judgments of God upon America will look like, if America does *not* heed His cry and turn back to him in time. Besides an economic collapse and greater natural disasters across America, will also see enemy attacks and war from shore to shore. Here are three prophetic pictures of what this will look like and why.

1. BIN LADEN—THE SEED FOR MANY

There was great celebration of Bin Laden being killed on May 2, 2011. But nine days later during prayer God spoke of Bin Laden and said:

"Bin Laden, Bin Laden, down trodden,
 Now cast into the sea, your enemy.
 But from him...within...your gates...enemies will arise.

"For you have cast one into the sea,
 But from him—many shall be.
 For I shall use your enemies," says the Lord.
"America, I shall use your enemies,
 Just as I did with Israel, to bring My judgments upon you.
 I shall raise up your enemies against you.
 I will use them just as I have throughout history
 To bring My judgments, and to bring this nation to its knees."

(You can access the full word in appendix F, "Bin Laden, Enemies Arise, and Word to Leaders," May 11, 2011.)

As we can see, God is saying many terrorist cells will rise from within America. Great fear will come upon this land. Many will be shaken—as with 9/11 the enemies shall come and they shall strike, but not just once.

This also aligns with the next two things we will share, to show just how serious things can get if America does not turn back to God quickly!

2. Three Enemies—Prepare For War!

Right now there is a growing split, a great divide inside our nation on many things; and this will lead to possible riots, civil unrest, maybe even civil war. But this would be just a prelude to what is to come. Remember how in the 2007 "America, America!" prophecy, God said,

> Enemies, enemies, enemies, they all want in!
> America, America! You are filled with sin.

Notice God said "enemies" three times. It was not until later in 2008 when we better understood why. He then revealed that *three different enemies* would be attacking America all at the same time from coast to coast.

Prophetic Vision and Word

Details of this revelation came in October 2008 during an intense time of prayer, another prophetic vision regarding war! God said that the economy would not be number one in the news anymore; it will instead be about war. God then said:

> They will call it a holy war
> And they will declare it from shore to shore.

He was speaking about terrorists declaring a holy war against America and cells rising up throughout the land. This directly relates to the prior "Bin Laden—the Seed for Many" word. We believe God then showed us that three enemies would attack:

1. Terrorist cells rising up from within and across our nation calling it a "holy war"
2. Attacking on the East Coast was Russia.
3. Attacking on the West Coast was an oriental looking country with olive (greenish brown) looking uniforms (possibly North Korea).

All three of these would lead to America being attacked on all fronts. God said they already have the plans in place and are waiting for the right opportunity. We shared all this October 5, 2010, on one of our ENews YouTube videos.[38]

Then in late 2012 God gave more details—some specifics which included subs, tanks, and missiles, also when Russia and Korea think the right time to attack will be.

Then the Lord said,

> But, I will help and protect you, if you turn to Me.
> I will turn back your enemies.
> But, if you persist in your lust and greed,
> In your abominations before Me,
> Then I will leave and the enemies will not retreat
> And their strikes will go deep.

Notice, God is pointing out key biblical and moral issues we addressed regarding the state of America (see chapter 5, "America—a Prodigal Nation").

Related Prophetic Timing Note: July 2008 during a time of prayer, God showed us America with her hands tied behind her back financially, with no way to escape. It seemed she was being driven to her knees; and in her weakened state, it was at that point her enemies wanted to attack. At that time America will have a decision to make: turn back to God or be left to her own ways and face devastation and destruction.

America's *only* hope will be turning back to God!

Update: Multiple confirmations

We can honestly say it was after the Lord revealed to us about the coming war, including the attacks/invasion from Russia, that we also heard of confirming words and visions from other servants of God. The two main ones were through the late great David Wilkerson and Henry Gruver.

We recently found out that David Wilkerson wrote in his prophetic 1985 book, *Set the Trumpet to Thy Mouth*, that there was coming a major attack from Russia upon America (New York and other major cities), and that the timing would be after America was greatly weakened by an economic collapse (as we just shared above in the related prophetic timing note).

> The great holocaust follows an economic collapse in America. The enemy will make its move when we are weak and helpless.[39]

We also heard of Henry Gruver's 1986 vision reporting he saw missiles coming out of many Russian submarines and hitting cities on the east coast.[40] He also saw missiles hitting the West Coast. Both the east and west coasts were attacked as we shared earlier.

These are just two of many confirmations out there. One other is a reported vision George Washington had in 1777 at Valley Forge of a coming Civil War (fulfilled about eighty years later); but he saw that the worst war would be far in the future with three enemies attacking/invading America at once (this also aligns with the "Three Enemies—Prepare For War!" section we shared earlier).

God in His great mercy has given America decades of clear warnings and time to repent. We pray she will come to her senses before these things happen!

3. OPENING THE DOOR TO WAR

Like pieces of a puzzle, this ties it all together. June 7, 2010, while in prayer, God gave more specifics regarding these enemy attacks and cells rising up across America. The following word came on the same day He warned of the coming "deadly storms" that began to hit the following spring, in 2011. You will see how this all ties into the "great sin" in America and in the church, previously mentioned in "The Gatekeepers," chapter 7, along with the Bin Laden word and the three enemy attacks.

God said that the door to war was opening and America will not be able to stop it from coming. Now, here are more details. Again, in this we see both the severity of God and the Fatherly aspect of God to awaken and bring us to our senses before destruction comes.

Opening the Door to War!
June 7, 2010, prophecy through Cindy deVille

"It is My hand that has held back the enemies from your land.
It has been My hand that has held them back.
But if you do not heed My voice, if you do not hear Me,
If My church does not hear Me,
If My church will not acknowledge Me,
If this land will not hear Me and acknowledge Me,
Then the enemies they will come in.
They will come ashore, they will come ashore, they will come ashore.
They already have the plans in place.
They await to come and disgrace America.

"You shall see cells rise up in your land,
You shall see war from shore to shore,
If I remove My hand of protection from you.
These are not things I desire to do," says the Spirit of God.

"The sin in your land is great, it is great.
The sin in My church, it is great.
Even many of those who lead
Those that feed My sheep, many are in gross sin.
They've opened the door, they've let it in.
Just as you see, as the political leaders of your land,

Much adultery, much sin, much perversion, much greed.
So these are in the lives of those who lead My sheep.
Many are trying to cover them up.
But I will come by My Spirit and expose,
So everyone knows," says the Spirit of God.

"For I am going to great lengths in these days,"
Says the Spirit of the Lord,
"To wake you up, to shake you up! To turn you back to Me,
To keep you from the destruction I see right before you.
If you continue to move in the path you have set,
In the ways you are going,
Destruction is imminent. Destruction will be.
There is no other way, but to turn back to Me,"
Says the Spirit of God.
"No other way!"

In all these we see why God warned in the "America, America!" prophecy:

Enemies, enemies, enemies, *they all want in!*
America, America! You are filled with sin....

So now, if you do not repent, I will leave as you have asked.
My protection shall leave you...
The enemies will come in and the devastation and destruction will begin.

THIS IS WHY!

This is one reason we have taken the time to clearly lay out what we believe God has been saying to America—so the church and America will know, and our nation's leaders will know, God *is* speaking and so you, God's leaders (the pulpits and pews) and America, will respond quickly to God's cry and answer, before greater judgment and destruction comes. *Now is the time to respond* before we see greater effects upon the economy, greater natural disasters, great calamity, greater civil unrest, and blood in our streets along with severe enemy attacks and war.

Sounding an alarm

We are doing our utmost to sound the alarm and communicate the severity of what we believe God has said. We have already seen negative effects on our economy and the natural disasters and deadly storms which God warned would come. But, the most devastating thing to come, if we do not hear His cry, is war and blood in our streets, and war from shore to shore.

Joel 2 is a biblical parallel for us right now of sounding the alarm to God's people and the nation warning of what's coming if the nation does not turn back to God in time.

Blow the ram's horn trumpet in Zion! Trumpet the alarm on my holy mountain! Shake the country up! God's Judgment's on its way—the Day's almost here!

—Joel 2:1, The Message

When God is warning a nation, He will make it clear by speaking what He is saying to many of His people. Thankfully, there are others also sounding an alarm. Again, since God's words to us came, we have also heard of many others having dreams, visions, and more of enemy attacks and war coming to America. This should be a red flag to the church that something is up.

Related warnings from Larry Stockstill and James Robison

In Larry Stockstill's book *The Remnant* (2008) he wrote:

With all of the public exposure of so many ministries, I am now more convinced than ever that God's judgment is imminent upon our nation. Early last year, James Robison from Dallas contacted me and encouraged me to read his article "Warning to America" He senses that we as a nation are moving toward either *humility or humiliation*. Our secret sins have brought us to a moment where God is ready to shake our nation in radical ways. James proposes that if we do not humble ourselves and repent, we could become a third-world nation living without electricity or running water.[41]

Then Larry and James both agreed that "the pastors of America are the key to stopping an awful judgment that is looming on the horizon of our great nation."[42]

Larry Stockstill's dream of enemy attacks upon America

In relation to this we also came across an article Pastor Larry Stockstill had done with *Charisma* in February 2008. He had a disturbing dream. He saw military trucks and armored vehicles getting in formation for a surprise strike on an American city. He felt alarmed, but when he tried to warn a pastor in his dream, the man ignored him. "I knew in my dream that a siege was going to happen the next day," Stockstill says. "The enemy was being positioned. But no one would listen to me."[43] He also said:

I believe we are facing a window of opportunity for repentance…Unless the pastors wake up to avert judgment, there will be judgment on America. If we don't respond we are going to lose this nation.[44]

Again, God is so rich in mercy that when there are delays people look at these kinds of prophetic dreams, visions, or words and dismiss and even mock them. But God's delays do not mean everything is OK; they can simply mean He is extended His mercy to allow time for repentance before destruction comes.

For those who cry out for mercy

Before or in the midst of these great judgments, some of God's people will cry out for "mercy." Scripture clearly tells us God is rich in mercy (Eph. 2:4) and He delights in mercy (Mic. 7:18). But He is saying that there are certain things that must be done because of His justice and certain things He must do to get our nation's attention so America will listen (Ps. 97:2).

As previously stated, only genuine repentance will lead to mercy. Once America genuinely repents and turns back to God, *only then* will mercy come. It has been proven over and over throughout history, when there is sincere national repentance, God responded.

> King Hezekiah and the people...they turned from their sins [repented first] and worshiped the LORD. They begged him for mercy. Then the LORD changed his mind about the terrible disaster he had pronounced against them.
>
> —JEREMIAH 26:19, NLT

Are We Mocking God?

Sadly, there are many in our culture in America, even in our churches, that are mocking God and saying, "No, God is not going to do this; it's just like before, were all going to get through this, everything will be fine." But *no!* This is *not* as before! This is not as before when God would send His messengers and speak and He would extend His mercy, and extend His mercy, and extend His mercy—this is not as before! His progressive warnings have been made known and greater judgment is standing right at the door. It's right at the door!

Sadly, many in our culture are self-deceived and convinced that God wouldn't do such a thing. But just as when Noah and Jeremiah *warned* the people *in their day* of great judgment coming—most everyone mocked them and said it'd never happen. But it did. And today God in His mercy is warning, sending progressive warnings to get America's attention; but it seems many are mocking and saying "it will never happen," even though it's already begun!

The day is coming when it will be evident to all that God's is speaking and divine judgment is coming upon America. Right now, we all have a decision to make—which path America will take.

12

AMERICA HAS A DECISION TO MAKE!

Today I have given you the choice.
—DEUTERONOMY 30:19, NLT

IT IS EVIDENT; the shadow of judgment is not only upon America but has begun to be progressively manifest in several ways.

1. Reaping What Has Been Sown

America is reaping much of what she has sown (spiritual, morally, socially, economically, etc.). We must remember, scripture clearly warns us not to be deceived, that God is not mocked, for whatever we sow we will reap (Gal. 6:7). America has been sowing seeds of great sin. It is just a matter of time before she reaps the dreaded harvest and fruit of her sinful ways.

2. The Hand of God

America has experienced God's progressive warnings and judgment to a certain level (economy, natural disasters, and some terrorist attacks, as previously highlighted).

3. What's Coming Next, If...

Greater warnings and severe judgments are coming if America stays on her current path (see previous chapter).

One reason we are writing this book is because we believe it is *not* too late to change our course and stop certain destruction from coming! *If the church and America will respond to God's cry and answer we reveal in this book*, we will see our nation turn from the path of destruction to the path of life and restoration.

TWO PATHS—TWO EAGLES

It has been said a picture is worth a thousand words. The two paths before us as a nation remind us of a dream/vision Cindy had in 1988 of two eagles. The dream/vision was of two separate portraits of an eagle positioned on what represented the front of the White House or Capital building. These portraits communicate consequences of choices we will make as a nation. (**Note:** These are very rough renditions from 1988, created by Darrel as Cindy describes what she saw.)

"America, America"

America has a Decision to Make
Which Path She Will Take
Images from 1988
©2008, Shekinah Today Ministries

Shekinah
TODAY

EAGLE 1

We have seen America's current course is in fact leading to…

PATH 1: JUDGMENT AND DESTRUCTION (AMERICA'S CURRENT PATH)

This will include:

+ God removing His goodness and protection
+ Greater natural disasters and storms
+ Economic collapse
+ Greater civil unrest, riots, and blood in the streets
+ Enemy attacks and war upon America
+ Greater Christian persecution
+ Increasing loss of liberties
+ The nation's destruction and demise

Imagine for a moment: War and bloodshed in our streets and invasion upon our shores; cities devastated; terror and tanks raging through our cities; bombs and sirens are going off while chaos and confusion seem to be everywhere. The banks and ATMs have been overrun. Electricity, gas, and other basic necessities such as clean water and food are scarce. And, the police and emergency response are too busy to come to your aid or protect you. Although this is horrifying for us as Americans even to consider, this is the path America is on. We must take this very seriously!

Now, please take a moment and ask yourself these two sobering questions:

+ Is Path 1 what I want to see in America?
+ Is this the legacy, the country I will leave for my children and my grandchildren?

We believe God can cause things (from Path 1) to culminate until America has nowhere to look but up to Him.

Eagle 2

Path 2: Repentance and Restoration (God's Path of Life)

Following God's Answer in the second half of this book will result in:

+ A Great Awakening all across America
+ Multitudes come to Christ and prodigals return
+ America on her knees turning back to God
+ A great cleansing in the land
+ God's healing, protection, and blessing returns
+ Economy fully restored
+ Great leadership
+ Opportunity for a great reformation
+ Restoration of the godly foundations

When America turns back to God then "Old Glory" will see a New Glory! (Many refer to the U.S. flag as "Old Glory.")

God's desire is repentance and restoration, not destruction!

The redeeming message from God's prophets of old and even the New Testament message of the Cross was: return to the Lord and He will forgive, restore, bless, and bring times of refreshing.

> Repent therefore, and turn back, that your sins may be blotted out, that times of refreshing may come from the presence of the Lord.
> —Acts 3:19–20, esv

There is great hope for America *if* we will listen, turn back to God, and do things His way. But the choice must be made. So we see the two paths laid before us as a nation—judgment and destruction or life and restoration. America has a decision to make, which path will she take? Until America does turn back, Path 1 will continue to build.

UNTIL AMERICA TURNS BACK...

Just two days before superstorm Sandy hit and devastated the Northeast Coast, a prophecy came that has been progressively occurring in the news since then. Again, this not considered "politically correct" but rather "biblically correct."

President Obama Note: First, please know this is not about race or political agendas; it's about serious moral and biblical issues destroying our nation. Second, please understand we pray for our president and we do not want to dishonor him in anyway. However, we cannot edit what we strongly believe is the word of the Lord because of the fear of man or in an attempt to be politically correct. Please pray for our president to hear God's cry, for he will stand before God and give an account before the Ruler and Judge of the universe for how he has ruled this nation.

Note: The original "America, America!" prophecy came in 2007 during George Bush's presidency. This shows we do not have a personal agenda against President Obama or any political leader. Rather it's about the God-rejecting, self-destructive path our nation and many of our leaders have chosen.

To America: Until You Bow Your Knee
October 27, 2012, through Cindy deVille

> During prayer I sensed a real heaviness as I prayed and wept for our nation. Then the Lord began to speak the following message which included our current president. As before, this is from a biblical standpoint, not a political one. During prayer the Lord said:
>
> Until America bows her knee in repentance and humility
> There will be peace no more.
> There will be no peace in the streets, no peace on your shores,
> But confusion and turmoil, more and more.

Note: We have seen this unfolding in the news since then—superstorm Sandy, public shootings (such as Sandy Hook Elementary), stabbings, bombings, political scandals, lawlessness, confusion and turmoil, great natural disasters, and extreme weather, etc. And as we were finishing this book, news of the civil riots in Ferguson, Missouri, began. All these things will continue to arise until America responds to God's cry.

Then God continued with *reasons why:*

> "As a nation you must turn from your perversion and greed.
> You continue to murder the infant that has no voice to speak.
> But, I hear their voices and I hear their cries.
> I hear them crying out day and night.
> Still you fight for your rights to kill and abort.
> I will have it no more," says the Lord.
> "I will have it no more.

"I Am the God and Judge of all the earth.
America, I am judging you.
You think I do not see your wicked and evil deeds.
I see, I see and you will soon have to answer to Me.

You fight, you fight for your gay rights.
You call them civil, but they are perverse before Me
And they will be your undoing!

You fight for that which is an abomination to Me,
And your president, Obama, has taken the lead.
An Obama nation is destroying you and destroying the foundations
    you once knew.
As a nation you have become even more vile and unclean before Me.
This is what I see," says the Lord!

"It is the prayers of the saints and their cries for mercy
That have held My great judgment back.
But, if you persist in your ways,
I have no choice, but to make you pay.
I am a just Judge and I will bring justice to you,
So I ask you now, what will you do?"

God's Word Is Clear

He is the just judge of the whole earth (Ps. 89:14). He still brings judgment today (2 Pet. 2:4–6). He is great in love and mercy but will not let sin go unpunished (Num. 14:18). He will answer great sin, injustice, and wickedness (Ezek. 7:3–9, 27). He can use economic woes, drought, extreme weather, and enemies to get a nation's attention or to punish wickedness (see 2 Chronicles 7:13; Job 37:11–13; Judges 2:14). These are just a few of many scriptures declaring these truths.

> Judgment shall return unto righteousness: and all the upright in heart shall follow it.
>
> —PSALM 94:15, KJV

God's judgments are coming to return our nation unto righteousness, one way or another! Our earnest prayer is America will heed God's cry and humbly turn back to Him before terrible judgment and destruction comes.

REALITY CHECK

In reality, how could this all play out? Will America respond to God's cry in time? Will we see great judgment or will we see instead a great outpouring of God's Spirit across this nation? We believe it will be both. The truth is, America is already under the judgment of God to a degree; but (at the time of this writing) much greater levels of judgment are coming, as the previous chapter has shown.

And, how quickly America truly turns back to God will determine how soon greater judgment is averted (or at least mitigated). Therefore, we may see some greater judgments come before we see the Great Awakening come. Again, how quickly we all respond to God's cry will determine much.

The reality is the turning back of America to God will be a process.

1. The American Church First

First it will take *you*—God's leaders and people—responding to and implementing God's Answer. How quickly you respond will determine how quickly or how strong the Great Awakening comes to bring America to her knees and back to God.

2. Then It's America's Leaders' Turn

Once the pulpits and churches of America respond to God's Answer, we believe it will *prepare the way* for our president and nation's leaders in Washington, DC, to heed God's voice and officially turn our nation back to God and His ways (see "A Call to America's Leaders," chapter 26, for more details including a national "new declaration").

The good news is we believe America *will* fall to her knees, turn back to God, and see a Great Awakening (Path 2). The bad news is, we (America) may have to first go through great judgment, calamity, chaos, and loss (current Path 1) and be greatly humbled before we awaken and come to our senses—like the prodigal in the pig pen.

The Reality Is...

Until America turns back to God, our nation will have to go through a very grueling time because of her great sin and pride. God will cause America to come to a place where there will be no way out, and she must cry out and abandon herself to Him.

Once America comes to her senses and truly turns back to God, then like the prodigal's father, He will run to her aid and begin to restore our nation.

America End-Time Note: Currently America has many parallels to Babylon spoken of in the Bible (Rev. 18); and for that reason (and others) many have come to the conclusion America will be destroyed and become insignificant in the end-time picture.

Personally, we believe God still has plans for America and that while great devastation and destruction may have to come before America turns back to God, it will result in *not the end* of America but rather a *new beginning!*

There are some reliable men of God we trust that also believe this: that America will go through a very hard time—like a crucible of purging and cleansing—but that a new America will rise from the ashes, like the mythical Phoenix (also see eagle 2) because God's has a destiny for this nation (end-time plans and purposes)![1]

The Other Reality

A humbling and more like Pharaoh and Egypt

Most of America's leaders may initially scoff and resist calls to turn back to God. So it may take a process similar to how God humbled once powerful Egypt and Pharaoh in Moses' day. It may take another enemy strike on a major city (such New York) to get America's attention before our nation and our leaders will listen to what God is saying. We pray this is not the case; yet, God will do what is necessary to get our nation's attention.

+ There also are certain national leaders that have mocked God and His Word or hardened their hearts. And we believe God may use all of this to greatly humble them for everyone to see.

+ We may also see the judgment of God upon certain cities in America known for debauchery and decades of great sin.

Note: God's protection for His people

For those Christians in certain cities and states across America, please stay very close to God so you can hear His direction and warnings if it's time to go, just as in Lot's day (Gen. 19).

Katrina example

We personally know of a Christian family that God told them to leave New Orleans weeks before Katrina hit. They obeyed and were spared.

Historic opportunity

The choice is clear, we all have a decision to make—from God's house, to the White House, to every house in America—which path we will take. The truth is, a historic opportunity stands before all of us to dramatically to change everything.

How quickly God's leaders and people respond and implement God's Answer will determine how quickly and how much judgment is averted and how much the floodgates are opened to the greatest awakening ever seen. God's Answer can change everything!

PART II

THE SOLUTION

GOD'S ANSWER FOR AMERICA

THIS CHANGES EVERYTHING

W E HAVE SEEN the desperate state of both our nation and the American church. Then we have shown from a biblical perspective how God often warns and deals with nations in great sin. We revealed exactly what God has spoken to America, what has happened so far as a result, and the coming devastating consequences if we do not change course.

Next we set up God's Answer by identifying the root problem and issues that must be dealt with before we will see lasting change. Then we share of the positive and dramatic changes coming to the church, including a special message to God's pastors and leaders.

SECTION 1:

PREPARING FOR CHANGE

13

Going to the Root of the Problem

14

Prepare for Radical Change!

15

God's Letter to His Pastors and Leaders

13
GOING TO THE ROOT OF THE PROBLEM

If the foundations be destroyed, what can the righteous do?
—Psalm 11:3, kjv

IT IS EVIDENT, that like the *Titanic*, America is on a collision course; but how do we stop it? Up to this point it appears all efforts have been in vain. Is it even possible to change the destructive course of an entire nation? If so, where do we begin and what kind of power and force will it take? What is the answer to bring lasting change for the good?

Will new political leaders or party do it?
Will new or better legislation do it?
Will better judges or court decisions do it?

The Fruit vs the Root

We believe the first half of this book makes it clear; America's current political, legislative, economic, and social issues are not the problem, but are rather the fruit of a much deeper root problem. Right now just changing a law or putting a new political party or person in place will be like putting a Band-Aid on a deeply rooted cancer. If we truly want to see real and lasting change, then we must first deal with the root of the problem—the heart and soul of the nation.

THE HEART AND SOUL OF A NATION

Overall, the fruit we are seeing throughout America is a reflection of the inward spiritual and moral condition of the people, like a cancer spreading throughout our nation. Real change that lasts begins in the hearts and souls of our nation. Our Lord Jesus Christ understood this truth and set the example of exactly how to bring real and lasting change.

Biblical Example: Jesus went to the heart of the problem

In the Gospels and the Book of Revelation, we see that Jesus always went straight to the heart and root of a problem or issue. A great example of this is how Christ began setting up His kingdom. He didn't come first to overthrow, reform, and set up His physical kingdom; but His first priority was to change and transform the hearts and souls of the people who would ultimately transform their outward lives and actions.

Jesus also began to teach the kingdom mindset we should have. In fact, it has been said that the kingdom of God is a revolution—a revolution of the heart.

This is exactly the kind of revolution America needs now, a revolution of the heart! Once deep-rooted change comes, then new fruit will naturally come.

Note: God's heart and rescue plan

God's Answer includes a rescue plan to rescue the souls of our nation. Right now many are focused on the political, economic, and legislative direction of our nation. These are important and God does care about the foundations, who rules, and our legislation. However, what is first and foremost on God's heart is the soul(s) of our nation. His heart's cry is for the multitude of souls racing towards eternity, for those deceived, in bondage, and the prodigals that need to come home. God's heart aches for these; yet do we? This must be a primary focus while not neglecting the other.

Changing the root: What is it going to take?

If we want to truly bring lasting change, then we must do as Jesus did—go straight to the root of the problem, the hearts and souls of our nation. For if the hearts and souls of America change, their actions will change, their ways will change, their fruit will change; then we will see a nation change. True change needs to begin from the inside out. But how can this happen? What must take place to bring about such a massive change?

The truth is—the depth of change America needs will take a divine move of God! Change will come when souls are so shaken under the convicting power of the Holy Spirit that their eyes are opened to see how great their sin, how great God's love, and how great their need is for Christ and His ways. It's going to take this happening on a scale that has never been seen before—a Great Awakening as we described previously in chapter 3.

Yes, only a Great Awakening, changing souls and hearts towards God, followed by a great reformation will *then* bring the lasting cultural and political change our nation desperately needs. For the truth is this: We can fight day and night to change laws and legislation, but only God can change the heart and soul of a nation.

God's change agent—the body of Christ—is the vessel to bring this Great Awakening and a great reformation. Many have been praying and working for it, but is there something that has held it back and us back?

WHAT HAS HELD US BACK?

The soul-changing move of God our nation so desperately needs will only come when God's leaders and people cooperate with Him. But exactly how? Many have been praying according to 2 Chronicles 7:14.

> If My people who are called by My name will humble themselves, and pray and seek My face, and turn from their wicked ways, then I will hear from heaven, and will forgive their sin and heal their land.
> —2 CHRONICLES 7:14

But why have things not really changed yet? Is God asking for something more? What has held us back?

Why Have We Not Seen a Great Reformation?

For years, many in the church have been praying for a Great Awakening and speaking of the need for a great reformation in every sphere that influences our society. These are known as the seven mountains: religion, family, education, government, business and finance, media, and arts and entertainment. And as salt and light we should be greatly influencing all these areas.

However, in spite of many great efforts and some positive results, overall it seems the American church has instead become more influenced and conformed to the culture and things in our nation continue to spiral downward. Why? We believe the following vision provides revealing insight as to exactly what has kept God's people from advancing into the promised land and truly impacting our nation in every area of society (the seven mountains).

Are You with Me?

Spring 2006 vision through Cindy deVille

While viewing a Christian program with several well-known ministers and prophetic people speaking about the seven mountains of society and possible strategies to reform them, I heard the Lord say:

"They're not ready yet."

After I heard this I had the following vision:

I saw a mighty Warrior; He was very big and tall and fully dressed and ready for battle (like in *Braveheart*). I didn't see His face as I was standing slightly behind Him and off to His right. He was looking with anticipation at a great land that stood before Him and His people.

This Warrior represented Christ, and He was ready to lead His army, His people, into the Promised Land. He said that everything He had promised His people was standing before them and that He longed to fulfill every plan, every dream, every promise that *He* had placed in their hearts, beyond what they even imagined. It was as though He couldn't wait to show them all He had in store. There was a great zeal that seemed to consume and radiate from Him.

He then turned His head and looked over His shoulder to His people and shouted:

"ARE YOU WITH ME?"

He was fully set to move quickly forward; but then, for a moment it was as though my eyes and my heart became His, and I saw what He saw and felt what He felt. It was heartbreaking and almost unbeliev-able. It's as though He was saying:

"Cindy, Look what they are doing."

Instead of His people standing with Him ready to go forward into battle, they all had their backs turned to Him. They were about ten feet away and all crouched down towards the ground. Each person had their arms wrapped around something, holding it close and affectionately, as if they loved it.

At first I couldn't tell what they were embracing, but God allowed me to see that they were "idols"—other lovers, sins, things of this world they loved more than God: wealth, status, pleasures, possessions, fame, success, the praise of man, the things of the world and of the flesh. They had turned away from their first love and were embracing idols.

Anything we exalt above Christ is considered an idol (idolatry).

Remember in chapter 6, "The State of the American Church," we shared about leaving our first love for other lovers and being lured away by the distractions and pleasures of the day. This vision reveals how these have held us back.

The second root problem

So we see that the heart and soul (spiritual and moral condition) of the nation is not the only root problem; but the very vessel God would use to be salt and light and be the *agent of change* and reform is also the problem. And until the American church changes, America will not change her course.

REFORMING OUR HOUSE FIRST

It's really important we understand this. We can fight and pray for change and the reformation of our nation all day long; but if many of the leaders in God's house and many of God's people are living in compromise, idolatry, disobedience, unrepentant sin, and not praying, we will not be able to change the nation. We (the American church) actually are part of the problem!

If we want to see radical change in our nation, we must first see radical change in our churches. Many in the church are telling the government, Hollywood, and the rest of America, "You are the problem; you need to clean up your act; you need to repent"; but God is pointing to the American church saying, "Church, YOU are the problem; YOU need clean up your act; YOU need to repent, *first!*"

Much of the church right now can't take a stand for righteousness in our land because they themselves are living in hidden sin and unrighteousness. Is it any wonder why the world looks at the current state of the American church and laughs at our calls for righteous change in our nation?

It's time for radical change

There must be a strong call for real repentance and a radical reformation in the church. What we need is a holy visitation from heaven—a cleansing and purifying fire that will hit our pulpits and send ripple effects throughout the pews and out into the city streets and to the multitudes!

It's time for the American church to fully surrender to God and allow Him to carry out an internal investigation and remove everything holding us back or standing in our way. For until we clean house and realign our ways with God's ways, we will not be able to fully change our nation.

With all this in mind, we point to Peter who declared that judgment must first begin in the house of God (1 Pet. 4:17). This does not mean a condemning judgment, but a purifying and purging that brings change. How will God deal with the great sin and compromise in His church and clean up His house? Next we share exactly how.

14

PREPARE FOR RADICAL CHANGE!

Suddenly I Will Come!

For the time has come for judgment to begin at the house of God ... it begins with us first.
—1 Peter 4:17

I F JUDGMENT MUST begin in the house of God, then it must first begin in the pulpits of America. It's time for a holy visitation, a separation, and consecration.

We have entered a critical and pivotal time in the history of our nation and the church. And, the truth is, the change we want to see in America must begin with us. God is calling His leaders and people everywhere to prepare for radical change.

As we shared in chapter 6, "The State of the American Church," Jesus still walks among His churches today; and He is coming to judge, to cleanse, and purify and to separate the precious from the vile. Before God does a great work *through* His church, He is going to do a great work *in* His church.

There are at two biblical parallels for what we are about to share in this chapter.

Biblical Parallel 1: Jesus Cleanses the Temple

One of the last things Jesus did in His ministry was like a prophetic parallel to what He is going to do again. Consumed with a great love and zeal for His Father's house, Jesus cleansed the temple. He overturned the tables of the money changers (those misusing His house) and reminded them, "My house shall be called a house of prayer" (Matt. 21:12–13). Then after He cleansed the temple, He proceeded to do great wonders and miracles in the temple (v. 14).

Biblical Parallel 2: A Sudden and Great Visitation

Like many prophecies in God's Word, Malachi 3:1–3 has two or more fulfillments. Often they have one close to the time it was given, another further into future. Malachi is such a book. The prophet Malachi speaks of God's Messenger coming to His temple suddenly to cleanse and purify. The *great visitation* we are about to share is prophetically parallel to this.

> "Behold, I send My messenger, And he will prepare the way before Me. And the Lord, whom you seek, Will *suddenly* come to His temple, Even the Messenger of the covenant, In whom you delight. Behold, He is coming," Says the LORD of hosts. "But who can endure the day of His coming? And who can stand when He appears? For He is like a *refiner's*

fire And like *launderers' soap*. He will sit as a refiner and a purifier of silver; He will *purify* the sons of Levi, And *purge* them as gold and silver, That they may offer to the LORD An offering in righteousness."

—MALACHI 3:1–3, EMPHASIS ADDED

The prophetic parallel:

1. Jesus Christ ("Messenger of the covenant") coming suddenly to His house (temple).

2. It will not be a casual visit but a very serious and powerful one ("who can endure the day of His coming?").

3. He will be doing a deep cleansing with the fire of His Spirit and power of His Word (water and *launderers' soap*) that will bring forth a shining glorious church as silver and gold (Eph. 5:26–27).

4. This will include a purification of God's leaders (represented by the "sons of Levi") for the good and benefit of His people (Eph. 4:11–16).

Now in direct relation to these two biblical parallels we share about the great visitation that is coming to God's house to put things in order and change everything.

The Great Visitation

January 20, 2008, prophecy through Cindy deVille

It was over a month after God had spoken the "America, America!" and "Shifting Economies" prophecies. We were in a time of intercession. I could see the condition of God's church. Many who had once known the presence and power of God were dying spiritually, anemic, backslidden, and had become prey to the enemy. But that was going to change.

"There is coming a great visitation to the earth.
A great visitation by My Spirit.
A visitation such as the earth has not seen or heard.
I will move in unprecedented ways!
I will visit My house
I will visit the White House
I will visit your house, O man of God!

"So prepare, O man of God, prepare!
Prepare everywhere, prepare!
For I will come with great power,
And I will cleanse and I will purify this hour.
I will separate the precious from the vile,
I will remove all things from My house that defile!

"I will, I will, I will," says the Spirit of God,
"I will fulfill all My will in the earth and in My church,
All My plans shall succeed.
I will have a glorious church,
And she will rise up and do great wonders in the earth!
Man has made his plans
But My purposes and plans shall prevail for I cannot fail!

"Tell Me, who can stop or stay My hand
When I decide to move throughout this land?
There is no power, no force, no government, no man
That can stand against My Spirit or My plans!

"So I am calling you, O man of God!
Rise up, rise up and take your place.
Rise up and seek My face.
It is a day of visitation so prepare,
Rise up and come to the holy place!

"It's time to cast aside every weight and sin
That would hold you back and pen you in.
Remove every impure and unclean thing before your eyes,
The enemy has sent them for your destruction and demise.

"Arise, O man of God, it is your day of visitation!
I am calling you to be Holy as I the Lord your God am Holy.
You must turn from and hate your sin,
Only then, I can begin to commune with you again!
Rise up out of your confusion and disgrace!
Rise up, O man of God, and seek My face!

"Rise up out of your slumber!
For the enemy of your souls,
He knows, he knows, he knows his days are numbered.
He has planted snares everywhere.
With a violence and a vengeance he has unleashed
Strong spirits of seduction, delusion, and deception
Upon My church and My people.
Spirits to draw you away and to devour you as his prey.

"It is the Day of Visitation so rise up,
O man of God, and draw your sword.
Wake up its time for war!
It's time to fight for your life!

"We are nearing the final round
And now starts the countdown.

You must get up off the floor,
You must get up and draw your sword!
I AM here, and there is a great cloud of witnesses cheering you on.
Don't give in, don't give up, we are so close to the end,
So rise up, rise up, rise up!"

We believe we are on the verge of the greatest move of God in history. And what is coming is going to totally revolutionize the church!

God's instructions in review

God is saying it's time to prepare, to prepare everywhere.

+ Prepare! Prepare yourself and get your church ready for what God is going to be doing.

+ He will come with great power, and He will cleanse and purify. (More about what this will bring in a moment.)

+ He is calling His leaders to rise up and seek His face. (This all ties in with God's Answer we will reveal soon.)

+ It's time to suit up and prepare for a great glorious battle that lies ahead! (We will touch on this more in the epilogue, "Entering a New Day: The Glorious Church.")

The Glory of God Will Bring Two Things

There is something to know and understand—God's day of visitation to His church will be both glorious and terrifying!

> For the day of the LORD is great and very terrible; Who can endure it?
> —JOEL 2:11 (SEE ALSO JOEL 2:31)

> But who can endure the day of His coming? And who can stand when He appears? For He is like a refiner's fire And like launderers' soap....He will purify the sons of Levi.
> —MALACHI 3:2–3

Notice Malachi 3:2 says, "Who can endure the day of his coming?" It's very, very important, pastor and Christian leader, that you prepare yourselves and your people. It is important that the church realize when this great visitation and outpouring comes it will bring two things—glory and judgment.

1. God's glory will bring astounding miracles such as in the Book of Acts, and even beyond. "For the glory of this latter house shall be greater than of the former" (Hag. 2:9, kjv).

2. At the same time there will be judgments in His house, and even some deaths in the pulpits for those leaders trying to minister in hidden sin or rebellion. The days of Ananias and Sapphira will return. As reflected in both Moses' day and in the Book of Acts,

the greater the level of God's glory in our midst, the greater the consequences and judgment upon sin in our midst. (Also see "Judgment Is Coming to the Pulpits of America" in appendix F).

As God reveals His glory, the awe and fear of the Lord will return to His house bringing many to their knees. Many will stand in awe of His works and fear the Lord. Again, our proper perspective should always be Hebrews 12:

> Therefore, since we are receiving a kingdom that cannot be shaken, let us be thankful, and so worship God acceptably with reverence and awe, for our "God is a consuming fire."
>
> —Hebrews 12:28–29, niv

We must allow the Spirit of God to go deep in our lives and burn up anything that is not of Him—burn up our agendas, our pride, envy, compromise, and complacency. Better to burn up those things built by the arm of the flesh—the wood, hay and stubble—now rather than when standing before His throne (1 Cor. 3:12–15)!

Is Your Church on the Rock and Ready?

Now is the time for pastors and churches all across the nation to prepare and position themselves for this great move and visitation of God. Pastor, Christian, church—you can position yourself now to be a part of the amazing work God is going to be doing, or be left behind in the wake of radical change. Church as usual is coming to an end. We are entering a time of great shaking when only that which is built by God, built His way, will remain standing (Heb. 12:25–29). And only those churches that build on the truth of God's Word, the Rock, and do things *His* way will be able to stand strong in the midst of the storms of turbulent times ahead; all others will be washed away (Matt. 7:24–25).

Rise up and lead the way!

God is calling you (pastors, Christian, church) to rise up in the midst of this present darkness and be the answer—Christ's victorious, glorious church! Are you ready to impact our nation and usher in the greatest awakening ever seen in your church and community and city?

If ever there was a time God needed His leaders and His people to surrender and submit themselves and their ministries to Him, that time is now. God needs strong leaders who will not compromise, that are fully devoted to Christ and to building His church His way. God needs you to arise! The body of Christ needs you to arise! The nation needs you to arise!

Reforming the nation starts with the church. Reforming the church starts with God's pastors and leaders. What kind of pastor and leader is God looking for? We answer that next.

15

GOD'S LETTER TO HIS PASTORS AND LEADERS

Unless the LORD builds the House, They labor in vain who build it.
—PSALM 127:1

RIGHT NOW, GOD is looking for strong pastors and leaders who have a heart after Him and will do things His way. He is looking for those who are willing to lay down everything, embrace His plans, then rise up and lead His people into great victory and help change a nation A related quote from E.M. Bounds echoes this:

> The church is looking for better methods; God is looking for better men.[1]

During a time of prayer God revealed His heart to us regarding His leaders (the five-fold ministry). It was as though He was showing us the kind of man and heart He was searching and looking for—someone to build His church, to lead, and to care for His sheep in these last days.

God Is Looking for a Man
January 12, 2008, prophecy through Cindy deVille

> "I am looking for a man, a man who will seek after and embrace My plan.
> A man who will build My church, My way."

I could hear Him say, "Who will do it My way?" God is *not* looking for a rock star. He is looking for a man who knows and pursues His heart! God is looking for a man that is humble and broken before Him. Then the Lord continued:

The land is filled with pastors who are building on sinking sand,
Building by the strength and reasoning of carnal man.
They read the books, statistics, and polls,
Yet Me and My ways they hardly know.

They embrace the latest fads and trends,
Yet where will it lead them in the end?
I know their clever marketing schemes,
But many of their hearts and ways are far from Me.

Is there a man who will cast aside
The ways of the world and all its foolish pride?

Is there a man who will come humbly before Me?
Who will pray a great price down on his knees?
Who will die to himself and take up his cross?
Who is willing to count all things of this world as loss!
Is there a man who will build My church?
Is there a man I can trust to obey,
A man who will do things My way?

Is there a man who will abandon his own plans and seek My ways?
For I AM the ancient of days,
I hold the mysteries of the universe and the wisdom of the ages.

Many have decided they are smarter than Me.
They have abandoned My ways and dug their own wells
Some of which will lead many souls to hell.
They are building by the wisdom of the world and its ways
And it will cause many of My people to be led astray.

God's ways may not always be popular but they will produce rich and lasting fruit. They will have eternal and everlasting results. They will produce life! Carnal, natural ways may appear to prosper in the day but they will always fall away. The fruit that seems to appear will rot on the vine. But not when it's done God's way, for His fruit will remain throughout all time! God is looking for those that will build *His* church *His* way rather than the American way.

Remembering whose house it is

It is a weighty thing to remember one day you will stand accountable before God as to your stewardship of His house. God will not be concerned about your popularity, how many Facebook or Twitter followers you had, how many books you wrote, how many people were in your church, or how many TV stations you were on. As the Head of His church, what He will want to know is whether you built His house *His* way or did you do it *your* own way, following the fads and trends of the day?

A lesson from three little pigs

Building man's way versus God's way is the difference between building a house of straw versus a house of brick (remember the three little pigs folktale). When the strong winds blew, the house of straw easily collapsed but the house of brick stood strong and steady.

The truth is the "house of straw" was quick, cheap, and easy to build; but it was devastatingly frail, weak, and easily destroyed by the big bad wolf (a parallel to Satan, the kingdom of darkness, and life's storms). On the other hand, the "house of brick" was costly and took time and hard work to build; but it withstood every attempt of the big bad wolf to destroy it.

If we build *God's* way, it will stand the storms and have eternal value (Luke

6:48; 1 Cor. 3:12–15). For God's ways are perfect, and His Word is proven true, and He is a shield to all who trust in Him (Ps. 18:30). God's ways can often seem at first foolish to carnal man; but the truth is God's ways are brilliant and far higher than ours (Isa. 55:9). We need to embrace His higher ways.

No guts, no glory—it's time

The truth is if we want to see the glory of God and a Great Awakening in our lives, our churches, and our nation, it will take guts; it will take great courage, conviction, and undying commitment and determination.

Right now we need courageous leaders and not cowards in our pulpits. We need leaders who fear God and not man, who will confront the sin that many are living in. We need men of valor and courage who won't back down, who won't compromise giving in to Satan's lies. We need real leaders who will feed the people milk and meat instead of just cotton candy and sweets. God needs real leaders who will raise up fully devoted, fearless followers of Christ—who know God, who know what they are fighting for, who know what they believe, and who boldly speak the truth in love!

It's time to shake things up and change the status quo in our churches, our nation, and even in our personal lives. It's time to stop settling for less than God's very best. If we will be willing and obedient to do what God is asking of us as His leaders and His people, we believe we will see His glory and the greatest awakening ever seen in our land.

A Changing of the Guard

There is coming a greater sifting, shifting, and repositioning as God tests and tries the hearts and motives of those in leadership. God will need to remove those in leadership who insist on building His church their own way. We are entering a new day and God's leaders in His house must hear His voice, move quickly, and do exactly what He says. He cannot have insubordinate leadership; this is rebellion and opens the door to confusion and every evil work, which will bring defeat and harm to His church. So God will remove them.

A great separation is coming. What will be left standing in His church will be leaders with a heart after God, who don't care about their reputations but are consumed with a desire to fulfill the purposes of God in the earth; leaders who have no agenda but God's agenda. They are fully devoted to Him, love truth, love His people, and are willing to lay down everything for His sake. The love of the world is not in them. They know who they serve and they count all else as loss!

An Internal Investigation for a New Day

A new day is dawning. Old things will pass away, the glorious church will arise. God is looking for warriors of the light who know how to stand and fight until the job is done.

Vision and Word through Cindy deVille

I see the Lord walking through His church. He's investigating, He's looking. He's saying: "I'll take you, and you, and you. I know you'll follow through, I know you'll do what I'm asking of you." He's walking and searching. He's saying, "I'll take you, and you."

He's sifting, He's sifting,
He's looking through all the troops.
He's deciding who will lead.
He's deciding who will feed His sheep.
He's making judgments:
Who will stand and fight for what is just and right.
Who will turn, run, and flee at the sight of the enemy.
He's sifting and looking.
He's been testing and trying and watching.

For He's raising up an army in these last days, with a fire in their eyes, and hearts full of zeal for Him and His house; an army who will not compromise or tolerate Satan's lies. An army with their eyes set on Christ, and the prize. There is a separation coming. The lines are being drawn in the sand.

When the Lines Are Drawn in the Sand

June 06, 2012, through Cindy deVille

This prophetic exhortation came as a poem:

When the lines are drawn in the sand,
On whose side will you stand?
Will you say, "As for me and my house, we will serve the Lord!"
Or will you compromise and lay down your sword?

God is looking for strong leaders in this hour,
Those that will not bow down or cower.
Not to money or to man,
But marching to the drumbeat of God's commands?

What will you do when the pressures on?
Will you stand tall or will you go AWOL?
Will you stand and fight or will you take flight?
It's time to decide who you will serve.
Will you follow the crowd,
Or will you live your faith out loud?
Will you hide it under a bushel, or set it on a hill?
Surely you know God's will!

It's time for the real body of Jesus Christ to wake up, stand up, and take our position in Christ as a warrior of light (Rom. 13:12; Eph. 6:10–20). It's time to decide on which side you will stand. For those who know their God shall be strong and do exploits (Dan. 11:32)!

God is looking for pastors and leaders to take the church to new levels and turn this nation back to Him. God is looking for leaders who will equip and prepare His people and churches for what's coming. God is looking for leaders that will embrace and do things His way. He wants strong leaders with a love and zeal for Him, His ways, His people, and souls. Will you be that man (or woman), and say, "Yes Lord! You can count on me!"? You can play a key role in God's Answer and help us make history.

SECTION 2:

GOD'S ANSWER

16

Mission Critical

17

The Pulpits Hold the Keys

18

Key 1: Opening the Door for Change

19

Key 2: The Power to Change Everything

20

Key 3: No Limits

21

Reviewing God's Answer

Section 2 Preface

The Stage Is Set

We have seen the desperate state of America and the American church and that we have two paths before us—destruction or restoration. We see that a historic opportunity stands before us to dramatically change everything in our churches and nation. The important question is, how do we begin this change? What is God saying it will take to bring the Great Awakening we must have to begin saving and changing our nation? God's Answer shows us exactly how next.

16

MISSION CRITICAL

Now thanks be to God who always leads us in triumph in Christ.
—2 CORINTHIANS 2:14

T'S UNDENIABLE; WE are in an epic battle for the soul(s) of our nation. And although it seems the forces of hell are advancing, we must remember that God reigns over kings and the kingdoms of men. He is not distraught, confused, or taken by surprise, and He is never without a plan. God operates in divine order, and He is a brilliant military strategist with all the forces, armies, and angels of heaven at His beck and call. Sometimes He is just looking for a man, like Moses, Joshua, or David, who will listen and take hold of His plan and run with Him.

God has a strategy and a plan

It is not a coincidence that David consistently experienced great victory in His battles. His secret? He always inquired of the Lord to gain insight, strategy, and timing. God was with him; but the real truth is he was *with* God and *aligned* himself with God's plan. He didn't just run off presumptuously and fight in His own strength. He got God's plan and remained under His command.

As we have sought God and labored much in prayer since 2007 regarding the condition of our nation, we believe God has revealed to us a divine plan and strategy we call God's Answer. This plan is biblical, powerful, yet very simplistic—like the gospel.

God is on a rescue mission; and right now, we believe God is uttering His voice before His army. We are presenting this plan and strategy to His leaders (the pulpits) and His people (the pews). And, we are calling His church to rally and unite under one plan (God's Answer) to save and change our nation. As in an effective military operation, we (the church) must be united, single-minded, fully engaged, and quick to obey in order to accomplish the mission.

THE MISSION

The mission is to usher in the greatest awakening ever seen, bringing America to her knees and back to God. Then advance a great reformation to transform America, restoring her godly foundations, and more. At the same time reforming and preparing our churches for the both intense and glorious days ahead.

The situation and what is at stake

This cannot be overemphasized! Remember the dire state our nation and churches are in. Remember God's progressive warnings and judgments we have seen so far to get our nation's attention. Remember Path 1. God warned that if America did not turn back to Him the consequences would be devastating. They would include economic collapse, greater natural disasters, enemy attacks, war and blood in our streets from shore to shore. The future of America is at stake—our families, our children, our churches, everything! One way or another everyone will be affected—everyone.

Mission Critical—Doing It God's Way

If we are going to accomplish our *mission* then we must do it God's way, for only He has the power to bring a nation to its knees. Only God has the *answer* to dramatically change everything.

A fundamental truth of God's Answer is that changing the nation begins with God's people—especially the pulpits of America—the leaders in God's house.

THE MISSION IN THREE STAGES OF OPERATION

Mission critical is an activity or element vital to the success of an organization or endeavor. Without it the result is failure. It is a term used in business and the military.

Stage 1: Mission Critical—the Pulpits and Pews

Critical to this mission is the fact that everything must begin with God's people (the pulpits and churches) across America. Also critical to this mission are three biblical keys. Turning these three keys will release the Spirit of God to flow from the pulpits, to the pew, then to the multitudes—bringing America to her knees in the Great Awakening. All three keys must be turned to initiate the Great Awakening in order to accomplish the mission.

Mission Critical Keys
The pulpits hold the keys. *It all begins here!*

Key 1: Opens the door to change (positions us for dramatic change)

Key 2: Releases the power to change everything (nation-changing key)

Key 3: Removes the limits (makes everything possible)

Important Note: As we reveal these keys, they may seem simple (even obvious); however, what makes God's Answer unique are His instructions on *how* these three keys are to be used. God's *prescribed* way makes all the difference (Prov. 2:6; 4:7).

Successful implementation of stage 1 (God's Answer: Mission critical with the three keys) will lead to stage 2 (the Great Awakening).

Stage 2: The Great Awakening—the Multitudes

The Great Awakening will sweep across our land from coast to coast (remember the "Glimpse of the Great Awakening" in chapter 3). It will help rescue souls, change lives, and change the course of the nation. This will include a prayer and action strategy highlighted in "The Call to Action," section 3.

Stage 2 (the Great Awakening) then sets up a window of opportunity for stage 3 (the great reformation).

Stage 3: The Great Reformation—Everything Changes

We can ensure lasting change by reforming all areas of America. We believe as the church unites under one focused plan we can help reform and transform the nation.

Failure is not an option! God is counting on us to embrace His answer, His plan, to rise up, and to lead the way into a new day.

Finally, we begin to reveal exactly what God's answer is to breakthrough into the greatest awakening and turn America back to Him and bring a great reformation. Then later we will share how God's Answer can be implemented from the pulpits to the pews both locally and nationwide.

Let us begin.

17

THE PULPITS HOLD THE KEYS

Where It Must Begin

Let the priests, who minister to the LORD, Weep
between the porch and the altar.
—JOEL 2:17

T IS WORTH repeating: There are times in history when God moves through His leaders and His people in such a way that everything changes. Right now we are in such a time as this—with the future of America hanging in the balance.

It's time to rise

We believe it is a new day and everything can change; and it all begins with you, the pulpits of America. You hold the keys to help change everything. God is counting on you as a leader in His house to do what He is asking of you. Now is the time to rise up and lead the way into a new day. God is ready to help you, and there is "a great cloud of witnesses in heaven cheering you on...so rise up, rise up, rise up!" (from "The Great Visitation" prophecy in chapter 14).

We share two biblical precedents for this *first critical step* of God's Answer we reveal in a moment.

Biblical Precedent 1

God tells the leaders how to bring change

From the start the prophet Joel spoke to the elders, the leaders of God's people. "Hear the word of the LORD...Hear this you elders...And all the inhabitants of the land" (Joel 1:1–2)."

Joel went on to highlight the natural disasters at a level they had not seen before, and how economic ruin was upon them. This is parallel to what America has been going through and where she is headed, as shared in previous chapters.

Then Joel called for the priests (spiritual leaders) to prepare themselves, to lead the people in what God was directing them to do. And how God promised them not only healing and restoration, but He would move greater than ever before (Joel 1:13; 2:19; 21–26).

Biblical Precedent 2

Doing it God's way—divine order

Only God's *prescribed way* will bring the real change we need and lasting results. Example:

Man's new cart vs God's way

King David wanted to bring up the ark of the covenant, representing the presence and glory of God (including His mercy, goodness, blessing, power, etc.). What church would not want the strong presence and glory of God abiding with them? David sure did.

Second Samuel 6 is one instance when David did not initially inquire of the Lord and it brought disastrous results. David tried to have the ark of the covenant (the presence and glory of God) brought in upon a "manmade" new cart. Surely it was the best new cart man could build; but it failed miserably because it was based on man's ways and reasonings rather than God's *prescribed* way. The same can be said for the American church today—our new shiny carts are not working! All our latest and greatest man made efforts are not working. God's glory (the Great Awakening) will only come *His way* and as we obey!

Learning from his mistake, David then inquired of the Lord and learned of God's prescribed way. David then called for the priests and Levites and said to them:

> You are the heads of the fathers' houses of the Levites; *sanctify your-selves*, you and your brethren, *that you may bring up the Ark* of the LORD God of Israel to the place I have prepared for it. For because you did not do it the first time, the LORD our God broke out against us, because we did not consult Him about the *proper order*.
>
> —1 CHRONICLES 15:12–13, EMPHASIS ADDED

God always has a *proper and divine order*, a *prescribed way* of doing things.

> So the priests and the Levites *sanctified themselves* to bring up the ark of the LORD God of Israel. And the children of the Levites *bore the ark* of God *on their shoulders*, by its poles, as Moses had commanded according to the Word of the LORD."
>
> —1 CHRONICLES 15:14–15, EMPHASIS ADDED

God's way for His presence and glory to be carried in is on the shoulders of His spiritual leaders, those that had consecrated and made themselves ready. They had the *critical role* and honor to begin changing everything. And when they did as God said, the result brought great rejoicing and God's presence and glory greater than ever before!

Once again (today), God is instructing His priests, the pulpits of America—the five-fold ministry—how to bring His presence and glory (the Great Awakening) to our churches and nation greater than ever before.

Remember in "The Course of a Nation," chapter 3, the amazing vision of a Great Awakening sweeping across America? We believe God has shown exactly how this will begin.

How the Greatest Awakening Will Begin!
July 12, 2010, through Cindy deVille

Eight days after July 4, 2010, during a focused time of prayer for America and the church, God brought forth a strong and heartfelt word with clear instructions on how to bring the greatest awakening and how to bring America to her knees and back to Him. We ask you to read this carefully and prayerfully. Our prayer is every pastor, every five-fold minister in America will hear God's cry and respond.

A Prophetic Word by God's Spirit

God is calling the pastors to their knees.
He's calling the five-fold ministry to their knees;
To their knees, to their knees in repentance, in unity, in humility.
Then we will see the glory of God come upon the church.
Then we will see the glory of God come upon the nation,
Come upon the nation.

God is waiting; God is waiting on His leaders.
God is waiting upon the leaders in His house.
He's waiting upon the five-fold ministry.

We will see such a Great Awakening across this land!
We will see the power of God and His mighty hand!
But it must begin with the five-fold ministry.
And God is calling them to their knees,
In repentance, in prayer, in humility, in unity.
And it will flow from the pulpits to the pew. And then it will flow like
    a massive river to the multitudes.
It will sweep across the land, greater than we have ever seen!

"There is NO OTHER WAY!" says the Spirit of God.
"For I am showing My church, I am showing My leaders
How to bring a nation to Me, how to bring a nation to Me!
How to bring this nation back to Me!
How to bring America to her knees in repentance, in prayer, in
    humility.
I am telling you and I am showing you how to bring America to Me."

And the Spirit of God would say,
"Will you cooperate with Me?
Will you do it My way?" says the Lord,
"Or will you insist on your own ways?
Your ways which have brought forth nothing.
Your ways which have brought forth no fruit."

(Overall the condition of America continues to grow worse.)

"Embrace," says the Spirit of God, "My ways!

Embrace, open your ears and hear,

Hear what I am saying to you, and do what I am asking of you.

Then you will see Me move," says the Spirit of the Most High.

God's Answer is not a political solution or a legislative solution, it is a holy solution.

God is showing us how to begin to turn America back to Him. It doesn't start in Washington, DC; it starts with the pulpits of America. The pulpits of America have played a key role as gatekeepers by opening the door to sin and compromise that has been defiling and destroying both the church and our nation. Now therefore, God is calling those in the pulpits to bring the solution. The pulpits (gatekeepers) will *unlock* the doors for the floodgates from heaven to flow like a massive river across our nation, greater than we ever seen!

God is calling for radical change

For over a decade there have been special events or days set aside for powerful and meaningful calls for repentance and prayer. We believe it is because of these God has extended mercy and held back greater judgment from our land. Things could be much worse right now had these not occurred. We also believe God has used these to help prepare the soil of our nation for what He will do. What we have seen so far has had some positive impact; but again, overall most of our churches have gone on with business as usual. This cannot be anymore. God is calling for radical change!

For us to see great breakthrough and the greatest awakening sweep across America it will require extraordinary action. Extraordinary action = extraordinary results! A one day or weeklong event will not suffice, unless it is the catalyst for massive church-wide transformation and reformation. It must become a movement in churches all across America.

GOD'S ANSWER—THE ESSENTIALS IN REVIEW

God is looking for an army of fully devoted and consecrated leaders and people to turn this nation back to Him and bring America to her knees in the greatest awakening ever. Will you answer the call? Multitudes of souls and a nation are hanging in the balance!

In review God showed:

1. It Begins with God's Leaders, the Gatekeepers

This is God's divine order, leaders first. Just as in biblical times, God is calling once again for His priests to prepare themselves and to lead the people, to help save and change a nation.

- God is calling His leaders (the five-fold ministry) to their knees, in repentance, in prayer, in humility and unity.

- God's divine designated order is from the pulpits to the pews, and then the multitudes (our nation)—from the top of the mountain (spiritually speaking) to everywhere else below.

Pulpits of America, five-fold ministry; changing the nation starts with *you*.

Remember "God's Letter to His Pastors and Leaders," chapter 15? Will you be one that will help lead the way into a new day for our churches and nation?

2. The Greatest Awakening Will Only Come His Way

The greatest awakening will *only come* if we do things God's *prescribed* way. And He is making it very clear—there is "no other way!" Too often we make the mistake of looking for a new cart or a "magic bullet" to solve everything, when the answer is right in front of us—doing things God's *prescribed* way but on a massive scale, as He is instructing. The greater the response the greater results we will see.

Changing our nation starts with changing the church, and this starts with the pulpits. Remember the coming "Great Visitation" in chapter 14—God is setting things up to take His leaders, His church, and our nation to a whole new level; but we must embrace and run with His answer. All our efforts will continue to fall short until His leaders and the church align with His way and do exactly what the Spirit of God is instructing. We must "cooperate" with Him.

Important Note: Great awakening will not come until... It is really important we understand that the Great Awakening will not come until the American church changes. God will not bring in a great harvest of souls to make them like we are now. He will only bring the great flood of souls when we have made ourselves ready, and we are ready to properly disciple them so they are passionate for God and fully devoted to Him and His kingdom purposes. We must get ready!

3. God's Spirit Will Flow Like a River

The results of obedience in the above prophecy are described by the great outpouring of His Spirit would be like a massive river:

We will see such a Great Awakening across this land!
We will see the power of God and His mighty hand...
And it will flow from the pulpits to the pew.
And then it will flow like a massive river to the multitudes.
It will sweep across the land, greater than we have ever seen!

This Great Awakening flowing like "a river" is parallel to the biblical "river of life."

- Revelation 22 describes a pure clean river of life proceeding from the throne of God and of the Lamb. And the leaves of the tress alongside this river of life are for healing of the nations.

- In John 7:38 Jesus said, "He who believes in Me...out of his heart will flow rivers of living water." Yes, rivers of living water can flow from God's people.

- Ezekiel 47 also foretells of the coming great temple of God and how water of life flows from it and becomes a deep massive river; and everywhere it goes it brings life, change, and restoration. The result also was a great multitude of fish (Ezek. 47:9), symbolic of a great harvest of souls!

God wants to release His river of life through His leaders (pulpits), His people (pews), and have it sweep across our land like a massive river of life—to save, heal, deliver, and bring great change to our nation. We will reveal soon in Key 2 the power that releases His river of life to flow!

4. How to Turn America Back to Him

God also said He is showing us how to bring America to Him. When you finish with this book, you will see not only how this is very possible, but also the magnitude of it all. Imagine such a sweeping move of God across our nation that it leads to multitudes turning to Christ and America turning back to God, like the Prodigal Son returning to his father. God is ready and waiting for His leaders to unite and respond!

5. Three Keys to Bring Change

In God's instructions we also see the three powerful *keys* the pulpits hold that will unlock the doors to begin great change in the churches and our nation. These keys are vital and powerful. We share exactly what these *three keys* are in the next three chapters.

It all begins with humility

As we proceed it will be clear that *God's Answer and* each *key* require "humility." Without humility we will not see judgment averted or the Great Awakening come. That is why God said healing and changing a nation starts with humility, "If My people...will *humble* themselves..." (2 Chron. 7:14, emphasis added).

As God's leaders we must truly humble ourselves and set aside our own agendas and fully submit to God and His ways, His plans. There will be no room and no place for pride or the flesh to operate in His house. God's ways are paved with humility.

URGENT! IT'S TIME FOR GOD'S LEADERS TO INTERVENE

We recall from a previous chapter, Larry Stockstill and James Robison's conclusion that "the pastors of America are the key to stopping an awful judgment that is looming on the horizon of our great nation."[1] Their conclusion confirms what God is saying. God's leaders will play a *critical role* in not only bringing the greatest awakening but they can also intervene to help avert greater judgment upon America, depending on how quickly they respond.

Biblical examples

1. Moses and Aaron urgently intervene

Judgment in the form of a plague had broken out against the children of Israel because of their great sin. Aaron (the high priest) had to respond to God's instructions quickly through Moses in order for the plague (judgment) to stop (Num. 16:46).

Likewise, God is instructing His leaders how to stop the increasing self-destruction and judgment of America. Five-fold ministry, God is counting on you to humbly unite and lead the way in turning America back to Him. (We share how this can be done in the upcoming "Call to Action," section 3). Time is of the essence! God is waiting on His leaders!

2. Joel's gives a call to the priests to lead the way

The prophet Joel's calls out to God's leaders "you who minister to my God" to prepare themselves, to unite, and to gather all the leaders and people to cry out to the Lord (Joel 1:13–14). Then he also said:

> Let the priests, who minister to the Lord, Weep between the porch and the altar.
>
> —Joel 2:17

This time of repentance and weeping was to be done publicly before the people. The leaders were called as an example to lead all the people in fasting, repentance, and prayer (Joel 2:12–17), as God is calling for once again today. (More about this later in "Call to Action," section 3.)

Related Prophetic Note to God's Leaders

Weeping at the altar or weeping in the streets?

We believe God is also saying: If the five-fold ministry (the priests) do not humbly unite and lead their churches and their people in humble genuine repentance and fervent prayer, then we will instead see weeping in the streets of America. We have already seen some weeping in the streets from public shootings, the Boston Marathon bombing, civil riots, natural disasters, and more.

If we do what God is saying, our humble obedience and prayer will begin to turn the tide. Then the weeping would only be on the inside of His house, at the altar; a weeping of intercession and prayer versus the weeping of pain and ruin in our nation's streets. We see this also reflected in Joel 2, to come before the Lord in heartfelt repentance before the calamity of judgment comes.

"Even now," declares the LORD, "return to Me with all your heart, with fasting and weeping and mourning. Rend your heart and not your garments. Return to the LORD your God, for He is gracious and compassionate, slow to anger and abounding in love, and He relents from sending calamity."

—JOEL 2:12–13, NIV

The foundation is set

Five-fold ministry (especially the pastors); this all starts with you! It's God's divine order and prescribed way. You will set the pace. As never before, our churches and our nation need strong and courageous leaders who will humbly unite, embrace, and run with God's Answer. Will you answer His call?

Pulpits of America—God is also saying:

I'm not coming to bring you condemnation.
I've come to show you how to change a nation.
I have the answers and I hold the keys,
But you must open your ears and listen to Me.

This chapter sets the foundation of *God's Answer for America*. Next we look at the first key that opens the door for everything to begin. Without it the other two keys will not work.

We close this chapter reminding you we are not waiting on God to move in our nation; He is waiting on us!

18

KEY 1: OPENING THE DOOR FOR CHANGE

Genuine Repentance—Nationwide

He who covers his sins will not prosper, But whoever
confesses and forsakes them will have mercy.
—PROVERBS 28:13

WE CANNOT STRESS enough how important this chapter is. Without this key, there is no hope of bringing the Great Awakening or averting the greater judgment of God upon our land. Chuck Colson accurately warns:

> No matter how fervently we pray, the Lord will not grant renewal to a nation that does not honor Him. First, we must repent.[1]

Genuine repentance is the critical first key that opens the door and sets the wheels of change in motion for our churches and our nation. Genuine repentance goes to the root of the problem—sin and rebellion in the heart and soul(s) of the nation. Without genuine repentance America will reap the bitter fruit of her rebellious ways. Without genuine repentance our nation will see greater natural disasters, economic collapse, greater civil unrest, war and blood in our streets, and multitudes of souls lost.

It is worth repeating Larry Stockstill's warning to the pastors of America:

> I believe we are facing a window of opportunity for repentance.... Unless the pastors wake up to avert judgment, there will be judgment on America. If we don't respond we are going to lose this nation.[2]

KEY 1: GENUINE REPENTANCE—NATIONWIDE

Imagine pastors and churches all across the nation on their knees in genuine repentance crying out for forgiveness for themselves and praying for their churches, the nation, our leaders, the prodigals, and the lost.

Then fast-forward months later to Washington, DC: envision America's leaders on their knees, along with people all over our nation on their knees, crying out to God in genuine repentance. Although some may think this impossible, we need to remember, "With God all things are possible" (Mark 10:27). The secret is *aligning* with God and *His* ways. We believe if God's leaders and people will *align* with His ways (implement God's Answer) *then* we will eventually see our nation on its knees and turning back to God!

It starts here

Only a baptism of genuine repentance sweeping like a wave across our churches will open the door to genuine change that lasts. God has instructed that it must begin with those in our pulpits bowing their knees in humble obedience, then leading the way for our churches and our nation. Without this wave of genuine repentance, our prayers and efforts are hindered and there will be no Great Awakening because the windows of heaven will remain shut. Turning this *first key* of *genuine repentance—nationwide* will open the door to genuinely change everything.

Genuine repentance puts us on God's side and aligns our hearts and our ways with Him and His ways. When we come into agreement and move with Him in effective prayer, the power of God's Spirit is released and glorious change is inevitable. This is why every past Great Awakening or great move of God has been proceeded by genuine repentance and great prayer.

> If My people…will humble themselves, and pray…and *turn* [repent] from *their* wicked ways, *then* I will *hear* from heaven, and will *forgive* their sin and *heal* their land.
>
> —2 Chronicles 7:14, emphasis added

Important Note: Scripture makes it clear that part of *the answer* to heal our land is when *we* (God's people) turn (repent) from *our* wicked ways. This truth applies to today and makes it very clear—changing and healing the nation starts with God's people.

The In-House Attack on "Repentance"

Not surprisingly, the enemy has worked hard the past several years to counter the importance, power, and need for genuine repentance. Through his crafty and deceptive ways, Satan has tried to nullify the truth and need for repentance through the well-meaning but distorted "hyper-grace" message (which we addressed in chapter 6, "The State of the American Church"). Some of these teachers claim there is no need for Christians to ever confess sin and repent, and that "repentance" is merely a "change of *mind*."

However, the truth is that repentance is so important, both Jesus and John the Baptist began their earthly ministries with the message of "repent" and "the kingdom of heaven is at hand" (Mark 1:15; Matt. 3:1). Then in Jesus' final message (Book of Revelation), He called for five of the seven the churches to "repent." His message to them was clearly about changing *their ways*, not just changing *their mind*! Repentance *is for us today*, and it produces powerful and wonderful results!

Genuine Repentance Is Powerful

Genuine "repentance" is not just a change of *mind*, but a radical change of *life* that experiences transformation. Genuine repentance is turning our back on sin and turning our hearts and lives completely back to God and in alignment with His ways. Genuine repentance restores our relationship and intimacy with God by removing those things hindering our communion with Him.

As we have seen, the consequences of abandoning, rebelling, and running from God and His righteous ways are very destructive. The only way to stop this dark harvest of destructive fruit in our personal lives and our nation is with the power of genuine repentance. When genuine repentance comes, the door to transformation is opened. The power of the Holy Spirit will come in and begin to turn around the multiple and destructive effects of our sin and rebellion. The power of God's Spirit breaks down strongholds and sets us free from the bondages of sin. The door opens for God's divine intervention and His power to bring healing, restoration, and reformation in our lives. God's response to genuine repentance is life changing and can be nation changing!

To see an illustrative example the power of genuine repentance in action, see "A Classic Example from Early America," appendix B.

WHAT DOES GENUINE REPENTANCE LOOK LIKE?

Genuine repentance comes when the Spirit of God opens our eyes to see the depth of our sin and the wickedness of our ways, from God's perspective. Then in our brokenness we are driven to our knees and crying out, "O God! Forgive me!" This is the kind of repentance we saw sweeping across our nation in the vision "A Glimpse of the Great Awakening" in chapter 3. Only the Spirit of God can open up blind eyes bringing the conviction of sin (John 16:8). Key 2 (next chapter) will be very instrumental in accomplishing this on a national level.

Genuine repentance begins with humility, goes to the root, and produces fruit. These are three things real repentance should always include.

1. Genuine Repentance Begins with Humility

True humility precedes true repentance. This is why God said, "If My people...will *humble* themselves, and pray...and *turn* [repent],...*then* I will *hear* from heaven, and will *forgive* their sin and *heal* their land" (2 Chron. 7:14, emphasis added).

Genuine repentance of a nation begins on a personal level for all of us. God resists the proud, so we must humbly draw close to God on bended knee in prayer and allow Him to search our hearts and transform our lives (James 4:6–8; Ps. 139:23–24).

2. Genuine Repentance Goes to the Root

Genuine repentance is a cleansing of the heart. It goes deep to the root—it is sincere and comes out of a heart of brokenness. A token prayer will not do. Genuine repentance happens when our eyes are truly opened, and we are humbled and broken before God because of our sin, then we pour out our hearts to Him.

David's Example: After Nathan the prophet confronted David's sin with Bathsheba, the king humbled himself before God and poured our His heart in genuine repentance. "Create in me a clean heart, O God, and renew a steadfast spirit within me" (Ps. 51:10; see also vv. 12, 17).

God seeks a true heart of repentance in godly sorrow and one ready to change starting from the inside out. "Return to me with all your heart....Rend your heart and not your garments" (Joel 2:12–13, NIV). We need to rend our hearts before God and then ask Him to search our hearts, our lives, our motives, and to expose any way in us that is not pleasing to Him.

> Search me, O God, and know my heart; test me and know my anxious thoughts. Point out anything in me that offends you, and lead me along the path of everlasting life.
> —PSALM 139:23–24, NLT

After this we need to honestly deal with anything God exposes as not pleasing to Him, remove anything unclean, and cast off every weight of sin (Heb. 12:1–2). His divine power (grace) will help us do this (2 Pet. 1:3).

3. Genuine Repentance Has Fruit

The evidence for genuine repentance is the fruit of a changed life (Acts 26:20). God's divine power (grace) empowers us to walk in obedience as children of light; but it is a choice. That is why Peter said:

> [Live] as children of obedience [to God]; do not conform yourselves to the evil desires [that governed you] in your former ignorance...But as the One Who called you is holy, you yourselves also be holy in all your conduct and manner of living. For it is written, "You shall be holy, for I am holy."
> —1 PETER 1:14–16, AMP

> His *divine power* has given us everything we need for a *godly life* through our knowledge of him who called us by his own glory and goodness.
> —2 PETER 1:3, NLT, EMPHASIS ADDED

God's divine power (empowering grace) helps us to:

+ Rise up in purity of heart, life, and motives
+ Rise up in humility carried out through obedience
+ Rise up in faith, in prayer, followed by action
+ Present our lives as a living sacrifice, holy and acceptable to God (Rom. 12:1–2)
+ Stay close to God, daily meditate in His word
+ Walk in His high ways and holiness, for His glory

Genuine Repentance = True Change = Not Church as Usual

Now, if we, God's people (the pulpits and pews), will truly humble ourselves and come before God in *genuine repentance* then the result will be *genuine change—not* going back to church as usual.

This genuine repentance must include *real* change starting with the pulpits of America, then in the pews. It is not enough to have representative repentance in the pulpit or at an event if most of God's people are not *really* changing *their own* ways. It starts with each of us on a personal level; but we also need godly leaders to rise up and lead by example.

We need some Daniels

Daniel was one of the few main characters the Bible with nothing negative said about him. He understood the times and he led the way on his knees—repenting and praying on behalf of his people (see Daniel 9). Daniel said, "We have sinned." He took the sins of God's people, the nation, upon his own shoulders and led the way.

God needs strong leaders to stand up set the example and lead the way. Our churches need to see true men of God in the pulpits on their knees in repentance, in humility, and in brokenness crying out for our churches and our nation. We need leaders who fear God more than man and will call for genuine repentance in the pulpits and pews, and then to our nation. Daniel was a man of great prayer (three times a day) and his heart was clearly seen in his prayer for his people (see Daniel 9). Will you be a Daniel for the church, a leader, an example for the people?

A PRAYER OF REPENTANCE

> O LORD, great and awesome God....we have sinned and committed iniquity, we have done wickedly and rebelled, even by departing from your [ways].
>
> —DANIEL 9:4–5

The following is a prayer of repentance example we offer on behalf of the American church.

> *O Righteous Father, in Your great mercy, please forgive us, for we have rejected You and rejected Your ways. As a nation we have lost our fear of You, and we have greatly dishonored Your name. In our arrogance and pride, we have not humbled ourselves and prayed; but instead we have foolishly clung to our own self-centered and carnal ways.*
>
> *Please forgive us for not being a fully devoted bride with a fiery love for You. We have not loved You with all our heart, our mind, our soul, and our strength. Instead, we have embraced other lovers and have allowed pleasures, other gods, and idols of this world to take Your place. Forgive*

us for living for ourselves rather than pursuing You, for not seeking first Your kingdom and Your righteousness.

We have drunk from the dark and polluted wells of the world instead of drinking from the rivers of life and Your cleansing, life changing Word. Please forgive us for not guarding our hearts and renewing our minds to Your glorious Word and higher ways.

Father, please forgive us for our great sin and compromise. We have not been holy as You have called us to be, but we instead have taken our sin lightly and have trampled on Your grace and mercy. Forgive us for our selfish pride, our envy, our strife, and our wicked ways. We have defiled Your house and helped defile our land.

Please forgive us for our complacency, not being the rich salt and bright light You have called us to be and that our nation so desperately needs! Forgive us for fearing man and not boldly speaking the truth in love; for allowing the forces of darkness to invade and ravage our land. Please forgive us for allowing our nation to forsake and abandon You and Your ways; and for opening the gates for great sin and perversion and allowing innocent blood to flood our nation.

Please forgive us for honoring man more than You and compromising Your holy Word. Forgive us for not building Your house Your way and for not making it the "house of prayer" You called it to be.

Please help us, O God, we pray! Come visit us—cleanse and purify us and Your house, that we may rise up and become Your glorious church in the earth, to be the glorious bride You are returning for.

And now, we earnestly pray, let the fire of Your Holy Spirit come and stir our hearts once again with a fiery love for You. Open our eyes to see how far we have fallen and how great our need is for You! Bring us and our nation to our knees in true brokenness and repentance.

Thank You for Your divine power to transform us and raise us up as Your glorious church—to advance Your will in the earth, to rescue souls, to disciple nations, and to impact eternity for Your kingdom and Your glory! Amen.

Genuine Repentance in Divine Order

Besides genuine repentance on a personal level, we believe God's divine order for genuine repentance of a nation involves 3 steps:

Step 1: The Pulpits

The five-fold ministry must lead the way. Their obedience will open the door for this wave of genuine repentance to sweep into our churches, then to the nation.

Step 2: The Pews

God is calling His people to follow the pulpits' lead and humble themselves in genuine repentance and obedience, which will prepare the way for the Spirit of God to flow out to our nation (see "Key 2: The Power to Change Everything," chapter 19). Our churches must change first, then our nation.

Step 3: The Multitudes

By the power of God's Spirit, America will "awaken" to see her need for God and turn from her sin and back to Him. We believe this step must include our national leaders turning our nation back to God and His ways with a "New Declaration" (see "A Call to America's Leaders," chapter 26).

Pulpits—five-fold ministry: you hold the keys! You must turn the *first key* of *genuine repentance—nationwide* to open the door, remove hindrances, and position us for genuine change. Then we need to then step through the door to walk out that change.

Once the first key opens the door, we are then positioned to release the power to change everything (the second key)!

KEY 2: THE POWER TO CHANGE EVERYTHING

Nation-Changing Prayer

I tell you, history could be altered and changed again if
people went to their knees in believing prayer.[1]
—BILLY GRAHAM

THE POWER TO change our nation is not in Washington, DC—it's in the pulpits and pews all across America, on their knees. True change in our nation will not come on the floor of the senate, but on the floor of the prayer closet across the nation and in our churches. And, only when we pray *God's way (with nation-changing prayer)* will we then see the change we desire in our churches, communities, political, and legislative. The church praying God's way can bring a monumental shift from coast to coast.

> Men may spurn our appeals, reject our message, oppose our arguments, despise our persons, but they are helpless against our prayers.[2]
>
> —J. SIDLOW BAXTER

A Paramount "Paradigm Shift!"

To see our churches and nation truly change—there *must* be a monumental "paradigm shift" in our churches regarding prayer; for until the church gets this right, we will continue to see failure or limited results in our efforts. God is wanting to turn America from great destruction and back to Him; but it must be a work of His Spirit: "'Not by might nor by power, but by My Spirit,' Says the LORD" (Zech. 4:6).

The *first key of genuine repentance (nationwide)* removes hindrances, opens the door, and positions us for deep and lasting change. The *second key* releases the power (God's Spirit) to bring a nation to its knees and begin changing everything. However, without this second key there will be no Great Awakening or reformation of our churches and nation.

Remember, only the Spirit of God can bring the kind of genuine repentance that we need to sweep across our nation. This will require what we call "nation-changing prayer." Next we share what this "nation-changing" prayer looks like and the power it has to change everything.

PROPHETIC WORD

Preface: It was the morning as we were praying in agreement with the National day of Prayer, May 7, 2009. (We encourage everyone to always participate in the National Day of Prayer.) As we were praying in agreement at home, God spoke a powerful word, describing what was required to change the course of the nation. He said this:

How to Change the Course of a Nation,
May 7, 2009, prophecy through Cindy deVille

> Tell them—the course of the nation is in their hands,
> If they will but pray...
> If their prayers would pour out like rain, like rain, like rain...
> If they will pray and press in, not just one day,
> But everyday—they will see everything change...
>
> They will see the things within their government changed.
> They will see things in high places moved, changed, rearranged,
> And come in line with what is divine.
> And come in line with what I am calling this nation to.
>
> If they will cause their prayers to pour forth like rain, like rain,
> Then I will pour down My presence upon this nation.
> I will pour down upon My church.
> I will pour down upon My people.
> And that which many have tried to do through the decades and have
>   failed,
> I shall do and I shall turn by My Spirit.
> I will change this nation.
>
> So I am calling My people to pray and to come to Me,
> For only I have the power,
> Only I contain the power to turn this nation back to Me.
>
> So tell them to come to Me, and to cry out to Me
> And to not let go, to not quit, to not back down,
> Until they see Me crown their efforts and their prayers with success.
> Until they see Me come and pour out My Spirit upon this nation.
> Tell them, tell them—the course of the nation is in their hands,
> If they will but pray!
>
> Turn, turning, turning from their own wicked ways.
> If they would turn—for it is the effectual and fervent prayer of the
>   righteous,
> The righteous, the righteous that will accomplish and avail much.
> It is the prayers of the righteous man and woman that stand before
>   Me.
> Those who are in right standing before Me.
> Those are the effectual and fervent prayers that will change this nation.

So do not come to Me and cry out with hidden sin in your heart,
With unforgiveness and hatred,
But come to Me as a holy people—for I am holy.
Come to Me as a righteous man and a righteous woman...
Then I will hear you, I will hear you, and I will answer you.

Do you not think I have the power to change a whole nation?
I do. But I am waiting upon you!
I am waiting upon you My church.
I am waiting upon you to turn to Me with all of your heart,
To lay aside all of your idols.
To lay aside all of the things that are coming between you and Me.
You must be doers of My Word
And not hearers only, deceiving yourselves.

These are not just dead words I speak to you today.
But I am showing you the way to turn this nation.
If you will but listen to Me and heed,
And do My word that I have spoken to you,
Then you will see everything change.

Note: We share more details of what this change will look like later in "The Results: Then We Will See...," chapter 25.

KEY 2: NATION-CHANGING PRAYER (MASSIVE)

Imagine the prayers of God's people being poured out like rain in our churches and homes all across America in such a way that the spiritual atmosphere over our churches, communities, cities, and the whole nation begins to shift and change.

Imagine God's people pouring out their prayers day and night, then the Spirit of God pouring down and breaking up the fallow ground of the hardened hearts and souls across America. Imagine the hearts and eyes of the lost, the bound and deceived, the prodigals and backslidden suddenly opening and them falling to their knees crying out in repentance and turning back to God. Then imagine people beginning to flood our churches because they want to know God and have their lives transformed.

Imagine in churches across our nation prayers pouring out like streams, then converging with other streams of prayer and becoming a massive river of prayer and intercession flowing throughout the land. Then imagine the Spirit of God descending and sweeping across our land from coast to coast bringing a nation to its knees in the greatest awakening ever seen. This is what God desires to do—He's just waiting on us!

Remember, this must begin with the five-fold ministry, for the pulpits hold the keys (chapter 16). God is calling His leaders and people to their knees in genuine repentance (Key 1) and massive nation-changing prayer (Key 2). Then the Spirit of God will flow like a massive river to the multitudes. It will sweep across the land greater than ever before.

A confirming word

We recently heard of a prophet of God from India. When he was visiting America in 2002, the Lord sent him a message that unless "rivers of intercession" flow in America, great judgment will come that will make 9/11 look like "child's play."[3]

Remember the severity of coming enemy attacks and war from shore to shore (see "What's Coming Next, If...," chapter 11). Yes, only "rivers of intercession" (Key 2) coupled with genuine repentance (Key 1) will help avert such great judgment.

Extreme times call for...

These "rivers of intercession" will only come as God's people pray every day (as instructed in the previous word "How to Change the Course of a Nation"). Some may consider this call for massive daily (day and night) prayer extreme; but it's been said that extreme times call for extreme measures. We are in such a time as this! The sin and deception in our nation is so great, and the depth of change needed is so deep it requires extraordinary prayer!

Jonathan Edwards was a key pastor and leader that helped bring the First Great Awakening to America that helped change the course of a young America, and prepare the people to make history with an extraordinary revolution that birthed a new nation. He said:

> When God has something very great to accomplish for His church, it is His will that there should precede it the extraordinary prayers of His people.[4]

Likewise before us stands an opportunity to make history—an extraordinary turning point for our nation. For us to change the course of a massive nation like America will require massive prayer—nation-changing prayer. In a moment we will share what constitutes "nation-changing prayer," but first let's review why prayer is so powerful and vital.

The Power and Benefits of Prayer

We need to renew our minds to the power and benefits of prayer. Throughout biblical and world history, prayer has shaped, saved, and changed people and nations. Our prayers can carry great spiritual force and the power of heaven to come upon earth.

Important Note: Every true "revival" and "Great Awakening" has been preceded by much prayer; but not one has ever started without it.

Scripture consistently reminds us of the need and even commands us to pray and not just a little bit. We are exhorted to pray without ceasing (1 Thess. 5:17), to let everything be done by prayer and supplication (Phil. 4:6), and also told that men ought always to pray and not to faint (Luke 18:1, KJV). To the casual Christian this may seem extreme, but this is how God's people are to operate. We are citizens of heaven. To us prayer should be as natural as breathing.

The following is just a short list of the power and benefits of prayer (individual and corporate).

+ Prayer connects us with heaven and aligns our hearts and minds with the heart, mind, and will of God (Matt. 6:9).

+ Then our prayers release God's divine will into the earth, as it is in heaven (Matt. 6:10).

+ Prayer brings God on the scene and into our circumstances.

+ From houses of prayer will spring forth the well of God's living water—the "river of life" (Ezek. 47; John 7:38).

+ Prayer releases the Spirit and power of God to move in our lives, our families, our circumstances, our church, our community, our city, and our nation like streams from heaven (Matt. 6:10).

+ Prayer pushes back and hinders the powers of darkness, as light dispels the darkness. The greater and purer the light, the greater the impact (Matt. 5:14–16).

+ Prayer releases God's Spirit and angels to go and work on our behalf (Acts 12:5–12).

+ Prayer not only changes *things*, prayer changes *us* (2 Cor. 3:18)

+ Prayer cultivates unity (Acts 1:14; 2:1).

The truth is, if God's people could see what truly happens in the spiritual realm when we pray, His people would be praying all the time. Our minds must be renewed (paradigm shift) to the power, glory, and importance of prayer—especially *nation-changing prayer!*

WHAT IS NATION-CHANGING PRAYER?

Nation-changing prayer will take shape in two ways:
Part 1: Pure, passionate, and persistent prayer
Part 2: Establish the "glorious house of prayer."

Reminder: Humility first

Again, humility is the starting point to nation-changing prayer. "If My people…will *humble* themselves *and pray*…" (2 Chron. 7:14, emphasis added). God opposes the proud but gives grace to the humble (James 4:6). Our prayers will be heard and our efforts will be successful only if we humbly submit and follow His ways. The first key of genuine repentance helps establish this.

Part 1: Pure, Passionate, and Persistent Prayer

God revealed in the prophetic word earlier in this chapter three components of prayer required to "change the course of our nation." Like a special formula, all three of these prayer components need to be in operation to have maximum effect and bring "nation-changing" results. These three prayer components are:

1. Pure prayer (unhindered)
2. Passionate prayer (fervent)
3. Persistent prayer (relentless)

Faith is the powerful force behind all these that can cause mountains to move and bring nations to their knees (Matt. 17:20).

Now, let us look at each of these:

1. Pure Prayer (Unhindered)

Effective and nation-changing prayer starts with us coming before God with pure hearts and clean hands (Ps. 24:3–4). The apostle Paul said, "Flee also youthful lusts; but pursue righteousness, faith, love, peace with those who call *on the Lord* out of a *pure* heart." (2 Tim. 2:22, emphasis added).

God is calling His people to purity in heart, in motive, in life, and in prayer (1 Thess. 4:7). This is where beginning with Key 1, genuine repentance, comes in—to cleanse our hearts and position us for pure and powerful prayer. This is not about perfection but allowing the true grace of God to empower us to walk holy before Him as His children, because our prayers can be hindered.

Three of the main ways prayers are hindered:

Sin hinders prayer

Living in hidden or unconfessed willful sin will hinder our prayers. It pollutes our relationship with God and causes a disconnect. "If My people will…turn from their wicked ways…then I will hear" (2 Chron. 7:14). "Your iniquities have made a separation between you and your God, and your sins have hidden his face from you so that he does not hear" (Isa. 59:2, ESV).

Unforgiveness hinders prayer

Unforgiveness is very serious (see Matthew 18:21–35). Unforgiveness will not only hinder our prayers but corrupt our hearts. "And when you stand praying, if you hold anything against anyone, forgive them, so that your Father in heaven may forgive you your sins." (Mark 11:25, NIV)

Dishonor, disunity, and pride hinder prayer

United prayer is powerful (such as gatherings of families or churches). Conversely, dishonor and disunity have the opposite effect. Peter also addressed this issue regarding marriage and prayer: "Likewise, husbands, live with your wives in an understanding way, showing honor to the woman as the weaker vessel, since they are heirs with you of the grace of life, so that your prayers may not be hindered" (1 Pet. 3:7, ESV)

Pure prayer positions us for powerful prayer. Those praying with hidden sin or unforgiveness in their hearts will be greatly hindered. It is important we allow God to first deal with the issues of our own heart. Those believers who are walking before God, empowered by His glorious grace and walking uprightly before Him will be heard by God and will be powerful and effective in prayer. James says it is the effective fervent prayer of the *righteous* that is powerful and effective (5:16, NIV).

Nation-changing prayer is pure and unhindered.

2. Passionate Prayer (Fervent)

God is calling for sincere, heartfelt, and fervent (intense) prayer.

> The effective *fervent* prayer of a righteous man avails much.
> —James 5:16, EMPHASIS ADDED

The word *fervent* means *intense, boiling hot,* like a furnace. You could say fervent is also passionate and heartfelt. Fervent prayer is fueled by great faith in God and His power to answer. Fervent prayer is also fueled with great purpose, even desperation—such as the state of our nation right now. Fervent prayer also comes from a heart of brokenness for the pastors, the church, and our nation. Our God is a consuming fire (Heb. 12:29); and when the fire of His Holy Spirit is in and upon us, our prayers will often carry a fervency and intensity.

Jesus' Example: Pressing in—a Defining Moment

Jesus, the night in the garden before His work on the cross, "prayed more earnestly" (Luke 22:44). He pressed in with fervency, with intensity, until the work was done in the Spirit that He would walk out the next day that began changing everything! It was a defining moment for Him.

Likewise, we also stand on the brink of a defining moment. The desperate need to change the destructive course of the American church and our nation should stir our hearts to massive action! Therefore, God is calling His people to "press in" to pour out our prayers every day, in purity and filled with faith. We must pour forth rivers of intercession across our nation—the magnitude of what must be changed requires it. Here is a reminder of what God said will happen when we do this:

> If they will pray and press in, not just one day,
> But everyday—they will see everything change.
> They will see the things within their government changed.
> They will see things in high places moved, changed, rearranged,
> And come in line with what is divine.
> And come in line with what I am calling this nation to.

We pray what God has promised will stir your soul. As you pray with purity, go deep and unstop the wells of life for streams and rivers to flow. Remember, Jesus said:

> He who believes in Me, as the Scripture has said, out of his heart will
> flow rivers of living water.
> —John 7:38

This brings us to the third component of prayer God is asking for. Nation-changing prayer must not only be *pure* and *passionate*, but it must also be *persistent*.

3. Persistent Prayer (Relentless)

Persistent prayer is relentless prayer. We must pour forth our prayers like rain, *until* we see God do what He has promised! His instructions were:

> So tell them to come to Me, and to cry out to Me
> And to not let go, to not quit, to not back down,
> Until they see Me crown their efforts and their prayers with success.
> Until they see Me come and pour out My Spirit upon this nation.

It takes great faith and a holy determination to persist in prayer, especially when we do not see things change immediately. God is a rewarder of those who *diligently* (in faith and persistence) seek Him (Heb. 11:6).

God wants and needs His people to "lock on" and not let go. We need to be praying day and night until we see everything change!

Daniel prayed *three times* a day. Even devote Muslims pray *five times* a day. Should not we, the church, pray *at least once or twice* a day for our churches and for our nation, including the lost and the prodigals?

Example of consistent prayer resulting in God's glory

Acts 1:14 accounts how the 120 all prayed continually, with one agenda—praying *until* they received the Promise of the Father. Then when they were in one accord and at the appointed time, the Spirit and glory of God came down and birthed the New Testament church.

Likewise, God is calling and instructing us to unite in one accord and pray continually *until* we see Him come and pour out His Spirit and glory upon our churches and upon our nation as He has promised.

Jesus told His disciples they should always pray and not give up (Luke 18:1, NIV). Then He said, "And will not God bring about justice for his chosen ones, who cry out to him day and night?" (v. 7, NIV).

Important Biblical Example: Elijah's Response

There had been a three-year drought in Israel. Once Elijah dealt with the source of the sin on Mt. Carmel, then God's people turned from Baal worship and turned back to the Lord (see 1 Kings 18:20–40). Once repentance came, it was then Elijah heard the sound of the "abundance of rain" in the spiritual realm ready to be released in the natural (v. 41). Repentance opened the door for the abundance of rain to come!

When Elijah heard the sound of the abundance of rain coming, what was his response? He did not sit down and just wait for it. He did not say, "God is sovereign; it will happen eventually." Rather, God was revealing to him what He would do if Elijah would release it through prayer. Elijah knew God's plan and he understood he had a significant part to play to bring it about. So Elijah partnered with God in pure, passionate, and persistent prayer (seven times) until he *saw* what he *heard* (by the Spirit of God) come to pass in the natural (vv. 42–44).

Our response

Just like Elijah, God is calling His leaders and people to partner with Him in pure, passionate, and persistent prayer until we *see* with our eyes what so many have *heard* by the Spirit of God—the sound of a coming Great Awakening that will pour down upon our land like rain! It is worth repeating once again what God promised earlier in this chapter:

> If they will pray and press in, not just one day,
> But everyday—they will see everything change…
>
> They will see the things within their government changed.
> They will see things in high places moved, changed, rearranged,
> And come in line with what is divine.
> And come in line with what I am calling this nation to.
>
> If they will cause their prayers to pour forth like rain, like rain…
> Then I will pour down My presence upon this nation….
>
> And that which many have tried to do through the decades and have
>   failed,
> I shall do and I shall turn by My Spirit.
> I will change this nation.

Whatever it takes

As the church we must add *persistence* to our *pure* and *passionate* prayers. If it takes us praying seven times, seven days, seven weeks, seven months, or seven years we must keep praying *until* we see this Great Awakening God has promised to "pour down" and flood our land with His presence and nation-changing power!

To birth a historic Great Awakening like never before will require prayers like never before—with the five-fold ministry leading the way. Day and night prayer that is pure (unhindered), passionate (fervent), and persistent (relentless) will provide the power to change everything.

Church-wide pure, passionate, and persistent prayer

Imagine God's people nationwide praying day and night. We would see such an outpouring and change in our nation it would defy description! And *this* is exactly what God is saying. This is *why* God is calling for our prayers to be pure, passionate, and persistent. Will you answer His call? Begin today!

Now, some will ask, "What specifically should we be praying for?" The focus of prayer should include prayer for both the church and the nation. We offer our Top 5 Prayer Guide in appendix A as a springboard to get you started.

Before we share part 2 of what "nation-changing prayer" includes, we offer some more encouraging and related prophetic insight.

RELATED PROPHETIC INSERT
GREAT ENCOURAGEMENT AND VISION

As God's people pray it is important we do what God is asking of us and not be discouraged if we do not see the answer when or how *we* want it. We must trust God will answer those prayers—that align with His will—in His time and His way. For God's ways are much higher than ours as He always sees the big vision and picture, not just the limited parts we see (Isa. 55:8–9).

God is collecting prayers to be poured out

Did you know there are prayers God collects to answer after a certain point is reached? Revelation 5:8 shows the prayers of the saints, like incense, can be collected into a vessel to be poured out when it becomes full. We believe this is exactly what will happen as God's people pray night and day; the vessels of heaven will begin to fill up, overflow, and then begin to be poured out upon our churches and upon our nation.

We all need to be reminded not to grow weary in well doing because we will reap in due season if we do not lose heart (Gal. 6:9). Many of God's people have been in a time of sowing, and many even in tears; but the time to reap will surely come, and a time of rejoicing, because God is always faithful to His Word (Ps. 126:6; Hosea 10:12).

In relation to this, God has given us several different kinds of imagery to portray what He is doing with the prayers of His saints and what will happen when they are answered. Besides the *river of life*, these have included a massive *dam* and a great *wave*.

A VISION: A GREAT DAM WITH PRAYERS

During a night of worship and prayer early 2013, our son Joshua shared a vision. He could see a massive dam holding back an ocean of water; as far as he could see, it seemed never ending. This water represented the prayers of the saints that were being stored up—prayers over the years and even generations for change in our churches, in our nation, for a great spiritual awakening and more.

The pressure on the dam was so great that little cracks started to form, and some of the water was spilling out here and there. The little cracks represented some positive change in America or a move of God here and there.

God wants to encourage His people and especially those heading up the prayer movements that God has heard every prayer and your efforts have not been in vain. When everything gets to a certain point, this dam will break forth and it will be like nothing we have ever seen. This is why the greater the number of people praying, the quicker it could burst or the greater it will be when it comes!

THE WAVE OF CHANGE

After the "Great Dam" vision, God also used the metaphor of a massive wave that will sweep across our land when the dam breaks. He showed us that:

- ✦ This great wave of His Spirit and glory will come and flood our land.
- ✦ He will use this wave to wash and cleanse the land.
- ✦ This wave will have such a force it will change the course of the church and the course of the nation.
- ✦ This wave will lift up and carry God's people up (those ready for it). They will ride this wave with His supernatural power and grace to do and fulfill His will in the earth.
- ✦ This wave will impact not only America, but nations will feel its power and force.

This supernatural wave is being created in prayer right now. Every prayer is adding to the water (symbolized by the wave, the great dam of water, and rain). So keep praying, keep on pressing through. Our prayers must be tenacious, not letting go until we see it!

We know God is calling us all to pure, passionate, and persistent prayer. The question now, is where? We can all pray at home, which is powerful; but God is calling churches to become a house of prayer (Mark 11:17). When we unite in prayer, everything is magnified. God's word tells us when two or three agree as touching anything on this earth it shall be done (Matt. 18:19). And that one puts a thousand to flight and two can put ten thousand to flight (Deut. 32:30). It's time to take our prayers to a whole new level!

PART 2: ESTABLISH THE GLORIOUS HOUSE OF PRAYER

Yes, we need a monumental "Paradigm Shift" on what God's house is intended to be a—"house of prayer for all nations" (Isa. 56:7; Mark 11:17). Prayer is to be at the very core of every church! Prayer is actually one of the highest forms of ministry because it brings God on the scene and releases His divine will into the earth.

We were greatly encouraged to see one of biggest and most influential churches in our city and America declare, "Prayer at Gateway Church is not something we do; it defines who we are…Prayer is engaging, exciting and rewarding."[5] This should be every church's decree.

In the days ahead the church must come to realize that our greatest work will be done on our knees—the supernatural transforming the natural. For without prayer most our efforts will be in vain and have little effect. As previously mentioned, for too long most of the church has had the cart before the horse. We believe this will be changing. We believe the day is coming that there will be houses of prayer everywhere. For the closer we draw to the Lord's return, the stronger the call and need for prayer will become.

Releasing Heaven and God's River of Life

With God's Word as the foundation, prayer is the furnace, the catalyst, the power source which empowers the church. Prayer provides the vital power connection with heaven—a gateway for the glory of God to come down and the river of life from His throne to flow to bring life, healing, and change to your people and surrounding communities (John 7:38; Ezek. 47; Rev. 22:1–2). Remember the word "How the Greatest Awakening Will Begin!" and how God's Spirit will flow like a massive river to the multitudes? But again, this will only come when we do it God's way.

Therefore, it is imperative that all churches give the highest importance to the ministry of prayer in order to provide a gateway (a connection to heaven). For it is God's desire to open up the floodgates and release heaven on earth to your communities, city, and the nation (Matt. 6:10).

Churches that do this God's way will be like an oasis in the desert with life-giving water and a place of refuge in the storm (Ps. 36:7–9). They will also become like that "city that is set on a hill" shining bright for all to see and glorify God (Matt. 5:14–16). They will become a powerful force to influence and transform.

A Glorious House

The church that is a "house of prayer" will also be a "house for God's glory" for His presence to dwell. God is coming back for a glorious church (Eph. 5:27). This is why we like to call the kind of churches God will be raising up as "glorious houses of prayer"—glorious in worship and prayer, rich and uncompromising in God's Word and truth, a lighthouse for God's glory to shine and His river of life to flow through. For in the days ahead the glory of God upon His house will be greater than the ever:

> "I will shake all nations, and…I will fill this temple with glory.…The glory of this latter temple shall be greater than the former," says the LORD of hosts.
>
> —HAGGAI 2:7, 9

One key element that brings God's glory and presence is worship.

The Dynamic of Worship and Prayer

Jesus made it clear the Father is seeking those that worship Him in Spirit and truth (John 4:24). A powerful dynamic to the "glorious house of prayer" is incorporating worship. When we look at Scripture we see the power of worship. In 2 Chronicles 20 it tells how the worshipers went before the army and how God defeated the enemy before them. God inhabits the praises of His people (Ps. 22:3, KJV). Worship or anointed music set an atmosphere for the presence of God (Ps. 100:4). God's throne is surrounded by continual worship and from His throne and presence the river of life flows (Rev. 22:1–2).

> And the twenty-four elders fell down before the Lamb. Each one had a *harp* and they were holding golden bowls full of incense, which are the *prayers* of God's people.
> —REVELATION 5:8, NIV, EMPHASIS ADDED

Notice they held *harps* for worship and bowls of *prayers*. Worship and prayer go hand in hand. We also see this in Psalm 149:6:

+ "Let the high praises of God be in their mouth [worship]."
+ "And a two-edged sword in their hand [God's Word]."

Praying God's Word and will is like a two-edged sword in our hand. Worship helps to:

+ Shake off and shut out the thoughts and distractions of everyday and helps us focus our attention on God (Ps. 100:4)
+ Positions us for sweet communion and powerful prayer
+ Prepares our hearts to hear the heartbeat of God and His will
+ Positions us to release God's kingdom and will into the earth (Matt. 6:10)

Worship and prayer together are powerful and dynamic on multiple levels. Worship-based prayer is a key to sustainable ongoing prayer in every church. One simple, insightful, and practical book explaining this is *The Praying Church* by Tom Grossman Sr. We also believe this worship-based prayer model is a form of restoring the "tabernacle of David" (worship, prayer, and glory of God) foretold of in Amos 9:11 and Acts 15:16. (The rich teaching of the tabernacle of David is beyond the scope of this book, so we encourage you to study it for yourself if you have not already.)

Life vs Lifeless

Without the high priority of prayer there will be no river of life flowing from our churches. Without prayer a church is spiritually lifeless; like an empty shell, no matter how large, polished, hip, loud, or grand it may appear—like the church at Sardis which Jesus said, "I know your works, that you have a name that you are alive, but you are dead" (Rev. 3:1).

It has been rightly said that prayer is the heartbeat of the church. Without prayer the church is spiritually dead and powerless.

This "glorious house of prayer" not only brings life but is also filled with great joy (Isa. 56:7). God wants His people and church to walk in "joy unspeakable and full of glory" (1 Pet. 1:8, KJV).

This is all just a glimpse of what His end-time church will look like. More about this later in the epilogue, "Entering a New Day: The Glorious Church."

Next is a powerful, insightful, and encouraging word that drives home what will happen to those churches that commit to become "glorious houses of prayer." It is also a cry from God's heart for His churches to be ready for what He is about to do.

Related Prophetic Word

Glorious House of Prayer—River Flow Out, Souls Flow In
April 30, 2014, through Cindy deVille

My house, My church must be ready to take them in,
Those that have been lost in sin,
They must be ready to take them in and disciple them.
My church must be ready.
For when I begin to move it will be like a mighty wave,
And many will be saved.
They will be saved, and the churches must be ready!
They must be ready.
Tell them—they need to be ready; they need to get ready,
They need to be ready get ready for what I am about to do.

In those cities, in those communities, in those churches,
In those places where My people are praying, where My house of
    prayer is,
Rivers are going to flow out of My house into the communities
And into the cities, and souls will flow in.
And prayers will flow out, and souls will pour in.
And I will begin to disciple, to transform, and to change.

Where the house of prayer is planted
Their prayers will be granted
And rivers will flow.
So many souls, so many don't know which way to go.
But as the prayers flow, as the prayers flow out,
It will cause the lost souls to turn, and they will know where to go.
They will go to where the rivers flow.

They will see the lighthouse,
And they will say to their family, "Come and go with me."

The house of prayer, My house,
Will be a lighthouse in the midst of dark and despair,
And many souls will turn, and they will know where to go—
Where the light is and where the rivers flow.
That is where they will go.
For they are not looking to be entertained
They are looking to be changed, to be changed.

This word included a vision:

Vision of a Fountain

through Cindy deVille

I see a big beautiful fountain in the middle of a city; and people, communities, and families are going to this fountain. They are all drawing water and drinking from this fountain. They are coming from all around drinking from the fountain (Ps. 36:7–9). Then God continued:

"This fountain will never run dry,
As the prayers of My saints are going forth day and night.
They will never turn out the light,
My lighthouse will shine day and night.
The fountain will flow day and night.
Prayer is the power that will keep the light shining bright.
Prayer is the power that will keep the fountains flowing.
The prayers will be what will draw them to Me," says the Lord.
"For it's not by might or by power but by My Spirit
Released with the intercession and the prayers
And the cries of the saints."

It will be amazing to see what God will do through those churches that align with His ways! "Glorious houses of prayer" will be easy to identify in the intense days ahead for they will be thriving—bringing life, light, and hope to their communities and cities.

We are on the threshold

We are standing on the threshold of the greatest outpouring we have ever seen, an outpouring of the glory of God in the church and then in the earth. God is calling for His people to come to Him, pouring out our prayers like rain until we see everything change. Will you join with us in nation-changing prayer and be a part of the greatest move of God in history? Our pure (unhindered), passionate (fervent), and persistent (relentless) prayers and "glorious houses of prayer" will release rivers from heaven to pave the way and bring forth a new day!

20

KEY 3: NO LIMITS

The Power of Unity

That they may be one just as We [Jesus and Father] are one.
—JOHN 17:22

GOD IS GETTING ready to take everything to a whole new level. Many have prayed for unity; and we believe when keys 1 and 2 are implemented, the Spirit of God will be released to bring His church to a level of unity we have never seen before. Think Acts 2 multiplied across the nation!

This is the critical third and final key from God's Answer of how to save and change our beloved nation. Without this key our efforts and results will continue to be limited. But, when we turn this final key there are no limits. With this final key nothing will be impossible for us and the results will be lasting!

Individual Efforts vs United Efforts

Our individual efforts, like one soldier in a battle, can only do so much. It takes an army working in unison under one plan to bring about great victory and change. Individual talent, anointing, or effort will only go so far. The only way we will see massive and lasting breakthrough in the nation is if we unite and work as one, in one accord, with Christ and His purposes at the center.

THE POWER OF ONE ACCORD

The power of unity is a principle demonstrated throughout God's Word. One accord = powerful results.

1. Nothing Is Impossible

In Genesis 11 we see in the story of the Tower of Babel that the people were united with one language and one heart and for one purpose. Even though their motives and reasons were wrong, God recognized their unity and said, "Nothing they plan to do will be impossible for them" (v. 6, NIV). So He stopped them by confusing their languages to bring disunity (vv. 7–8).

2. The Priests Made Way for the Glory of God to Come

In 2 Chronicles 5:11–14 we read where all the priests sanctified themselves, set aside their usual divisions, united their voice, and made way for the glory of God to come down and fill the temple.

3. The Birth of the Church

Two thousand years ago, the power of unity and one accord was once again demonstrated:

> When the Day...had fully come, they were all with one accord in one place. And suddenly there came a sound from heaven, as of a rushing mighty wind, and it filled the whole house.
>
> —ACTS 2:1–2

When the 120 disciples were in "one place" at the right time in "one accord," then suddenly God moved mightily.

4. Dynamic Multiplication Factor of Unity

There is in fact a dynamic multiplication factor when we unify our efforts. God's Word also tells us that one can put 1,000 to flight, but two can put 10,000 to flight (Deut. 32:30). That's a ten-fold factor. We are many times more effective when we work together in unity!

We revealed in the "The Pulpits Hold the Keys," chapter 17, of God's Answer that He was calling His leaders to their knees in repentance, in prayer, in humility, in "unity." Now we will look more specifically at the kind of unity and humility for which we believe God is calling.

KEY 3: UNITE—WORK AS ONE

Imagine God's leaders and people uniting together with one heart, one mind, one purpose, and one united divine plan to change and reform our churches and our nation. Unity in great humility and prayer, as the 120 did in the Book of Acts, ushered in the birth of the church and a whole new era.

Just as the Founding Fathers united and as a result everything changed and a new nation was born, God is calling His leaders and people to humbly unify our efforts, follow His answer—His instructions to save and change our nation, and at the same time birth a new era of the church (the glorious church). It will be a work of the Holy Spirit, but it will also be an act of humble obedience from His leaders.

The Decree: Unity in My house—Work as One

There is a decree going forth from the throne of God, a "call for unity" in His house. God is decreeing what must begin to take place for His church to be strong and effective for the days we are entering. (Remember the word "Days of Wonder and Days of Dread...Ahead" in chapter 10.)

God's glorious Son, Jesus Christ, has a work that must be done. Therefore, God is decreeing:

- It's time to come in line with the Divine; with His ways, plans, and timing.

+ His body will see how great her need is to function as one; that we will need each other to function, to flow, and to grow.

+ It's time to become one so the work can be done. It can't be fully done until we unite as one—one body that will rise up in the earth, His glorious church. It's time for us to become one to rise up and run.

Imagine a united glorious church in one accord, working as one, like a mighty supernatural army. It's coming; and the call is going out to see who will be a part of it. We say "part" of it because we believe this kind of unity will actually come out of separation. We explain why in the "Reality Check" later in this chapter.

We firmly believe as pastors and churches across the nation take hold of God's Answer and seriously implement keys 1 and 2, the Spirit of God will powerfully be released to do what we have failed to do in our own strength for decades. The Spirit of God will breathe upon the church and we will rise up in unity of spirit likened unto the vision Ezekiel had in the valley of dry bones (Ezek. 37:1–14).

WHAT IS REQUIRED TO UNITE

True unity is a work of the Holy Spirit and can only take place as we surrender our hearts and lives to Christ, allowing Him to work in us. Following are five things we believe will bring about the kind of unity God needs in His church for these last days.

1. Unity Through Humility

True unity requires true humility. In the greatest kingdom, the kingdom of God, unity starts with humility. God's Word says we are to be "clothed with humility, for 'God resists the proud, But gives grace to the humble'" (1 Pet. 5:5). The Lord Jesus Christ is our ultimate example as He humbled Himself even unto death (Phil. 2:8). And His heart cry to the Father was "not My will, but Yours, be done" (Luke 22:42).

One of the secrets to unity is dying to self and selfish ambition. We must become more "kingdom of God" minded. We must live for the fame of *His* name instead of our own. Paul exhorts us to be

> Like-minded, having the same love, *being of one accord, of one mind.* Let nothing be done through selfish ambition or conceit, but in lowliness of mind let each esteem others better than himself. Let each of you look out not only for his own interests, but also for the interests of others.
>
> —PHILIPPIANS 2:2–4, EMPHASIS ADDED

Humility also helps us keep our motives pure and keeps us from jostling for position, keeping us within God's call for our lives. As we truly humble ourselves and set aside our own agendas and fully submit to God and His ways, His plans, nothing will be impossible for us! The day of the Christian superstar is fading and a new day is dawning!

2. Unity Through Dynamic Covenant Love

The Puritans, who helped establish the godly foundations of early America, believed the kingdom of God could come to earth and change every area of society through Christian truth and principles. But they saw this only being possible through their lives of covenant—being total commitment to God (vertical) and with each other (horizontal). Again, this required great humility and total commitment. They took covenant very seriously and knew it must begin with the leadership. This covenant thinking is based up the two greatest commandments.

Vertical relationship and covenant:

> You shall love the Lord your God with all your heart, with all your soul, and with all your mind.
> —Matthew 22:37

Horizontal relationship and covenant:

> You shall love your neighbor as yourself.
> —Matthew 22:39

Humility with this kind of (vertical-horizontal) love and commitment centered around our Lord Jesus Christ creates a culture of great unity. Jesus said, "By this all will know that you are My disciples, if you love one another" (John 13:35). We are destined to come into the unity of the faith (Eph. 4:13); and true faith works through love (Gal. 5:6).

3. Unity Through Obedience

Closely linked with humility and love is obedience. If we are going to unite and flow together as one body and army under the direction of our Lord Jesus Christ, our Commander and Chief, then it is important that we are quick to hear and follow His orders. Every member must be in its place, doing what they were created and instructed to do. If soldiers in an army rebel choosing to go their own way, it can bring disorder, chaos, and even a great loss to the entire army. Obedience is critical if we are going to obtain victory. Jesus said if we love Him we will obey Him (John 14:15).

4. Unity Through Praying Together in One Accord

The 120 in the upper room demonstrated the power of praying together in one accord. Corporate prayer is very powerful! As we pray together in our churches and across the nation, our hearts become aligned with one another and with the Spirit of God, bringing about a great unity and power to bring change. Remember the "glorious house of prayer" in Key 2.

5. United Plan, Strategies, and Action

America exists today because our Founding Fathers united under one vision and plan (the Declaration of Independence, then the Constitution), pledging their lives, their fortunes, and their sacred honor. It was because of this that everything changed and a new nation was born.

Could you imagine the powerful result from leaders all across the body of Christ humbly uniting as one? Imagine what could be accomplished if the majority of the body of Christ operated as one; not just in a general sense, but working together like an army with very specific plans and strategies that greatly affect and even reform America. We offer a glimpse at such a proposed plan later in the implementing of God's Answer (See the call to action in "Step 3: The National Level," chapter 24).

REALITY CHECK

A GIDEON'S ARMY—UNITY FROM SEPARATION

We believe there will be a great work of unity by the Spirit of God in His church. However, we will also see unity emerging from a time of separation, as God searches to see, "Who is really with Me?" There is a line being drawn in the sand, and those that are fully devoted to Christ and are willing to lay down their life and do church God's way are going to be on one side. Those unwilling to hear what the Spirit of God is saying and doing will be on the other side. Remember, in "God's Letter to His Pastors and Leaders," chapter 15, we shared at the end: "When the lines are drawn in the sand, On whose side will you stand?"

Gideon's army is a scriptural example of strategic separation. God is investigating the troops, testing and trying the hearts and motives of His people to see who is ready. God needs to know who is "all in" and willing to follow Him and who He can trust to get the job done. These are the ones who will lead the church into victory.

> Those that know God and will be strong and do exploits
> Those who are fully devoted and surrendered to Him
> Those who have laid down their lives as living, holy sacrifices
> Those who are living for His pleasure and not their own
> Those who are walking in purity and humility in heart, life, and
>   motive
> Those who will fight for what is just and right
> Those who will not compromise

Scripture also tells us, "Many are called, but few are chosen" (Matt. 22:14). Few are willing pay the price. Like a Special Forces unit in the military there will be times of vigorous testing to be sure we are equipped and ready. God is preparing an army to rise up.

Like Gideon's army, God will strip away; He will separate those that are truly His from those just playing church or not cooperating with Him. Those that remain will come into great unity, for they will be of one heart, one mind, and one purpose. Their hearts are fixed upon God and His will. Those are the ones He will raise up and use to reveal His glory, to shine bright in the days ahead (see Isaiah 60). Remember "The Great Visitation" word in chapter 14 about God separating the real from the false and out of that His glorious church would rise. (Also, for more details you can access a word called "A Great Sword of Separation" from 2009 in appendix F.)

It's time to unite

We believe God is calling all of us as His leaders and people at this very critical time to humble ourselves and unite under one divine plan to bring America to her knees in a great awakening and reformation. We propose the outline of such a plan in chapter 24, "Step 3: The National Level."

God, by His Spirit, is pulling together and fashioning a glorious army that will rise up together with one mind, one heart, one purpose, and one voice to help bring change to His church and this nation and to impact nations around the world as never before. We believe God is looking for the kind of unity witnessed in Acts 2 to once again usher His people (His church) into a whole new era.

May Jesus' prayer, "Father…that they may be one just as We are one" (John 17:21–22), echo in our ears, minds, and hearts! For the church to be truly effective, we must come together and operate as one body (Eph. 4:15–16). Then the things the church has tried to accomplish through the decades God will do by the power of His Spirit—*if* we will *unite* together as *one* and run with God's Answer.

Together we can save and change the nation!

21

REVIEWING GOD'S ANSWER

WE STATED IN chapter 1 that God's Answer is critical to the future of America. And what we do right now will determine the course of our nation—great judgment and destruction or great awakening and restoration. God is counting on His leaders and people to embrace His answer, to rise up, and lead the way into a new day for our churches and our nation.

God's Answer is more than a message—it needs to become a movement in churches all across America!

MISSION CRITICAL

The Pulpits Hold the Keys and Lead the Way

The Great Awakening *and changing the nation begins here!*

God is calling the five-fold ministry to humbly lead the way—in repentance, prayer, and unity. Then change will begin to flow like a massive river from the pulpits, to the pews, then to the multitudes of America. This must include three keys that will bring lasting change.

Key 1: Genuine Repentance—Nationwide

Only a baptism of genuine repentance sweeping like a wave across our churches will open the door to genuine change that lasts. This must begin with the pulpits (and the pews) of America. This *key* positions us to release the power to change everything.

Key 2: Nation-Changing Prayer (Massive)

God is instructing His people *how* to pray to release His power to change everything in our nation. Nation-changing prayer will take shape in two ways:

Part 1: Begin Pure, Passionate, and Persistent Prayer

- Pure—no hidden sin or unforgiveness
- Passionate—fervent prayer of the righteous is very effective
- Persistent—relentless until will see the answers

God's is calling His people everywhere pouring out their prayers like rain every day (day and night) until God pours out His Spirit across this nation and we see everything change (Zech. 4:6). "Rivers of intercession" (our prayers) from the West Coast to the East Coast will alter the course of this nation, bringing America to her knees and back to God.

Part 2: Establish "Glorious Houses of Prayer" Everywhere

God's mandate is for His house to be a "house of prayer" (Isa. 56:7; Matt. 21:13; Luke 19:46; Mark 11:17)—to be a light house with God's Word, worship, and prayer at its very core.

We need churches all across America connecting with heaven and releasing God's rivers of life (Ezek. 47; Rev. 22), healing, and restoration into their communities, cities, and the nation for sweeping and lasting change to come. Rivers of prayer will flow out and souls will flow in.

Key 3: Unite—Work as One

United as one there will be no limits! We must unite in one accord with one purpose within one focused plan to bring forth a nation-shaking awakening and reformation. We will share how this can realistically be done, even with a Gideon's army.

Also, God is calling for a whole new level of unity to bring forth a new day and raise up His glorious church in the earth (Isa. 60:1–3; Eph. 5:27).

God's Answer, a holy solution

God's Answer is not a political solution or a legislative solution, it is a holy solution. When we (God's leaders and people) do what God is instructing, America will see the greatest awakening in history and true solutions for our nation will come. Everything can change!

There is no other way! If the pulpits of America, the five-fold ministry, will not embrace and follow God's Answer, we will not see the breakthrough, but overall things will get worse and greater judgment will instead need to come to bring the change. However, if we will cooperate with God and do things His way, the results will astound us! God will change everything!

We must implement God's Answer now!

We must remember, one way or another God will bring America to her knees and back to Him. How this happens (great judgment, a Great Awakening, or both) will be determined by how quickly God's pastors, leaders, and churches respond to His answer. Time is running out, and there is no other way.

Next we begin to share how God's Answer can be implemented in the pulpits (every pastor with the rest of the five-fold ministry), by every local church, and then on a national scale, church-wide. Do not wait another day, begin now!

SECTION 3:

THE CALL TO ACTION

Implementing God's Answer: Turning the Keys

22

Step 1: The Pulpit Level

23

Step 2: The Local Church Level

24

Step 3: The National Level

25

The Results: Then We Will See...

26

A Call to America's Leaders

27

A Final Word

A CALL TO UNITE AND BEGIN NOW

W E STAND ON the threshold of the greatest move of God America has ever seen. We have the historic opportunity of a lifetime before us to greatly change our churches and the self-destructive course of our nation.

If we truly want to avert the greater judgment of God and bring forth a Great Awakening, then it is time for pastors, ministries, and churches across America to engage and do what God is instructing. You (the pulpits) hold the keys; and now is the time to unlock the doors to begin this Great Awakening and great change!

Biblical Example: Hezekiah's call for urgent action

Hezekiah became king in a time when the nation was broken, idolatry was rampant, and God's house was compromised, defiled, and closed. Enemies had also ravaged the land, with many killed or taken captive. This was because their leaders had rejected God and His righteous ways. (This is the same path America is progressing down today!)

Once Hezekiah became king, he did not waste any time. He was passionate and completely dedicated about the change his nation so desperately needed (2 Chron. 29–32). In his very first month as king, he made dramatic changes. He began rebuilding and changing everything. We believe this is the kind of heart and attitude God needs and wants His leaders to have: do it now; don't delay; start today! This is also the kind of leadership we need in our nation. Hezekiah got his nation back on the right path by the following, which we believe are parallel to what we must also do for our nation:

1. Cleansing and Restoring God's House

Change began with the spiritual leaders. Hezekiah gathered the priests and Levites and called them to first sanctify themselves and then cleanse and sanctify God's house. They were to first prepare themselves and remove everything that was defiling God's house. God's leaders arose and acted quickly to do as instructed.

2. A Call to Nation's Leaders

Once God's house had been prepared and cleansed, then Hezekiah called the nation's rulers to return to God and the ways of God. When they did, it opened the door to national reformation.

3. Then Came Great Reformation

Once the spiritual and national leaders responded, Hezekiah then brought great reformation to the nation. This included destroying and removing all the altars and idols that were allowed to come into the land. He took a stand against the wickedness in the land.

All this resulted in both God's house and the nation being greatly restored, blessed, prospered, and victorious over their enemies. It is also noteworthy that as a result Hezekiah was highly esteemed and honored (2 Chron. 32:27).

This all happened quickly because God's leaders were unified in heart and action. We believe the pattern and process will be the same for America as we implement God's Answer.

IMPLEMENTING GOD'S ANSWER

Implementing God's Answer on a massive scale will be a process, as it was with Hezekiah.

Step 1: Pulpit Level

It starts on a personal level with every pastor and ministry (and Christian) hearing God's answer and responding to the call to prepare and sanctify and consecrate themselves for what God is about to do (Key 1).

Step 2: Local Church Level

Then it is time for pastors all across America to begin implementing God's Answer into their churches. It's time to respond to God's cry—to prepare and sanctify and consecrate the people for what God is about to do. It's time to cleanse God's house from anything that would defile or hold us back. This includes establishing a "glorious house of prayer" (Key 2) to begin changing your communities, cities, and the nation.

Step 3: National Level

Now, let us work as one within a united plan—a nationwide campaign to bring the Great Awakening, turn America back to God, and then reform the nation (Key 3). This would include a call to America's leaders to return to God and His ways, His path of life and restoration, before greater judgment comes.

God is counting on you, His church, to rise up and seize this moment! We cannot stay still or silent, we must act now! Begin today! God is waiting on you! A nation is waiting on you!

STEP 1: THE PULPIT LEVEL

All the priests who were there had consecrated themselves, regardless of their divisions...and...the glory of the LORD filled the temple of God.
—2 CHRONICLES 5:11, 14, NIV

Please note that while this chapter is addressed to the pastors of America, every five-fold minister can adopt this for their ministry. We also exhort every Christian to do the first four steps.

GOD'S ANSWER HAS made it clear: the birth of an historic Great Awakening that will dramatically save and change our nation begins with you—five-fold ministry!

It's Time to Get Yourself and Your Church Ready!

Now is the time to embrace and run with God's Answer—because lives, families, churches, and our nation are hanging in the balance; much is at stake. At this critical time God's leaders must align and cooperate with Him, lest they be left behind in the wake of radical change. For church as usual is about to come to an end.

God is preparing to do a greater work *in* you, so He can do a greater work *through* you! And right now the Spirit of God wants to come along side and help you prepare and lead the way for a new day.

PREPARING FOR A NEW DAY—EIGHT STEPS

God is calling His pastors and leaders to their knees, to humbly draw near to Him and prepare for a time of great shaking, great visitation, and great awakening (Hag. 2; 6-9; Heb. 12:26-29)!

Following are eight steps we believe are critical to help prepare and position you (pastors, five-fold ministry) to be ready for what God is about to do. God wants to prepare you first and then your church to go to a whole new level for the intense days ahead and at the same time help save and change our nation. Remember, God is saying it is time to "Prepare, O man of God, prepare everywhere" ("Great Visitation" in chapter 14)."

Note: If you have personally already walked through this process, and believe you are ready for what's coming, then please help pass on God's Answer along with the following eight steps to every pastor, five-fold minister you know.

Before walking through these steps, we encourage you to go back and review

"The Great Visitation" prophecy in chapter 14, "God's Letter to His Pastors and Leaders," chapter 15, and "The Pulpits Hold the Keys," chapter 17.

Step 1: Meeting with God

This is a critical time, and more than anything else right now God needs your undivided attention.

Years ago, during what became a turning point in our lives, God needed our attention to speak to us. He then gave us the following vision that you may relate to:

> We were seated at a long dining room table. It was covered will all kinds of things, many were tall and piled high. These represented all the things in our life, things we thought we needed to be doing for God and ourselves. In the vision God was on the other side of the table and He wanted to talk to us, but He couldn't because all these "things" and distractions were in the way.
>
> Then with a jealous zeal, the Spirit of God, with one great swipe, knocked everything off the table. It was clear He wanted nothing between us—no distractions! He wanted clear communication, because He had something very important to say.

Likewise, we believe God has something important to say to you. This can be a major turning point for you, your church, and ministry. Therefore, we exhort you to:

A. Set aside at least one to two days to get away and to meet alone with God, without distraction. Part of the answer for us and our nation is humbly *seeking His face.* "If My people...will humble themselves and pray and *seek My face...*" (2 Chron. 7:14, emphasis added).

B. Do not hesitate. Make this a top priority and adjust your schedule to make this happen. God is waiting on you.

As you clear the table and draw near to Him, He will draw near to you (James 4:8), which leads us to the next step.

Step 2: An Internal Investigation

This is a time to encounter God and invite Him to come in and conduct an internal investigation of your heart, life, and ministry. Let David's prayer in Psalm 139:23–24 be yours:

> Search me, O God, and know my heart: try me, and know my thoughts: And see if there be any wicked way in me, and lead me in the way everlasting.

This is a time to:

A. Humbly lay everything before God—your life, your ministry, your church. Let your prayer be, "Not my will but Your will be done. Not my way but Your way, Lord."

B. Allow the Holy Spirit to investigate and evaluate everything you are doing—everything. Allow Him to show you what to let go of and what to keep. He wants to help you remove everything that would hold you back or slow you down.

Consider also these self-examining questions as you go before Him:

+ Am I truly walking and communing with God, as Jesus did, or has He merely become a means to an end?

+ Have I put up walls because of hurts, offenses, or disappointment in ministry? (This is a time to allow the Holy Spirit to minister to you, bring healing and restoration.)

+ Are my motives for ministry truly pure, or have I allowed pride, selfish ambition, or greed to creep in?

+ Am I truly seeking God's heart, direction, and ways; or am I just following the crowd and the culture?

+ Have I compromised the truth of God's Word because of fear, or to gain popularity and offerings?

+ Am I living a holy and godly life, or have I allowed hidden sin to creep in?

It's time to cast aside any weight and sin that would hold you back and pen you in (Heb. 12:1). This is a time, right now, that the Spirit of God wants to come in and help you remove all the extra baggage and weight you were not meant or anointed to carry. God is saying, "Come and embrace My ways. 'Come and take My yoke upon you...For My yoke is easy and My burden is light'" (Matt. 11:29–30). His way is light and refreshing. Again, Jesus set the example; He did only those things the Father showed Him to do (John 5:19). During this special time aside also commit to do the next steps 3 through 8.

We pray this will be a time of great cleansing, healing, refreshing, and renewed vision.

Step 3: Commit to Your Greatest Call—Walking with God

God does not want you to be another casualty in ministry. God is calling us in very close to Him. As never before we need to hear His voice, for these are days of great distraction and deception and there is great pressure to compromise. He needs His leaders to be strong and walk in victory. Daniel 11:32 says those that know their God will be strong and do exploits. Staying very close to God will be vital in the days ahead.

In the days in which we live it's easy to get buried in all the details of everyday ministry and forget the most critical thing—time with God. We also need to remind ourselves:

A. **To Know Him:** Our number one ministry is unto the Lord first, then to the people. Our greatest call and highest priority is God and fellowship with Him, not a church or organization. Knowing Him is life's greatest pursuit and pleasure (Ps. 16:11). Therefore, no matter how busy you are, the number one thing you will do every day is when you come aside, seek His face, and pray and connect with Him. He has everything we need for life and ministry.

B. **Your Power Source:** Everything we need flows from Him; for Christ is the Vine (power source), we are the branches (John 15:5). When we are vitally connected with Him and His Word, He will impart His life to us; His wisdom, His power, His grace for life and ministry. Waiting upon God brings strength and refreshing (Isa. 40:31). From His throne flows divine guidance, inspiration, wisdom, insight, understanding, ideas, and messages—it's all there in His secret place. For "He is a rewarder of those who diligently seek Him" (Heb. 11:6).

C. **Your Greatest Work:** Your greatest work will be done on your knees. Prayer paves the way to be effective and fruitful in everything we do. Therefore, our lives need to go beyond devotional and study time and be lives of prayer, like our greatest example, Jesus. Prayer supernaturally paved the way for everything He did. Everything He did and taught came from His time with the Father (John 5:19; 8:28).

The New Testament leaders understood the high priority and power of giving themselves continually to prayer and ministry of the Word. It greatly affected their city (Acts 6:4, 7).

Those who are vitally connected to Him, walking in humility, walking in obedience, and walking in faith; these will be the agents of change and will release heaven into the earth. They will have fresh manna from heaven to feed God's people and the multitudes. In staying vitally connected and very close to Him, you will hear His heartbeat for His people and hear what He wants to say and do.

Satan knows your power source and will work to keep you from it; therefore you must become vigilant and jealous for your time with God.

Step 4: Commit to a Higher Standard

The American church overall has lowered its standards to align with the culture of the world rather than the culture of God's kingdom. God is calling His leaders to raise the standard back up to align with His Word and His higher ways. Jesus is returning for a glorious bride (Eph. 5:27), and the five-fold ministry is called to help prepare His bride (Eph. 4:11–13). Therefore:

A. We all need to remember, God's church is not a democracy. We have King that has set standards for His kingdom. Let's rise to His kingdom standards and show them the straight and narrow path that leads to life (Matt. 7:13–14).

B. In this day and hour, we the church must have a passion for purity (see Ps. 24:3-4; Matt. 5:8; Phil. 4:8; 1 Tim. 4:12)! Besides humility, God is calling His leaders and people to a place of purity—purity in heart, in mind, in motive, in life, and in message.

C. As never before God's leaders must stay vigilant and alert, guard against compromise, and make a commitment to walking on God's highway of holiness. Satan knows his time is short and he is doing everything he can to defile God's people (remember "The State of the American Church," chapter 6).

Important Reminder: Living a pure, holy life is *not* legalism. Living holy is *love* in its purest form and *life* at its highest level (1 Pet. 1:15–16). True holiness and obedience are a natural extension of our love relationship with God, walking close to Him (Step 3).

Step 5: Commit to Build His Way

In chapter 15 in the "God Is Looking for a Man" prophecy, God said, "I am looking for a man, a man who will seek after and embrace My plan. A man who will build My church, My way." God is calling pastors all across America to hear His voice and begin to build His way to impact their communities, cities and nation and bring forth lasting fruit.

Every pastor must make a choice—God's way or man's way?

Building God's Way = Survive and Thrive

- Jesus said, "I will build *My* church, and the gates of Hades shall not prevail against it (Matt. 16:18, emphasis added)." It is very important to remember it is *His* church (not ours). Therefore, it is critical we build it *His* way and according to *His* blueprint and specifications.

- Only those churches built God's way will survive and thrive in the intense days ahead (remember "Days of Wonder and Dread…Ahead" in chapter 10).

Building Man's Way = Washed Away

+ The biblical account of Isaac and Ishmael demonstrates the trouble the flesh can cause—doing things our own way versus doing things *God's* way (and in His timing).

+ When we build in the arm of the flesh (without God's direction or guidance), we then have to sustain what we've built by the arm of the flesh. This is why so many pastors are burning out; they are building and doing things God never told them to build or do. Thus they do not have the empowering grace to carry it out.

+ Without divine inspiration, all of man's grand ideas and plans are like building that house on sand that can be easily washed away (Matt. 7:24–27).

Prayer helps build God's way

If we are going to build God's house His way, then we must be men and women of prayer, for we must know His heart and what He is saying (Step 3). We must know how He wants us to build His house; otherwise we will give way to the trends of the day and build by the arm of the flesh and natural reasoning. And our churches will become like those castles in the sand that will be blown away by the storms of the day (Matt. 7:24–27), and our people will become prey for the enemy (1 Pet. 5:8).

Step 6: Commit to a Glorious House of Prayer

As previously stated, building God's house His way must include His foundational blueprint—a glorious "house of prayer" (Isa. 56:7; Mark 11:17; Eph. 5:27). Remember, in the intense days ahead those churches that are truly God's will be easy to identify: they will be praying churches, "glorious houses of prayer" (as previously described in Key 2, chapter 19).

+ They will be thriving as conduits releasing rivers of life from heaven into the earth into your church and into your community.

+ Prayer is paramount there. Therefore, the supernatural power of God (and His angels) will pave the way and help them move forward in everything He has called them to do.

If it is not already, begin to wisely turn your church into a "glorious house of prayer" today, do not delay! We share in the next chapter some ways to help you do that.

Step 7: Commit to the Uncompromising Word of God

Scripture warns that we are in days of great deception (1 Tim. 4:1). Therefore, as a pastor in God's house, it is essential to be a lover of God's Word, which is truth.

We are in a time when we can no longer settle for preaching only philosophy, success, motivational and leadership principles, we must make sure we preach the fullness of God's Word with balance (2 Tim. 2:15; 4:2)! Because the Word of God is alive and active and powerful, it has the power to save, to heal, to convict, and to set people free; and it brings life and instructs in righteousness.

Therefore, we exhort you to prayerfully evaluate your messages:

+ Are they one sided? Are they balanced with both the goodness and severity of God? Are they communicating the full character of God, both the Lion and the Lamb? God's people need the full meal—the meat with the sweet.

+ Are you softening your message so no one will be offended? You do *not* want to stand before God one day and have Him point out to you lives and families that were led astray or allowed to become prey because you watered down His Word in order to appease people.

+ Are you sharing strong truth balanced in love? Are your words bringing condemnation or conviction? It is essential to speak the truth in love, and that out of a heart of true brokenness that comes only through prayer—connecting with God and getting His heart for the people (Step 3).

+ Are you doing as Paul instructed Timothy? "Preach the word" and "correct, rebuke, and encourage" (2 Tim. 4:2, niv). We must also ensure we are rightly dividing and studying the Word of God (2:15), for teachers will be judged stricter and held in higher account because of our great influence.

God knows what the people need to hear. And as never before He needs strong leaders to lead His people in these last days. But when we follow the polls and trends to see what to preach, we cease to be a leader and instead become a follower. There is nothing wrong with getting understanding of the culture, but the Holy Spirit is the One we should be following. We need pastors and leaders with backbone who will stand up and say this is the way, this is what God is saying!

Boldly Stand Up—Speak the Truth in Love

Are you speaking up about the moral and social issues of the day? Remember in "The State of the American Church," chapter 6, the research that showed 90 percent of pastors are afraid to speak up and confront social issues of the day.[1] God's Word is truth and light. Matthew 5:15 says that you put a light on a stand so it can give light to the whole house. Likewise, God wants His leaders and people to stand up and give light to their communities and to the nation. But when we bury the truth or refuse to stand up and speak up, we are putting our light under a basket rather than on a hill, and we allow the darkness to fill the void.

We cannot cower down and be silent! (Please see "I Will Not Be Silent!" at the end of Appendix E.) We need praying men of God in our pulpits who are bold and courageous. We cannot let fear of losing tax-exempt status compromise the church's responsibility to stand up for righteousness and speak the truth. People need to hear the truth—it's what sets them free (John 8:32)!

The pulpits in early America spoke freely and passionately like this, and they helped strengthen and inspire a nation to stand up for what was right and fight for freedom.

Step 8: Pastors' Pledge and Commitment—Raising the Standard

As a leader in God's house (five-fold ministry), you will be accountable for how you respond to the message of this book. God is looking for leaders who are fully devoted to Christ and committed to do things His way, which will bring forth a new day.

We invite every pastor to take the following pledge:

Pastors' "Next-Level Church" Pledge

By the grace of God which empowers me:

1. I will be the pastor and leader He has called and needs me to be.

2. I commit to a life of prayer for it is my greatest call. I will make my appointment with God the most important of each day. Everything I do flows out of my divine connection with Him. He is the vine I am the branch (John 15:5).

3. I commit myself to be pure in life, heart, mind, motive, life, and ministry, walking in humility and faith.

4. I commit to build God's house His way, which is superior to man's ways. In all my ways I acknowledge God, and He will direct my paths (Prov. 3:6).

5. I commit to make our church a "glorious house of prayer" and make prayer our number one ministry. This church/ministry will be a conduit for heaven to release God's will and a "river of life" to flood our community, city, and nation.

6. I commit to teach and speak the full uncompromising Word of God. For the Word of God is alive and active, powerful, brings life, convicts of sin and instructs in righteousness, and sets people free.

7. I commit to stand up for righteousness and speak the truth in love in my church, my city, and my nation. I will let the light of God and His truth shine bright!

8. I will embrace God's Answer and implement it into my church and ministry, to help bring forth the greatest awakening ever seen and a righteous reformation. Saving and changing our nation and turning America back to God, starts with me!

Commit to pray, obey, stay focused

We also want to pass on to you three directives God gave us years ago that have served us well. These will help you stay on track. He instructed us to simply "pray, obey, and stay focused." As we "pray" we get His heart and instructions to "obey." Then it is a matter of "staying focused" to finish those assignments through prayer and obedience until they are done.

The most important things you can do are simply "pray, obey, and stay focused." That way your load will be only what God has given you, not man's ideas of what you should do.

A PROMISE AND WARNING

As we close this chapter, we leave you with this promise and warning:

The Promise: Those pastors who will embrace God's Answer (and the steps in this chapter); take it, run with it, and prepare yourselves and your churches will be greatly rewarded on many levels. You will see great fruit in your life and your ministry. God is able to do exceedingly abundantly above all you can ask or think (Eph. 3:20).

The Warning: We must remember, God is zealous for His house and He needs pastors and leaders today who will fully cooperate with Him to do things His way and follow His instructions. However, those who persist in their own ways will be in danger of being removed. God is coming to visit His house and judgment *is* coming to the pulpits of America. This is very serious; God is not playing games! We cannot stress this enough—those churches (no matter how big) that will not make God's uncompromising Word and prayer top priority (a "glorious house of prayer") will not be able to stand and will be in danger of being washed away by the coming storm (Matt. 7:24–27). (For more details see "Judgment Is Coming to the Pulpits of America" in appendix F and the word "Days of Wonder and Days of Dread...Ahead" in chapter 10.)

In closing, for those ready to run with God, our greatest days are ahead, as He prepares to raise up His glorious, victorious church.

Pastor, once you have walked through this process (the eight steps in this chapter) you will be ready to implement Step 2 of God's Answer into the local church. This is a time to position your church to help bring forth a Great Awakening to transform your church, community, city, and our nation.

23

STEP 2: THE LOCAL CHURCH LEVEL

Consecrate yourselves, for tomorrow the LORD will do wonders among you.
—JOSHUA 3:5, NAS

IT WAS A defining time. Joshua and the leaders were preparing God's people to miraculously cross the Jordan River and enter into everything God had promised them. As the priests were preparing to carry the ark of the covenant and lead the people, Joshua commanded the people to *prepare* and "consecrate" themselves, for tomorrow the God was about to do great wonders among them (Josh. 3:5).

This is what God is saying to His people right now: *prepare* and "consecrate" yourselves, for I am about do great "wonders" among you! As most know, to "consecrate" means to "be set apart" for a sacred purpose. Again, if pastors across the nation will implement God's Answer, we believe will we see an unprecedented Great Awakening in our churches and across our nation.

You and your church are called to be part of God's Answer for America, and it's time prepare your fields for rain and a great harvest.

PREPARE YOUR FIELDS FOR RAIN AND HARVEST!

Right now, if across America on prime-time TV there was a great message calling for our nation to turn back to God, it would probably be scoffed and mocked by most, including national leaders. Why? Because the soil and soul(s) of the nation must be first prepared, for so many hearts are hardened and deceived because of sin.

Young Destiny's vision and word

Several years ago, a special moment occurred for us as a family. We had been helping a ministry one Wednesday night in the media team offices. Towards the end of youth service worship, our daughter, Destiny (eleven years old at the time), walked slowly and quietly into the room. We turned to greet her and noticed she had been weeping and was trembling as it seemed the Spirit of God was heavy upon her.

She said, "Mom and Dad, God just spoke to me and told me to come and tell you something." This really caught our attention, for at this time it was not something she normally did; so we asked in anticipation what God had said. She shared how she had a vision of a massive wheat field ready for harvest, and that God instructed her to tell us:

Prepare your fields for rain, for I am coming!

This was a very meaningful word to us. First, it came from our precious daughter (Joel 2:28); second, it reminded us of many things God had spoken to us, including "The Great Visitation" we shared earlier in chapter 14. And God is saying the same thing to His pastors and the church today—"Prepare your fields for rain, for I am coming!" He is coming to visit, get His house in order (Mal. 3:1–3), and ready for the great harvest to come. We must prepare and be ready!

How do we prepare our fields for rain?

The farmer works hard to plow and soften the soil so it's ready for the seeds he will plant. Then God does His part by bringing the sun and rain, and bring forth the harvest in due time. The prophet Hosea spoke regarding this:

> Sow for yourselves righteousness; Reap in mercy; Break up your fallow ground, For it is time to seek the LORD, Till He comes and rains righteousness on you.
>
> —HOSEA 10:12

"Sow for yourselves righteousness" and "break up your fallow ground." We prepare the soil of our churches, our communities, and our nation in genuine repentance, a time of holy consecration (Key 1), and nation-changing prayer (Key 2). We sow righteousness by doing things God's way.

"For it is time to seek the LORD" relates to a time of holy consecration, an internal investigation, and seeking God's instructions (personal or corporate). This includes continuing in nation-changing prayer.

"Till He comes and rains righteousness on you" relates to rain from heaven that will bring forth the harvest we desire to see throughout our nation; just as God promised (Key 2) that He would pour out upon us, our churches, and our nation if we would pour out our prayers like rain, night and day.

IMPLEMENTING GOD'S ANSWER IN YOUR LOCAL CHURCH

As the pastor, we pray you have taken the eight steps from the previous "Step 1: The Pulpit Level" chapter, commit to embrace God's Answer and run with it. As you can see, this plan is not just about changing a nation; it's about first changing our churches. It is also about beginning to awaken and raise up the glorious church (Eph.5:27). If you will implement the following steps in your local church and stick with it, we believe you will not only see all God has promised in your church, your community, and your city; but your church will also be a part of the greatest awakening in history.

Here is our recommended way to implement God's Answer into your local church.

1. Share God's Answer with Your Leaders and Church

It is essential that all local church leadership and their people have a clear understanding of:

+ The Situation: The seriousness of the situation, what is at stake (the two paths before us), and the urgency of the hour.
+ The Solution: What God's Answer is to bring the Great Awakening to our nation and begin changing everything.

Go through this book together as staff and a leadership team so you can all be in agreement moving forward. Then share God's Answer with your church. Keep before them the vision and magnitude of what God has promised He will do, if we simply follow His instructions.

Encourage your leaders and people to pass God's Answer on to everyone they know so churches all across the nation can unite in implementing it and prepare for what God is about to do.

Note: Assign someone to help implement God's Answer.

Pastor, Christian leader; we know you are busy and you don't have to do it all. We recommend assigning someone that has a heart and passion for prayer, your church, and the nation to help oversee the implementation of God's Answer into your local church and city and also to unite with other churches in your community or city.

2. Call a Sacred Assembly (a Turning Point Event)

One way to introduce and implement God's Answer to your church is to schedule an initial night of corporate worship and prayer, such as a sacred assembly (see Joel 2:15–17).

Let the people know how important this is. Let them know this will be a life, church, and nation-changing event that no one should miss—the beginning of a new day; a time to cast great vision and a time of consecration and a time to prepare for all the amazing things God is about to do in our churches and nation! This is also based on Joel 2 that occurred during a critical time in his nation:

> Consecrate a fast, Call a sacred assembly; Gather the people, Sanctify the congregation, Assemble the elders, Gather the children.... Let the priests, who minister to the Lord, Weep between the porch and the altar.
>
> —Joel 2:15–17

Begin with a time of worship; then:

A. Share the Message and Vision of God's Answer with Your Church.

Make clear the seriousness of the situation in our nation and the two paths set before us. Then share God's Answer (chapters 16–20) that will open the door to a nation-shaking Great Awakening and reformation.

Share how you believe this will take your church to a whole new level to be ready for the days ahead and at the same time have greater impact up your community, your city, and also help change the nation.

B. Have a Time of Repentance and Consecration.

Starting with the leaders in your church on the platform, leading by example for all to follow, repent and consecrate yourselves. We recommend you first review with them Key 1, what "genuine repentance" is and involves.

C. Corporately Commit to Make Prayer a Top Priority.

As the pastor, let them know you are committed to build God's house His way, and that this will include following God's blueprint for a house of prayer for all nations (Isa. 56:7; Matt. 21:13; Luke 19:46; Mark 11:17).

Note: If your church is already praying, then this is a good time to take prayer to the next level.

Share Key 2: what God has said will change everything and what nation-changing prayer is.

+ Let them know their greatest work will be done on their knees, releasing the Spirit of God to pave the way for a new day. Then follow up prayer with action (faith with works, James 2:17).

+ Let them know that God's Word, prayer, and worship are at the very core of every true house of God and everything else flows from there; that through this you will establish a glorious connection with heaven to flow like a river of life, healing and restoration into your communities, cities, and the nation (see Ezekiel 47; Revelation 22).

+ Let them know this church will shine bright like a lighthouse in the darkness, for their prayers will be like adding flames to this fire that are keeping the lighthouse lit and will cause it to burn brighter and brighter.

+ Let them know rivers of prayer will flow out and souls will flow in (and to be ready for this).

+ Let them know God will be raising up "glorious houses of prayer" everywhere that will play a critical role in these last days, and your church will be part of it!

Note: We suggest you lay out clear direction how this will be implemented in your church—what and when. Before this special service, designate places and times of prayer and share these with your people at this event.

D. Begin Nation-Changing Prayer.

During this event include a time of corporate focused prayer for your church, and the nation. We encourage you to use our Top 5 Prayer Guide in appendix A as a starting point.

By doing this as a church you will be helping set in motion the birthing of the Great Awakening and position your church for the amazing things God will be doing (Josh. 3:5)!

3. BECOME A GLORIOUS HOUSE OF PRAYER

Begin praying daily and weekly (if you haven't already). Be praying for your church, your city, the body of Christ, and the nation (for specifics see the Top 5 Prayer Guide in appendix A).

Remember the importance of *worship-based prayer*—undergirding your prayer with worship or anointed music as much as possible to help set an atmosphere for the presence of God (Ps. 100:4; 22:3; Rev. 5:8). Worship and prayer go hand in hand. Again, this also aligns with God's Word that foretells the restoring of the tabernacle of David (worship, prayer, and the glory of God) (Amos 9:11; Acts 15:16).

Following are ways to help make your church a "glorious house of prayer" for God's glory to dwell in and flow through:

+ Have daily united prayer with staff, pastors, and leaders.

+ Open up your church to daily prayer (ideally day and night).

+ Encourage daily prayer by every church member.

+ Have a weekly corporate prayer service.

+ Take the 12 O'clock Prayer Challenge (see next chapter). Encourage everyone to unite in prayer with the body of Christ across the nation by taking the 12 O'clock Prayer Challenge we will highlight in the next chapter.

+ Get the youth and children involved in praying for your church and America.

+ At the beginning or conclusion of every service, home group, Sunday school, or Bible class, take a moment to unite and pray for your church and the nation.

+ Encourage prayer walks at your church, around government buildings, schools, and throughout the city.

Note: We suggest contacting already well-known houses of prayer in the nation and ask them for more details on implementing a house of prayer. You can also go to shekinahtoday.org for more information and resources.

To the measure we humble ourselves and pray is the same measure God will move in our churches, our communities, and our nation.

+ No Prayer = No Power, No Change

+ Little Prayer = Little Power, Little Change
+ Massive Prayer = Massive Power, Massive Change

Everyone needs to engage

Everyone needs to be engaged and praying. Many think the pastor or intercessory team is responsible to do most of the praying for the church and the nation; but every Christian has a role to play. Every Christian is a priest unto God (Rev. 1:6). All the saints are part of a royal priesthood, a holy nation (1 Pet. 2:9). Every believer has the responsibility to pray. Really, for a true Christian, prayer should be a lifestyle and become as natural as breathing.

To Christian households

Pastors, we exhort you to ask your people to do the following:

Imagine Christian families in homes all across America praying nightly for our pastors, our churches, and our nation. Yes, we encourage every Christian to make your home a "house of prayer!"

There are many "Christians" (especially the men) who have fallen into the American routine: get up, go to work, come home, eat, and sit down all night watching TV and/or play video games. God has so much more for us in life!

It's time for change and to prepare for what God wants to do. We encourage families to pick a time to turn off all media and come together sometime in the evening to pray for their pastors, their churches, and the nation (see Matthew 26:40). Prayer together cultivates unity and strengthens families.

Those families that do this will see multiple benefits. We encourage families all across America to begin doing this with your family today. Together we can help change a nation!

4. Teach about the Power and Benefits of Prayer

It is worth repeating: if God's people could see what happens in the spiritual world when we pray, His people would be praying all the time! It's time for that major "paradigm shift" regarding prayer.

Pastor, five-fold minister; it is critical your people understand the power and benefits of prayer that will stir and motivate them to pray. If you have not done so already, we highly recommend you do or revisit a series of messages on the importance and power of prayer—personal and corporate. Show how repentance and prayer has impacted people, cities, and nations in biblical times and in world history. Also share messages and examples of prayer in American history, from the Pilgrims and Puritans to the Great Awakenings that helped shape and impact our nation (there are many examples).

Important Teaching Note: Jesus' disciples observed Jesus' prayer life—how He often rose up early to go pray and then went out to the minister. They saw the power and effects of His prayers. This is why He was asked, "Lord, teach us to pray" (Luke 11:1). Notice, they did not ask Him to teach them to "teach," to "preach," to "heal," or to do "miracles," because they saw the *prayer empowered* the teaching and preaching and the ministry gifts. Prayer is paramount!

5. SHARE GOD'S ANSWER WITH OTHERS

Please pass *God's Answer for America* on to other pastors and churches you know to help bring the Great Awakening and change our churches and our nation before great judgment comes.

6. UNITE (KEY 3) AND PRAY WITH OTHER PASTORS AND CHURCHES

We recommend you come together with other pastors in your city and pray with and for each other regularly, if you are not already. Consider a monthly or regular prayer gathering with other pastors and also with churches in your area, praying for your city and praying through the Top 5 Prayer Guide (Appendix A). Consider being a host church.

7. PREPARE FOR THE GREAT HARVEST AND GROWTH

Your church must be ready to take in the great harvest, for when God begins to move it will be like a mighty wave and many will be saved.

Imagine 100 people showing up at church ready to get saved and discipled, then 100 more next week, and the next week; are you ready? While we may be exaggerating with 100 each week to make a point, it could become a reality. The point is we must be ready for souls to start flooding our churches.

Remember the powerful prophetic word at the end of Key 2, "Glorious House of Prayer—River Flow Out, Souls Flow In." God's said where His house of prayer is—rivers of God's Spirit are going to flow out into the communities and into the cities and souls will flow in. Prayers will pour out, and souls will pour in. And God will begin to transform and change them. Remember, they are not looking to be entertained—they are looking to be changed. And you will need to be ready to disciple them!

Be expecting great results! When the *dam* breaks (see Key 2) and the *wave* of God's Spirit begins to move greatly across our land, we believe God will honor those churches that have been obedient and praying, with a great harvest of souls flooding our churches.

Prepare your church for this great harvest now, making sure you have a strong "discipleship program" ready for when they come. As you know, it is very important new believers become well grounded in God's Word and spiritually grow to help advance the kingdom of God. "Prepare your fields for rain" for the great outpouring is coming! A great harvest of souls is coming!

OTHER BENEFITS TO YOUR CHURCH

Your leadership and obedience to God's Answer and instructions will again not only help change a nation but will also positively affect your church, your community, families, men, women, teens, and children; along with a great harvest of souls and growth. We believe besides all these there are two other benefits for running with God's Answer:

1. Keys to the City

Those churches that build and operate God's way will rise up and lead in their communities. They will be the rich salt and a bright light they were meant to be—a city on a hill for all to see (Matt. 5:14).

Many will be looking for answers, direction, and hope. And if you will build God's house His way, that's what your church will be in these last days. We believe implementing God's Answer will also give you access to the keys to your city—the souls, lives, families, and leaders in your community.

2. Psalm 91: A Place of Protection and Refuge

If the church and America does not respond to God's cry quickly enough, we will see the destructive things unfold we have described coming upon our nation. However, we believe God will protect His people; but with a condition, for protection is promised for only those who stay very close to Him (Ps. 91). God knows how to protect His people. In Goshen He protected His people in the midst of great judgments upon Egypt (Exod. 8:23). We also see demonstrated in Ezekiel 9 intercessors were marked for protection in the midst of calamity and judgment (Ezek. 9:4–6). God will honor those who honor, obey Him, and are praying.

Final note

Once you commit to implement the keys of God's Answer and build God's house His way, be aware the enemy (Satan) will attempt to frustrate you and cause you to abandon this mission, just as Sanballat tried to distract and stop Nehemiah from rebuilding the walls (see Nehemiah 4, 6). You must be determined to follow through, no matter what. You must remember, God is building for eternity and what matters most is you build His house, His way. This cannot be a "let's try this out and see if it works"; you must be "all in" through thick and thin. God rewards faith and diligence (Heb. 11:6).

Keep the vision of the mission and the joy of the results before you—the greatest awakening ever seen, our churches and nation radically changed. God will greatly reward the faithful. So we encourage you to—pray, obey, stay focused!

Next we offer how to implement God's Answer on a national scale—how we can accomplish all three stages of the mission from the Great Awakening to a great reformation!

Connect with us

If you are or will be implementing God's Answer into your churches and ministries, we would love to know who you are and connect with you. We can also communicate with you further as things progress in our nation. You can contact us at shekinahtoday.org

24

STEP 3: THE NATIONAL LEVEL

A United Nationwide Call to Action

Commit your actions to the LORD, and your plans will succeed.
—PROVERBS 16:3, NLT

OVER 200 YEARS ago during a critical time in our nation's history, the Founding Fathers, with their nation hanging in the balance, saw the two paths and the opportunity before them. What did they do? They united in one accord; and with one voice they famously declared, "We mutually pledge our lives, our fortunes, and our sacred honor."[1] They united under one vision and plan (the Declaration of Independence, then the Constitution), and committed everything to make it happen; and a new nation was born.

Now the future of our nation hangs in the balance once again. So we must ask ourselves: "What are we willing to do?" The price for complacency would be devastating to this nation. There is so much at stake and God is counting on all of us (His leaders and people) to follow through.

Time to Unite—One Vision, One Plan

We believe, like never before, God is calling His people to unite with one vision and with one plan to reach, save, and transform our nation.

While some may say, this just isn't possible; we know that *with* God, all things are possible (Matt. 19:26). When we align ourselves *with* God's heart, His vision, and His strategy; cities and nations can be brought to their knees. Sometimes, all God needs is someone who will believe and then do what He is asking, just as Moses did.

To carry out such a great vision we know will require a great plan, great resources, and a great team (a united body of Christ). We believe this can be a church-wide, unified effort across denominational lines. Although we may have some theological or doctrinal differences, the uniting factor is God's Answer to save and change our nation.

As God's people humbly unite together within one focused plan, we can see great breakthrough much stronger and quicker than ever before (remember Key 3).

Important Note: Begin steps 1 and 2 now—don't wait! We believe now is the time for every pastor and church in America to begin implementing God's Answer—Step 1 (pulpit level) and Step 2 (local church level). Don't wait for this third step (the national level). Help set the example and lead the way today.

A Plan to Transform Our Churches and America

This plan will help fully implement God's Answer nationwide in order to bring the Great Awakening and lasting reformation.

As God provides the team and the resources, this proposed plan would include:

1. Unite key leaders—to pray, strategize, and lead the way.
2. A church-wide campaign—to implement God's Answer
3. A national campaign—to turn America back to God

We believe the results of this will include taking our churches to a whole new level, turning America back to God, and "multitudes" of souls coming to Christ. At the end of this chapter and book, we will show how together we can begin moving forward with this plan.

Now, following are more details regarding this proposed plan. Again, we see God's divine order: it all begins with the "pulpits," then goes to the "pews," then to the "multitudes" (the nation).

1. Unite Key Leaders (the Pulpits)

We believe there is a godly remnant of ministers that are grieved over the direction of our churches and nation—let us unite and lead the way to bring forth a new day!

Our first objective is to get this message of God's answer out to every pastor, minister, church, and Christian across America.

As we reach out to leaders we believe the Spirit of God will divinely orchestrate and draw key leaders to the table. Together we will unite with within one plan for one purpose—to save and transform our nation through a Great Awakening and reformation. These leaders will have the same heart, vision, and passion for our churches and nation.

Leaders Strategic Summit

Our proposed plan is to schedule a Leaders Strategic Summit to gather together these "key leaders" to pray, plan, strategize, and then go forward with a great power and purpose. We would prayerfully unite our forces, our resources, our gifts, and our talents to accomplish the mission. We also believe God has already prepared key leaders and ministries anointed for certain areas, like specialists in a military operation, for such a time as this. But we need to unite and work together for maximum effect (as previously described in Key 3).

This Leaders Strategic Summit would include:

A. Reaching Pastors and Churches across America

Prayer, plans, and strategy to prepare for the great visitation and Great Awakening God wants to bring: This would include a strategy to reach every pastor and church in America and help them to fully implement God's Answer to bring about the greatest results. This would include plans for the church-wide campaign we offer below.

B. Reaching the Nation

Prayer, plans, and strategy for a "national campaign" to reach out to America and her leaders: This would include a plan and strategy for great prayer and action until America turns back to God and a great reformation takes place.

C. A Great Reformation Action Plan

Prayer, plans, and strategy for a great reformation action plan to impact every sphere of society: Then strategize how to best implement this plan within the window of time we will have once the Great Awakening begins to sweep across the land.

Imagine God's leaders working together in such an extraordinary way! Only God can put this together by His Spirit.

2. Church-Wide Campaign (the Pews)

One way to help implement God's Answer church-wide and share next level plans to transform America, is with a church-wide event. This event would serve to unite pastors and churches across America in a time of holy consecration, preparation, and strategic operation. This event could include:

+ A church-wide simulcast with pastors and churches all across America, casting a short, clear vision of what is at stake and God's Answer, and exhorting pastors and churches to implement God's Answer into their churches (if they have not already).

+ A time for the church to corporately, humbly unite in holy consecration—preparation for the amazing things God wants to do.

+ Exhort every church to become a glorious house of prayer as part of the "nation-changing prayer" movement to pave the way for the Great Awakening and reformation. This would include uniting in the 12 O'clock Prayer Challenge we will share later in this chapter.

This prayer movement will also help prepare the way for of our nation to hear and see God's message and cry to America. (See the upcoming national campaign.)

+ Cast a vision and share plans and details of how every church can help prepare in prayer and action for the national campaign to reach America—a nationwide campaign to turn America back to God and bring a great reformation.

+ Set up to reveal next level plans and strategies.

3. A National Campaign (the Multitudes)

Once churches across the nation are implementing God's Answer, then the stage will be set to begin a national "God's Answer for America" campaign to our nation; for God not only *is the* Answer, He *has* all the answers America needs and is searching for.

A National Campaign—to Turn America Back to God

+ Media campaign—message to America

+ A national event—a call to America

+ A call to America's leaders

+ Prayer and action

+ A great reformation

The Goal

The goal of this "national campaign" is to reach and pierce the heart and soul of America and her leaders with a powerful and convicting message of truth and hope, calling them to their knees in repentance and back to God and her godly foundations. Again, this can only be possible and effective when God's people are flooding our cities with nation-changing prayer (pure, passionate, and persistent prayer, Key 2).

Once again, with God's leaders and people uniting forces, resources, gifts, and talents, this national campaign would include:

A. Prepare with Nation-Changing Prayer

The church-wide campaign event would include launching daily church-wide prayer for the national event and campaign. This national campaign will be saturated in prayer to prepare the soil and soul(s) of our nation to hear and see God's message and cry to America.

B. Media Campaign

The world has used the media to destroy the soul of our nation; it's time to take it back and use media to turn the soul(s) of our nation (communities and cities) back to God—speaking the truth in love.

We would use every form of media and social networking to clearly communicate God's message to our nation. This would include an engaging, anointed, and compelling media message to America. This media campaign would continue until America turns back to God and everything changes.

C. A National "God's Answer for America" Campaign Event

This national campaign would include a powerful event and compelling message, showing the two paths before our nation, and to turn back to God for He is America's only hope. We believe the church-wide prayers (Key 2) will help open the ears of the nation to hear.

We envision this event in Washington, DC, and including key church leaders across denominations coming together to pray and speak to America. We will share more details of what, where, when at the Leaders Strategic Summit meeting, and eventually on our website at: shekinahtoday.org.

Note: this event would be part of the campaign that would continue with prayer, media, and more until America turns back to God and the great reformation is complete.

This event would also be a launching pad for what follows.

D. A National "Call to America's Leaders"

After this national "event," key designated church leaders would meet with the top national leaders offering to pray for and with them; and speaking truth in love, imploring them to return America back to God's ways as when she was young to bring healing and restoration and avert self-destruction and severe judgment.

NOTE: SPEAKING TRUTH IN LOVE

It is more important than ever today that we speak the truth, because so many are deceived. However, we must remember to speak the truth in sincere love, by the Spirit of God, and not out of a cold, condemning heart. This can only happen when we stay close to Christ on our knees, allowing Him to break our hearts for the lost and the deceived.

This would also include key leaders, pastors, churches, and ministries in every state praying for and then going to their local and state leaders, as well their senators and representatives in the house; praying with them and exhorting them to turn back to God and embrace His righteous ways of life, blessing, and protection. We believe this will eventually include the Spirit of God using His people to give mayors and governors answers they are seeking (see "The Results: Then We Will See...," chapter 25). But again, this must all be preceded by and saturated in nation-changing prayer (Key 2), then in action. The following shows how to do this.

E. Prayer and Action

Throughout all this both prayer and action will be critical. We have already shared the power of prayer, but God's Word also exhorts believers that true faith is coupled with action (James 2:14–26).

It is important to remember, every Great Awakening was preceded by extraordinary prayer, which then lead to significant action. Again, the First Great Awakening united and prepared the people to stand against tyranny and injustice. The Second Great Awakening brought sweeping social reforms, including and a just fight for those in slavery. We believe this Third Great Awakening will do likewise, include nation-changing prayer turned into nation-changing action.

God's way to pray and fight (action)

As God's people obey and pray, press in and intercede for our nation, God will fight in the heavenlies and prepare the way for His people (Eph. 6:12). Then as we rise up and go forward, speaking the truth in love and fighting for what is just and right in our communities, our schools, our cities, our states, Washington, DC, and the halls of Congress, the enemies will retreat and we will begin to see everything change. Again, this will *only* happen when we (the American church) pour out our prayers like rain, day and night. The battle will be won first on our knees!

Prayer would also pave the way for God to raise up righteous leaders and judges throughout the land, and do His will.

F. The Great Reformation

The Great Awakening will set up a great reformation that can completely restore the godly foundations and transform America. However, we believe the great reformation can begin even now (to a certain degree), as God's people begin to implement God's Answer with the kind of prayer and action we just previously described.

REALITY CHECK AND PROPHETIC PERSPECTIVE

God's fully devoted ones will rise

While it may be a reality that every pastor and church in America will *not* heed God's Answer or unite within this plan, we believe there are many who have the same heart and burden for our churches and nation that will respond. They will be like that Gideon's army that brought great victory for a nation, or the devoted disciples that stayed in the upper room and became united in one accord and ushered in a whole new era.

The call is going out, and the lines are being drawn in the sand; on which side will you stand?

Once again, unity will come from a time of separation. And in the end God will have an army of fully devoted ones who will rise up and run as never seen before, and they will help usher in the glorious church for God's end-time purposes and at the same time help save and change our nation. (In relation to this we encourage you to access the prophecy called, "My Fully Devoted Ones" in appendix F.)

Right now we can all begin praying together daily across the nation by joining us in the 12 O'clock Prayer Challenge.

Special Section: The 12 O'clock Prayer Challenge

Several years ago God's instructions of "How to Change the Course of a Nation" (Key 2) stirred our hearts to call for daily prayer. In 2010 we began calling the 12 O'clock Prayer Challenge. It was after this we became aware of a similar call from over 150 years ago in America.

Historical prelude

In New York in 1857, a great financial crisis caused widespread panic. Many believed the dire moral and spiritual condition had combined to bring about this crash. (Remember how economic woes are one way how God gets people's attention; see chapter 9). In response, a businessman, Jeremiah Lanphier, sent out the invitation to join him at twelve o'clock noon every Wednesday in earnest prayer for the city and situation.

The account is, what began with six people praying every Wednesday eventually became ten thousand praying every day in New York. This flood of prayer began to overflow to the churches praying in the evenings. As this daily prayer movement spread, church bells would ring as a signal for people to unite in prayer at 8:00 a.m., twelve o'clock noon, and 6:00 p.m. The result: millions were saved and the launch of moral and social reforms.[2]

While we can pray anytime, united prayer at a certain time everyday is powerful. We propose twelve o'clock noon as that time (as a minimum) for a time of prayer in your church, your home, your ministry, your office, or wherever you are in public at the time.

Consider delaying lunch until after you pray. Pray before you eat; for willful hunger adds the dimension of sacrifice, fasting, and power to your prayers. Imagine what God will do and what power will be released!

- Imagine people all across the nation stopping to pray at noon—pouring out their hearts in nation-changing prayer! In America, each hour would be like a four-hour wave of prayer sweeping across the nation, hour by hour, from the West Coast to the East Coast—everyday (plus Alaska and Hawaii).

- Imagine people all across the nation praying at flag poles with the American flag (representing our nation); praying at flag poles at schools, government buildings, and businesses from coast to coast. (Praying old glory will see a new glory—God's glory!)

- Imagine every Sunday at noon every church across America joining in nation-changing prayer for God to visit His church, pour out His Spirit across our nation, turn America back to Him, and bring the change we urgently need, praying also for our nation's leaders to heed God's cry, humble themselves, and follow His ways.

Imagine how powerful this could be! Remember the vision of the Great Awakening sweeping across our nation from coast to coast we shared in chapter 3, "The Course of a Nation"? It's worth sharing once again!

Cindy:

> I saw a map of America. I first saw youth gathering at schools around flag poles, then I saw the same thing happening at universities and colleges. I began to see prayer sweeping across the nation from coast to coast. I saw people praying outside of government buildings, in businesses, financial districts, on Wall Street, and in Hollywood. As I saw this vision, I kept hearing what seems like a loud cry from heaven, "Pray, America! Pray!"
>
> Then, I saw the Spirit of God descend upon the nation, and I saw people begin running into the streets, crying out in repentance and for salvation, as they fell under the convicting power of the Holy Spirit. What I saw swept over every sector of society in America. It was a nation-shaking move of the Holy Spirit that began changing everything.

This is what God's Answer will bring!

Also the next chapter, "The Results: Then We Will See...," provides more details of what will happen if we will do this. In relation to all this, the national campaign and the 12 O'clock Prayer Challenge, we share another word of great encouragement.

PROPHETIC WORD

Prepare the Way for Change

October 19, 2012, through Cindy deVille

> Following my 12:00 prayer time today, Spirit of the Lord came upon me and He began to prophecy, with great authority:
>
> Let the voice of My people be heard.
> Tell them to proclaim My truth, My Word!
>
> No more will My people run into the closet and hide.
> But, I will provide a platform and a place.
> I shall give them a voice that they will raise,
> And they shall declare My Word, My truth;
> And a nation will be set free from the lies of the enemy!
>
> For the enemy has perpetrated His lies,
> But now, he will be the one who will run and hide,
> Into the closet to lick his wounds.

For My glory is coming, it's coming soon.
Continue, continue to pray at noon, at noon each day.

Tell everyone, everywhere,
It is their prayers that will prepare and make the way!
It is the prayers of the saints, night and day,
That will cause the enemy to run away.
It is the prayers that will stop his deceitful lies,
It is the prayers that will turn the tide!

Tell them, don't let up or give in,
For they are about to win a great victory.
Tell them to keep their eyes on Me,
For I have the power to change everything!

A new day is coming!

Remember the tenacity of Elijah the prophet, who would not cease to pray *until* He saw the cloud of rain. We need to have this kind of tenacity, staying on our knees *until* we see the cloud of His glory revealed over this nation and His wave of change sweeps throughout America, from sea to shining sea.

We must not fall into complacency or be moved by what we see. No matter how hard the battle gets, we must never stop; we must never give up until we see all God has promised. We must pray, then stand up and fight for what is just and what is right!

If God's people will pray and unite as never before, we will then see God move as never before! So let us humbly unite and cry out to Him—pray, America pray—then we *will* see a new day!

Unite with us

We are calling God's leaders and people to unite under one plan to reach, save, and transform our nation. Therefore, we are asking every pastor and Christian leader who desires to see our churches changed and America turning back to God to connect with us by going to shekinahtoday.org and look for the "God's Answer for America" link. Together we can save and change the nation!

25

THE RESULTS: THEN WE WILL SEE . . .

Looking unto Jesus, the author and finisher of our faith, who for the joy that was set before Him endured the cross.
—HEBREWS 12:2

N OW WE WANT to give you a glimpse of the power, depth, and magnitude of change God's Answer will bring when implemented. The vision of the results we have revealed so far in this book have been from a big picture view; this chapter will provide more details we believe that will inspire you and give great joy and hope. But it is very important we remember these will only happen when God's leaders and people embrace and implement God's Answer—fully cooperating with Him.

The joy set before us

Joy set before us helps strengthen our resolve to endure and push through when it gets tough, when it seems nothing is happening (maybe even seems worse). The greater the battle, the sweeter the victory. Like a woman during pregnancy; the joy of knowing the baby will come gives her the strength to endure months of carrying the weight of baby inside and preparing for it's coming, then eventually with great labor and force bringing the baby forth. And finally, when the mothers holds the baby in her arms, great joy floods her heart and washes away the pain and extreme effort it took during pregnancy and birthing process. We believe this is what the birthing of the Great Awakening (and a new era for the church) will be like.

Our ultimate example of this truth is our Lord Jesus Christ. What He had to endure and push through is unimaginable, but now His joy and His eternal prize are unequaled!

We have devoted this chapter to help set a vision of great joy before you, and show the magnitude of what can be accomplished if we will simply obey God's instructions revealed in His answer. When God's people obey, the results will be incredible!

THE RESULTS

AN OVERVIEW OF WHAT WE WILL SEE

The prophet Joel gave us a glimpse of how God responds to His people who heed His instructions. He said He would bring them an abundance of harvest and restore the years that the locust has eaten (see Joel 2:18–25).

Now, regarding America, we list some main things we believe God said He will do and restore if we simply heed His answer:

- We will see the greatest awakening sweep across our land.
- It will flow like a massive river to the multitudes.
- Prayers will flow out, souls will pour in.
- God will breathe upon His church and this nation.
- God will cleanse, purify, and raise up His glorious church.
- God will far exceed our prayers!
- He will complete what His church has tried so hard to do for decades.
- He will do a deep work and it will take root.
- Mayors and governors will bow before Him.
- There will be a great reformation.
- There will be a return to the foundations from previous generations.
- There will be a great harvest and a new day.
- God's Spirit will move into even the dark places of our land to break through, reach, and turn those in the homosexual community and the pornography industry.
- The church will have the answers and great influence in the coming days.
- God will unfold plans and unveil secrets to His leaders.
- God will show His leaders how to win cities in a day!

"Tell My pastors, tell My people, it's time to pray.
The tide is about to turn,
Things are about to change."

God is just waiting for us to embrace and run with His answer. Will you answer the call? Begin today!

Special Prophetic Update: America's government will be shaken and changed

As we were working to finish up this book, God spoke to us that as His people obey and pray, there will be *change* in our government. We believe the "change" God is speaking of will include:

- The process of real change in our government for the better will at first be very hard to go through, but the end result will be worth it.

+ There will be a great shaking of our foundations, but they will stand.

+ There will be a plucking up and rooting out of corruption that is throughout our government.

+ God will strip away get rid of the fat our government is carrying, and it will become lean. The "fat cats" will be removed.

+ There is coming a cleansing in the land. It will begin in the high places, the names and the faces many know and see. The high and lofty ones (prideful ones doing damage) will be brought down. God will remove them.

+ As God's people pray He will make the way for the righteous to be set up as leaders and judges in this land, and they will be His hand and His mouthpiece.

Remember what God said in Key 2:

If they will pray and press in, not just one day,
But everyday—they will see everything change.

They will see the things within their government changed.
They will see things in high places moved, changed, rearranged,
And come in line with what is divine.
And come in line with what I am calling this nation to.

If they will cause their prayers to pour forth like rain, like rain...
That which many have tried to do through the decades and have failed,
I shall do and I shall turn by My Spirit.
I will change this nation.

As God's leaders and people do what He says (God's Answer), we will be amazed at what will take place! Everything really will change, just as God said.

The Church Will Have the Answers

The time is coming when the leaders of our nation will come to the church for answers. Because the church is praying, God will be giving His people answers and solutions for the nation. They will come to get the answers they need, just as Pharaoh inquired of Joseph and the kings of Babylon sought Daniel's wisdom and insight. And of course Solomon's wisdom from God was sought by rulers of nations. "The fear of the LORD is the beginning of wisdom, And knowledge of the Holy One is understanding" (Prov. 9:10).

God is setting it up to exalt Christ and turn many to Him. God's people will have solutions for cities, governors, and mayors.

The Results: More Details

To see more details of what we believe God will be doing see "Mayors and Governors Will Come" and "Going into the Dark Places" in Appendix F. Also see a prophetic news making event towards the end of Appendix E. These are all encouraging words and visions that reveal a sense of the vast, deep work God will do if His leaders and people will rise up and implement God's Answer (and all three keys). One such vision follows:

Prophetic Vision: College Campus Vision of God's Outpouring

Cindy: In the fall of 2012, it was actually during a cycling spin class I was taking at the gym. Typically I am in an attitude of prayer as I am listening to worship music and cycling. I often looked out the window, as I was up on the second floor, and outside the window was a local college, and I could hardly take my eyes off of it.

Then I saw a vision of young people gathering for prayer in the top floor (upper room). I then saw the roof of the college being lifted up from one side and I saw the Spirit of God being poured out through the roof into the college. I just kept seeing this and sensed the Holy Spirit showing me this is what He would be doing across our nation.

We believe young people will play a major part of what God is wanting to do in His church and the nations.

We conclude this chapter with a peek at the magnitude God will work through His leaders and church when we implement God's Answer.

PROPHETIC WORD

Preface: Saturday afternoon we were sitting in the living room as a family a couple hours before church that night when the Spirit of God came on Cindy rather suddenly—first praying in the Spirit and then the Spirit of God spoke powerfully. The utterances came in waves over the next hour. The following is part of what came forth.

Things Are About to Change

June 21, 2008, prophecy through Cindy deVille

God said:

For this nation is Mine,
I've had a purpose for it throughout time,
I've had a purpose," says the Spirit of God.

"My leaders, the five-fold ministry; if they will repent and turn
back to Me,
And do things My way,
I will use them, I will use them mightily.

I will use them to influence—leaders, governors, senators.
I will use them to influence this nation.
I will use them to turn back—things, laws, legislation.
I will use them—they will have great influence.

"Tell My church they must speak the truth.
They must not compromise,
They must not back down,
They must not change the truth.
They must speak the truth.
If they will speak the truth and if they will speak it in *love*,
They will see change.
They will see hearts change, they will see hearts turn,
They will see a nation turn.
But they must rise up and speak the truth.
They must speak it in love, in the spirit of love.

"NO MORE! No more of the world influencing the church.
No more, no more, no more.
There's going to be a turn, there's going to be a turn,
And the church, the church, the church,
My church, done My way.
She will be the influencer in these coming days.
She will influence the culture.
She will influence the culture, she will!

"This can only happen if she does it My way.
My way, My way, My way," says the Spirit of God.
"For I AM the God of the universe,
I hold the secrets, the plans, the strategies, the techniques.

"In Me—tell, tell My leaders, tell them,
Everything they need will be found in Me—everything, everything!
Tell them—do not go to the world,
Tell them—come to Me,
And they will be amazed at what they see!
For I will unfold to them plans.
I will unveil secrets to them.
I will show them how to win cities in a day.
But it *must* be done *My way*.

"So tell My pastors, tell My people,
It's time to pray.
It's *time* to pray.
The tide is about to turn;
Things are about to change."

Amazing! Pastors, five-fold ministry, Christian; God is casting a strong vision and clear instructions. You can be a part of bringing forth great change in our churches and nation!

We pray this chapter has greatly stirred your heart and helps motivate you to take action—to embrace and run with God's Answer. God is waiting! Our nation is waiting!

26

A CALL TO AMERICA'S LEADERS

*Those who honor me I will honor, but those
who despise me will be disdained.*
—1 SAMUEL 2:30, NIV

SPECIAL **NOTE:** THIS chapter is to America's civil leaders (executive, congressional, judicial, governors, and mayors).

Note: Once God's leaders and people respond to God's Answer, the responsibility to respond to God will then shift to America's national leaders—federal, state, and local.

Mr. President and all of America's civic leaders and judges, we humbly submit the message in this chapter to you. We are sincerely praying for you, that you would wisely honor God and rule and judge righteously for the good of the whole nation (Mic. 6:8; Prov. 14:34). We also ask you to please read what we believe is a compassionate cry from the heart of God to you and the nation called "America, America!" from 2007 (chapter 2). God speaks of what has been unfolding in our news since then and foretells what is coming and why. The good news is, if you will truly turn America back to honoring God in all our ways, then we will all see a new day of restoration in our nation. However, He also warned:

But you have turned Me away again and again—
Away from your schools, away from your children.
You have turned Me away from rule, from your government.
You have rejected Me, and you have given place to other gods.

So now, if you do not repent, I will leave as you have asked.
My protection shall leave you,
My goodness and mercy shall leave,
And My glory shall leave you.
You shall be left to your own ways.
The enemies will come in
And the devastation and destruction will begin.
—"AMERICA, AMERICA!" PROPHECY DECEMBER 5, 2007

This is the path our beloved nation is racing down—a path of self-destruction!

Wise American Leaders Acknowledged God's Authority and Rule

Our Founding Fathers and many of America's great leaders have honored and feared God. They boldly declared in the Declaration of Independence that the "Supreme Judge of the World" has endowed us with certain unalienable rights.[1] And they recognized that God rules in the kingdoms of men and knows how to humble kings and nations (see Daniel 4). They knew honoring God and His righteous ways exalts a nation (Prov. 14:34). They knew the fear of the Lord is the beginning of wisdom, and all who follow His ways and instructions have sound understanding (Ps. 111:10). Today it appears most of America's leaders have forgotten these truths and instead are doing what is right in their own eyes.

> There is a way that seems right to man, But its end is the way of death [destruction].
>
> —Proverbs 14:12

And, it seems as if President Abraham Lincoln was speaking directly to America today when in the midst of civil war he declared (with the approval of Congress):

> We have forgotten God. We have forgotten the gracious hand which preserved us in peace, and multiplied and enriched and strengthened us; and we have vainly imagined, in the deceitfulness of our hearts, that all these blessings were produced by some superior wisdom and virtue of our own.[2]

President Lincoln (and Congress) also wisely declared in this same proclamation:

> It is the duty of nations...to own their dependence upon the overruling power of God, to confess their sins and transgressions, in humble sorrow, yet with assured hope...that genuine repentance will lead to mercy...Truth, announced in the Holy Scriptures and proven by all history, that those nations only are blessed whose God is the Lord.[3]

God's Ways and Laws Are Supreme

God is the Supreme Being and Judge of all the earth (Gen. 18:25), and His universal laws supersede all the laws of our land.

Mr. President and all of America's civic leaders and judges, please understand; God's ways are supreme to man's ways (Isa. 55:8–9). The fact is, God's ways are so supreme and brilliant that they can at first appear almost foolish to man because man's vision and understanding are limited. It is actually very unwise for man to think God's ways are no longer "relevant" and that we know better than Him how to rule a nation and bring great prosperity and peace. When we honor Him and His ways, then we will see blessing and favor on the land once again, for "blessed is the nation whose God is the Lord" (Ps. 33:12).

President George Washington (with Congress), acknowledged this truth and that it was therefore their "duty" to honor and obey God, the source of America's blessings and strength:

It is the duty of all nations to acknowledge the providence of Almighty God, to obey His will, to be grateful for His benefits, and humbly to implore His protection and favor.[4]

A MESSAGE TO AMERICA'S LEADERS

Mr. President and all of America's civic leaders and judges, God is calling America back to Him and His ways (the Founder and foundations of our nation).

Remember, America's great leaders before you declared it is our "duty" to honor and obey the will God as the "overruling power" of nations. This is why we see the founding documents of our nation based on God's ways and universal laws. "Righteousness exalts a nation" and that is why our nation rose to power so quickly and was so strong and blessed (Prov. 14:34). However, the progressive abandoning of God and His ways through anti-biblical legislation, judicial decisions, and even some executive actions are having the exact opposite effect. Is it any wonder why our troubles and problems continue to multiply and escalate?

Sadly, for decades America has been steadily rejecting God and His righteous ways (that lead to life, peace, and blessing), and that is why America is now eating the fruit of her *own* ways leading down a path of great sin, self-destruction, and devastating judgment. The reality is, if America does not change course quickly, we will see…

What's coming next, if…

+ Economic collapse
+ Greater natural disasters and storms
+ Greater civil unrest, riots, and blood in our streets
+ Enemy attacks and war from shore to shore
+ The nation's destruction and demise

(To understand why, please see the first half of the book, especially chapters 2 and 11).

Will these things happen on your watch and under your governing? Or will you be instrumental in helping to restore righteousness and the favor and blessings of God upon our land? We pray it is the latter! The truth is, until America turns back to her true Founder (God), these things (listed above) are going to escalate and culminate together to bring our nation to its knees.

America's Only Hope

God will do whatever He must do to get our nation's attention and bring America to her knees and back to Him (see the above "What's Coming Next, If…" list or chapters 11 and 12). And, God is saying to you, and the nation:

> A nation has looked to a man for hope.
> True hope and change begins with Me.
> Come in unity, in humility before Me.

When you bow your knee and seek to honor and please Me in all
things,
Then I will bless your land.

If you, America's leaders, will call for true national repentance (as President Abraham Lincoln did) and return to God and His ways, only then will God turn your enemies back, calm the storms, and restore and bless America again. We share later what we believe this should include a "new declaration" for a new day.

HONOR VS DISHONOR

President George Washington wisely declared during his inauguration that God's favor and goodness will not remain on a nation that dishonors His eternal standards and ways: "The propitious smiles of Heaven, can never be expected on a nation that disregard the eternal rules of order and right, which Heaven itself has ordained."[5]

A Promise: If You Will Honor God and His Ways

We humbly implore you to honor God and His ways for the sake and good of the nation (Prov. 14:34). For God is saying to you:

If you want to see My favor upon you as a leader,
Then you must favor Me and My ways.
You must honor Me and My ways,
And I will honor you and lift you up before the nation.

If you will honor God and His ways, then He will open up the floodgates of restoration and blessing and you will be honored as well. God is also saying:

If you will honor Me and you will honor My ways,
I will bring forth a new day in this nation. A new day.
But until you do, things...will not change.
You want to progress, but you will only digress.
For you have not addressed the issues that need to be addressed;
This is why your economy has been under such great stress.

Note: These "issues that need to be addressed" we highlighted in chapter 3, "America—A Prodigal Nation," and in the "new declaration" later in this chapter.

Dishonoring God and His Ways

On the other hand, the more the progressive agenda (anti-God, anti-biblical laws and rulings) are forced upon this nation, the more the progressive warnings and judgments of God will increase (see the above "What's Coming Next, If..." list or chapters 11 and 12). He is making it clear America is moving in the wrong direction, a path leading to self-destruction.

We should remember, God resists the proud and gives grace to the humble, and He has the power to raise up and to bring down; God has the power to remove one's crown (1 Pet. 5:5–6; Ps. 75:7; Dan. 5:21).

You have a decision to make

Mr. President and all of America's civic leaders, you face a great opportunity—honor God and His ways and He will honor you as great leaders that helped change and restore a nation (1 Sam. 2:30). However, if you choose to continue to dishonor God, rejecting His righteous ways, and if you harden your hearts like Pharaoh did, then God will have no recourse but to in turn dishonor and greatly humble you.

Earlier in the book we quoted Daniel Webster, the famous orator and political figure who served in the house, senate, and as secretary of state for three presidents. It is worth repeating his admonishment regarding the rewards of honoring God versus consequences of dishonoring Him:

> If we abide by the principles taught in the Bible, our country will go on prospering and to prosper...if we and [future generations] shall live always in the fear of God and shall respect His Commandments...we may have the highest hopes of the future fortunes of our country....But if we and our [future generations] neglect religious instruction and authority; violate the rules of eternal justice, trifle with the injunctions of morality, and recklessly destroy the political constitution which holds us together, no man can tell how sudden a catastrophe may overwhelm us and bury all our glory in profound obscurity.[6]

The man considered the greatest, most honored, and respected president of our times understood the value of honoring God's ways:

> Our faith in God is a mighty source of strength....The morality and values such faith implies are deeply embedded in our national character. Our country embraces those principles by design, and we abandon them at our peril.[7]
>
> —RONALD REAGAN

President Reagan also warned:

> Without God, democracy will not and cannot long endure. If we ever forget that we're one nation under God, then we will be a nation gone under.[8]

Mr. President and all of America's civic leaders, you have a choice; the easy way or the hard way. Please do not wait until America ends up like the prodigal in the pigpen with no other way out before coming to your senses. We humbly and urgently implore you to rise up like the great American leaders who have gone before you and lead this nation in humble and genuine repentance, then once again honor God and His ways. The following shows how to begin doing this.

WHAT MUST HAPPEN

In order to stop the self-destruction of our nation and greater judgments of God to cease, America *must* do three things:

1. Turn Back to God in Genuine Repentance

President Lincoln's (and Congress') leadership example is worth repeating:

> It is the duty of nations...to own their dependence upon the overruling power of God, to confess their sins and transgressions, in humble sorrow, yet with assured hope...that genuine repentance will lead to mercy....Truth, announced in the Holy Scriptures and proven by all history, that those nations only are blessed whose God is the Lord....It behooves us then, to humble ourselves before the offended Power, to confess our national sins, and to pray for clemency and forgiveness.[9]

2. Commit to Honor God and His ways

Just as God has called the leaders in His house (the American church) to their knees in humble repentance and prayer and to do things His way, God is also calling those in the White House and our government to their knees in humble repentance and to lead our nation back to Him and His righteous ways. We will outline what we believe this renewed commitment should include in a "new declaration" we present in a moment.

3. Stand with Israel

The other thing America *must* be very careful to do is to strongly support Israel, especially regarding Jerusalem (the "apple of God's eye," [Zech. 2:8–9]). For God will bless those who bless her, and be against those that are against her (Gen. 12:3).

One of the reasons God raised America up was to be an ally and protection for Israel. We must also realize Israel and Jerusalem are not just the Jews' land and city; it's the very land and city Yeshua, Jesus Christ, will reign from when He returns. It is *His* land and *His* city, no one else's! So those that oppose or try to divide Israel and Jerusalem are opposing God.

Important Warning: America, it would be very unwise trying to force or trick Israel to divide land, especially Jerusalem. There have been many prophetic voices warning if that America is instrumental in dividing Israel, then God will divide America (some prophetic voices have seen this as a literal dividing of America down the Mississippi River area).

It must be real

Mr. President and all of America's civic leaders, we believe the time will come when you will be compelled to stand before the nation to acknowledge and turn back to God. But it must be more than just words in a time of desperation or a token announcement for a day of prayer. This cannot be just a time for speeches and back to your own ways in few weeks. There must be genuine repentance that is heartfelt and followed by serious and significant action, demonstrating the fruits of repentance in a lasting way (Acts 26:20). There must be a seismic shift back to the godly foundations and biblical fundamentals this nation was birthed and built upon—something monumental such as a new national *declaration*.

A New Declaration to Restore the Foundations Our Founding Fathers fashioned our nation's Declaration of Independence by acknowledging God as "Creator" and "with a firm reliance on the protection of Divine Providence."[10] America's turning back to God should also be an official act, a new declaration; not of *independence* but a "declaration of dependence upon Almighty God,"[11] as once phrased by Billy Graham. This echoed what President Abraham Lincoln (and Congress) said earlier (emphasis added):

> It is the duty of nations...to own their *dependence* upon the overruling power of God.[12]

The truth is America has a legacy of dependence upon God. From the Pilgrims to our Founding Fathers to Congress in 1954 when they voted to add the phrase "under God" to the Pledge of Allegiance, as they did this Congress declared "the dependence of our people and our Government upon the moral directions of the Creator."[13] Also our currency already declares "In God We Trust."[14]

Once again, America needs to return to her legacy of "dependence upon God." America needs a "new declaration" that acknowledges Almighty God and His Son Jesus Christ and our true *dependence* is upon Him, as our Founding Fathers once did—an official declaration so as a nation we will never forget or depart from God and His ways again, a "new declaration" that includes:

+ To restore original intent, declaring "the separation of church and state" as a term to keep government out of God's house and affairs, not to separate God from our governmental, judicial, and civil duties—to seek God's wisdom and operate in His ways, for as proven throughout history, God's ways bring true life and true liberty, blessing, and happiness that lasts.

+ Declare the restoration to freely honor God, the name of Jesus Christ, and biblical truth and values in our government, in our courts, and in our schools—the freedom to include these and honor God without hindrance.

+ To restore prayer in our schools, acknowledging our dependence upon Almighty God and thanking Him for His goodness, blessings, and protection upon us, our parents, our teachers, and our country—the freedom to pray without hindrance.

+ To restore God's Word (Holy Bible and Ten Commandments) to a place of honor in our schools, the public arena, and our courts—the freedom to read or display these without hindrance.

+ To restore the sanctity and protection of human life inside and outside the womb; this must include national repentance and pleading for God's mercy and forgiveness for allowing the murder and bloodshed of over fifty-five million innocent and defenseless children in the womb—ending legal abortion in America immediately, demonstrating the fruit of true repentance.

+ To restore the sanctity and the definition of marriage as only between one man and one woman, just as God designed it and His Son Jesus Christ declared it was from the beginning of creation (Matt. 19:4).

+ Declaring the pursuit of obeying the two greatest commandments; to love God and honor Him in every way and to love people, which includes helping the poor, needy, sick, broken, orphan, and widows in a biblical way.

+ Declaring we will pray and seek God's wisdom regarding issues such as fair healthcare, and fair taxation. **Note:** When we honor God, honor life, and His ways, then the solutions we need as a nation will come. God has all the answers!

+ Declaring our unwavering support for Israel.

Mr. President and Congress, again we humbly implore you; please don't wait until the economy has collapsed, greater natural disasters are ravaging the land, enemies attack our cities, tanks are in the streets, and there is war from shore to shore destroying and overtaking our nation and America has no other way out but to turn back to God. The sooner you respond and turn back to God and His righteous ways, the sooner God will rush in to save our nation and bring healing and restoration!

To the Governors and Mayors of America

You do not have to wait until Washington, DC, (representing America) turns back to God. Do it now! Gather the governmental and Christian leaders of your state or city and answer God's cry and message from this book. God will honor those who honor Him (1 Sam. 2:30). Set examples of what leadership and patriotism look like for God and country. In relation to this, remember the very encouraging word we previously shared called "Mayors and Governors Will Come…" in "The Results: Then We Will See…," chapter 25.

SPECIAL SECTION: AMERICA'S LEADERS— YOU WILL STAND ACCOUNTABLE

We remind you, Mr. President, Congress, judges, governors, and mayors, biblically you are public servants of God (see Romans 13:3–7). Therefore, you as leaders are accountable before Him to govern and judge righteously according to His standards and not according to your own.

As an elected official you may say, "I have to answer to my constituents. I have to answer to Americans. I have to answer to my party." But we want to remind you; in the end, there is One greater than all of them that you will have to answer to—God the "Supreme Judge of the World"[15] as our Founding Fathers proclaimed Him to be in our nation's Declaration of Independence. You will stand before Him and give an account as to how you governed and ruled in this nation (not your constituents or political party). Did you bow before Him and His ways or did you bow down to your party and their agenda? You are accountable first and foremost to Him, to judge and do justly and walk humbly before Him (Mic. 6:8).

Becoming an enemy of God

It is very important that you see things the way God sees and not as man sees or judges. God does not judge based upon political affiliation or skin color and neither is He worried about poll numbers or being "politically correct." God judges according to His Word and righteous ways. No matter who we are or what title we hold, if in your pride you choose to cast aside God's Word and defiantly champion, celebrate, and promote the very things He is against, then you have positioned yourselves as an enemy of God (James 4:4, 6).

When you choose to oppose God and His ways, you become His enemy and have already lost. He is able to humble nations and kings (and presidents) with a word. We see how He brought Pharaoh king of Egypt to His knees through devastating judgment, and drove King Nebuchadnezzar out of his mind because of his pride. He can humble and dethrone those who continue to defiantly oppose Him.

God is ready to help those who humbly honor Him and His righteous ways that lead to the path of life.

Two Paths, One Choice

Mr. President and all of America's civic leaders and judges, we once again humbly implore you to take very seriously how you respond to God's message to you (this chapter and book). You have a decision to make; which path America will take—judgment and destruction or repentance and restoration.

Our earnest prayer is America will not have to be decimated as Egypt was; but that all of us will instead quickly and humbly heed and return to God and His path of restoration, life, blessing, protection, prosperity, and peace. The truth is, judgment is standing right at the door. God is waiting on you. What will you do?

27

A FINAL WORD

Then Jesus said, "Did I not tell you that if you
believe, you will see the glory of God?"
—John 11:40, NIV

WE PRAY THIS book has captured your attention and left you with a great sense of sobriety and urgency, as well as stirred your heart with great faith and anticipation for what we all can do together to help save and change both our churches and nation. God has the answer America is looking for and He has set before us a path of great vision, hope, and change—if we will take it!

What are you going to do?

Now, you have a decision to make. You can put this book down, be a hearer only, and do nothing; or you can link arms with us and with pastors and churches all across your city and America and do what God is instructing to save and transform this nation.

God is ready to take you—His leaders, His church, His people—to a whole new level; but we must hear, embrace, and do what He is saying. If we will do this, then we will see a new day in our churches and a new day in our nation.

As we wrap up this message, we pray the following final word will also bring you great hope and encourage you to rise up and run with God's Answer for America.

A SONG AND WORD OF THE LORD

Preface: During morning prayer the following came as a prophetic song from the heart of God for our nation. It brought us tremendous encouragement; and we believe it will encourage you, especially those who have been already praying.

Awakening

November 1, 2012, through Cindy deVille

"A Great Awakening is coming to our shores, a Great Awakening.
More and more will awake as I shake the nation.

"A Great Awakening, a Great Awakening, and many will come to Me,
And many on bended knee I see,
And they will come and they will say,
'Please show me the way.
Show me how to be saved, show me the way.'

"Many will come and they will bow down before Me,"
Says the Lord, "from shore to shore, from sea to shining sea,

I see them bowing their knee, I see them coming back to Me.

"For your labor has not been in vain,
For all the trials and all the pain,
For all the tears and all the years, for all the prayers,
When you think I did not hear through all the years.
For the prayers of the saints, they're making a way for a new,
A brand new day.

"So do not be afraid of what's to come,
Just know My will, it will be done.
I will bring your nation to its knees, I will turn it back to Me.
For I have heard the prayers of My people.

"I," says the Lord, "have stirred their hearts to pray,
I am the one who wants to bring a new day.
So I have stirred the hearts of My people;
I have caused you to hear My cries so you would come
And cry out to Me day and night.

"Continue to pray, press into Me,
Cry out to Me night and day.
Continue in faith and know that I hear you,
That I am moving and I'll do what I have promised you."

Like a Baby in the Womb

I would not plant this seed in you and allow it to grow,
Like a baby in the womb and not bring it forth.

Continue to pray, pray at noon, pray at noon,
Pray at noon each day, continue to cry out
And you will see this awakening delivered.
Like a baby hidden in the womb,
It will come forth and all will see it.
You have been giving birth to a Great Awakening.

Giving Birth to a Great Awakening!

God's metaphors are amazing and insightful regarding what He has promised He will bring when we run with His answer.

+ Pour out like rain = pour down His presence and glory.
+ Dam bursting = prayers being collected to flood the land.
+ Wave of change = sweep, wash, and cleanse.
+ Baby to birth = the process, effort, and joy to bring it forth.

The Great Awakening is like a baby being developed in the womb. It is being developed through nation-changing prayer—our pure (unhindered), passionate (fervent), and persistent (relentless) prayers. As with pregnancy, the signs of it coming will become more obvious the closer it gets. Then when it's time for it to come, it will take a great pushing to bring it forth. And when it comes, the joy it brings will be worth every ounce of effort and every prayer!

God also said to keep praying "at noon." This is where the 12 O'clock Prayer Challenge comes in. Go to shekinahtoday.org to let us know you are joining with us.

Our Greatest Days Are Ahead

The days ahead will become the church's finest hour. As we said at the beginning of God's Answer, there are times in history when God moves through His leaders and His people in such a way that everything changes. This is such a time! Will you be a history maker for the kingdom of God and for our nation?

It's time for the church to rise up and be God's voice to this nation. It is a time for her to fulfill her destiny. Let us unite as never before and call America to its knees—first from the pulpits, then the pews, and then to the multitudes (the nation). Then we will see a brand new day! We must not delay. Begin today!

God is waiting on us. America is waiting on us. What will you do? Time is running out. We need every Christian engaged. Great judgment is standing at the door. A nation and multitudes hang in the balance! The Great Awakening is waiting to be born! Once again, for those of you who embrace and run with God's Answer, you will help make history—in your church, your community, your city, and our nation.

Our Prayer

We pray the message of the book and God's words resound in your heart. May the Spirit of pure (holy), passionate (fervent), and persistent (relentless) intercession fall on the pulpits and pews of America. And may there remain no rest for our souls *until* we see God's Spirit poured out and flood our churches and our nation with His nation-changing power and glory. We pray God's Answer will become a movement in churches all across America that will not stop, to the honor and glory of Yeshua, Jesus Christ our Lord, Amen!

Together with God's Answer, we can save and change our nation!

HELP US GET THE NATION-CHANGING MESSAGE OF THIS BOOK TO EVERY PASTOR AND CHRISTIAN YOU KNOW.

Our prayer is every pastor in America reads this book, gets this message, and embraces God's Answer for America that will not only begin to transform our nation's churches but also change the course of America and then spread to other nations. Please pass this book on to your leaders and everyone you know.

Connect with us

If you are or will be implementing God's Answer into your churches and ministries, we would love to know who you are and connect with you. We can also communicate with you further as things progress in our nation. You can contact us at shekinahtoday.org.

Epilogue

ENTERING A NEW DAY: THE GLORIOUS CHURCH

*For thus says the LORD of hosts: "Once more (it is a little while) I
will shake heaven and earth, the sea and dry land; and I will shake
all nations, and they shall come to the Desire of All Nations, and
I will fill this temple with glory... The glory of this latter temple
shall be greater than the former," says the LORD of hosts.*
—HAGGAI 2:6–7, 9

YES, THIS BOOK is not only God's answer for America, but it is also God's
answer for His church and a catalyst to awaken, arise, and be glorious in
the earth.

It is the first stages of the glorious church rising up in the earth for these end
times (Eph. 5). God wants to release His glory as never before in the earth; but
it will only come through His glorious church that has been cleansed, purified,
and become a "glorious house of prayer" and do things God's way. The prayers
of the saints will be paving the way for a new day. This will become so evident
that there will begin to be "glorious houses of prayer" everywhere.

As pastors and Christian leaders across America implement God's Answer
with the *three keys* revealed in this book, we are going to see the glorious church
begin to arise like a great last days' army, as God breathes upon His church.

The Light of the World

Jesus is the "light of the world" (John 8:12), and He has called His people to
display and radiate His light (Matt. 5:14). The day is coming when His glorious
church will be a light shining bright in the midst of great darkness and multitudes will come to the last great harvest. We will see what the prophet Isaiah
described begin to unfold before us:

> Arise, shine;
> For your light has come!
> And the glory of the LORD is risen upon you.
> For behold, the darkness shall cover the earth,
> And deep darkness the people;
> But the LORD will arise over you,
> And His glory will be seen upon you.
> The Gentiles shall come to your light,
> And kings to the brightness of your rising.
>
> —ISAIAH 60:1–3

The separation between Christ's kingdom of light and Satan's kingdom of darkness will become more distinct and obvious. We will see the days of Elijah return. As things shift and intensify, God wants His church to arise and shine bright in the midst of coming darkness (as described in Isaiah 60:1–2).

God's Glorious Church Will Rise and Light the Way

Church as usual is coming to an end. Like a Gideon's army, God will separate those that are truly His from the rest. Those truly obedient to God's voice will come into great unity, for they will be of one heart, one mind, and one purpose, and they will rise up and be glorious in the earth (Eph. 5:27). Their churches and ministries will not only survive but thrive and shine bright in the intense days we are entering.

As things intensify and get darker, God will cause His people to know the way. They will be the ones that have the answers. Those who are walking in the light will have great insight, great understanding. But those in the darkness will be confused and defused; they won't know which way to go. And those that once thought of God's people as fools will see them raised up. We have much more to say about the coming glorious church, but that is for another time and another book.

The stage is being set

It's worth repeating one more time; for those pastors and churches that implement God's Answer, you will not only transform your churches, save and change a nation, you will also have positioned yourselves for great victory and the most intense and glorious days ahead. Will you be ready for what's coming?

God is setting the stage for the church's finest hour, as she casts her net into the sea of humanity rescuing souls, multitudes for eternity, and as she prepares for a "kingdom change" with the return of the King of kings.

> Behold, I am coming quickly, and My reward is with Me, to give to every one according to his work. I am the Alpha and the Omega, the Beginning and the End, the First and the Last.
>
> —Revelation 22:12–13

And of His kingdom there will be no end.

—Luke 1:33

SPECIAL NOTE TO THE PRODIGAL, BACKSLIDDEN, OR THOSE WHO HAVE NEVER ACCEPTED CHRIST

GOD'S LOVE AND His plan for your life have not changed. Today He is extending His love, His forgiveness, and new life to you through His Son Jesus Christ. Scripture tells us that if we confess our sins, that He is *faithful* and *just* to forgive us and to cleanse us from all unrighteousness (1 John 1:9).

> If you confess with your mouth the Lord Jesus and believe in your heart that God has raised Him from the dead, you will be saved. For with the heart one believes unto righteousness, and with the mouth confession is made unto salvation.
>
> —ROMANS 10:9–10

> Jesus said…"I am the way, the truth, and the life. No one comes to the Father except through Me.
>
> —JOHN 14:6

Like the father in the story of the Prodigal Son in the Bible, if you will turn and cry out and run into the arms of God, His arms are wide open and He is standing and crying out for you to come.

Don't wait, let today be a new beginning; a new and glorious life for you awaits in Christ!

Appendix A

TOP 5 PRAYER GUIDE

W E SHARED HOW part of God's Answer includes nation-changing prayer that must be:

+ Pure—no hidden sin or unforgiveness

+ Passionate—fervent prayer of the righteous = very effective

+ Persistent—relentless = until will see the answers!

Imagine, from the West Coast to the East Coast churches praying (and fasting) day and night in unity! We must unite in one heart and one voice!

Now, what should we specifically be praying for? The focus of prayer for every Christian should include prayer for both the church and the nation. We will offer the following in our Top 5 Prayer Guide

The Power Prayer of Agreement

This Top 5 Prayer Guide also offers the prayer of agreement. There's power in agreement (Key 3; Matt. 18:19–20; Deut. 32:30). The 12 O'clock Prayer Challenge is one way we can unite together in prayer everyday (see chapter 24).

We exhort you to pray with us every day. Pray these as the Holy Spirit leads you, but we do highly recommend you regularly pray for each of the five main areas we list below. You could take each one of the five areas to pray for each day of the week. The main thing is we are covering each of these areas regularly with pure, fervent, and relentless prayer; praying in faith—believe it, pray it, then see it!

THIS TOP 5 PRAYER GUIDE IS:

1. Pray for a Great Awakening across America

Pray for the convicting power of the Spirit of God to sweep across our nation from God's house, to the White House, and throughout every city and town in our land. Pray for the glory of God and His Spirit to be poured out like rain in our churches, in our nation, and throughout the earth. Pray God will awaken the nation!

2. Pray for the Five-Fold Ministry (the Pulpits)

Pray for a great awakening and cleansing across the pulpits and ministries of America. Pray for a genuine heart of repentance and brokenness on behalf of our churches and our nation. Pray for purity, humility, faith, and unity to work together in one accord. Pray the pulpits and pews of America will boldly stand up for righteousness and speak God's truth in love.

3. Pray for the Church (the Pews)

Pray that churches all across America would become "glorious houses of prayer," making prayer high priority. Pray for genuine repentance and a great cleansing and purifying throughout, to prepare the glorious church to rise up and be salt and light, impacting America and the nations.

4. Pray for the Nation (the Multitudes)

Pray for our nation's leaders at all levels, for all civil servants, and for those in our military (1 Tim. 2:1–2). Pray America would fall to her knees under the convicting power of the Holy Spirit from the West Coast to the East Coast. Pray she would humble herself before God in genuine repentance and prayer and that her eyes would be opened to see how great her sin, how great God's love is, and how desperate her need is for Christ and His ways.

Pray for the souls of our nation, for the prodigals to come home and for the multitudes racing towards eternity to come to Christ. Pray for a great reformation across the nation, in our churches and throughout depths and fabric of America. Pray for the godly foundations to be restored, in our government, in education, in our families, and in every area of our culture—along with righteousness, honor, truth, and the fear of the Lord.

Pray that greed and corruption be rooted out of our government, political, judicial, and financial systems. Pray that integrity, righteousness, and justice will prevail in our land.

5. Pray for Israel and Jerusalem

Pray our leaders and America will fully support Israel. Pray for the peace of Jerusalem. Pray wisdom, grace, and strength for Israel's leaders.

Imagine Christians and churches across America pouring out their prayers! Remember, chapter 25 provides some details of the results we will see if we will embrace and run with God's Answer.

You can go to shekinahtoday.org to access a more detailed Top 5 Prayer Guide and also let us know you are taking the 12 O'clock Prayer Challenge.

A CLASSIC EXAMPLE FROM EARLY AMERICA

T HE BIBLICAL PATTERN of three ways God uses to get a nation's attention (see chapter 9) has actually been played out in early America. Amazingly, there are many sobering parallels to what we have been seeing in our nation today. We will also see within this account hints of some of the keys included in *God's Answer for America* (see chapters 18–20).

A Key Time in Early America

It was 1675 in New England, over fifty years since the Pilgrims had first settled there. They had started so strong in faith, in covenant, and trust with God (see "Where We Began: America's Godly Foundations," chapter 4). But years of prosperity and comfort turned into spiritual apathy, with sin and disobedience becoming more open and prominent (like the pattern throughout Israel's history). Part of the problem was that parents were failing to pass on their faith to the younger generation. And all this was leading to a gradual drifting from God and opening the door for more sin; much like what has happened in America today.

As the spiritual condition digressed, the biblical pattern of natural calamities, such as drought, weak crops, sickness, and economic woes got progressively worse. During these times of calamity, there would be calls and gatherings for repentance and prayer. Then God in His great mercy would relent or rein back His warnings or judgment.

However, over the years the repentance and prayers of the people became less and less sincere, and they would quickly return to their old sinful ways. And so God also began to relent less and less, with His warnings and judgments often continuing, but at a lesser degree. Some in the pulpits were trying to warn the people what was happening and why; but most of the people's hearts grew more hardened towards the warnings and cry of God.

Now after years of warnings and progressive natural and economic problems, something much more serious was about to happen and get their attention as never before. Greater judgment was at the door! The first Indian attacks came in 1675—it was a wakeup call.

Peter Marshall and David Manuel tell the rest of this account best in their excellent expanded edition of *The Light and the Glory*. The following are a string of direct excerpts about what happened after the first Indian attacks:

> Almost immediately a fast day was declared in Massachusetts but no sooner had the service ended that reports of fresh disasters arrived.

Clearly this time God's judgment was not going to be turned aside by one day's worth of repentance.

It was manifestly clear…that God was not going to be satisfied with superficial or temporary change. What He now demanded is what He had been calling for all along: nothing less than a complete amendment of life. This would necessitate a rooting out of sin and dealing with it to a degree that had not been seen on the eastern seaboard for nearly fifty years.

At first, the people, frightened and badly shaken though they were, still did not take the [ministers] warnings seriously; they had heard it all before so many times. But, the war news got steadily worse. And it obviously was war now; practically every Indian tribe in New England had donned war paint and was collecting scalps.

Finally, people began to heed their ministers. The Bay Colony's churches filled, and people who had not attended church in years stood in the aisles and joined in the prayers. For they had come to see that the battle was a spiritual one, and even the most pragmatic among them had accepted that fact.[1]

This reminded us in part of after 9/11 when America's churches were flooded the following weekend. But there was not real change. The story continues:

God's patience with the colonists' hypocritical ways had come to an end. He was not about to relent and restore the saving grace that had so long protected them and that they had so long taken for granted, unless New England had a change of heart.

Many of the families and settlements now being hardest hit had long ago removed themselves from the churches, physically as well as spiritually. Moreover, many of these families had incorporated themselves into a town without first gathering a church.[2]

God's Faithfulness in the Midst of Judgment

As we share in the "Where We Began: America's Godly Foundations" in the chapter 4, early Pilgrim and Puritan settlements were often built around a church, symbolizing God at the center of their lives. But for those who do not, but rather abandoned Him, how can they expect His hand of blessing and protection to remain? The story continues:

But where settlements, even the most isolated ones, had striven to keep faith with God and with one another, God kept faith with them. According to a history of the town of Sudbury, the reason that Sudbury rather than Concord was chosen by the Indians as their next point of attack was that the Indians feared the influence that Concord's minister, Edward Bulkeley, had with the Great Spirit. The history quotes an old Indian chronicle as follows: "We no prosper if we burn Concord," said they. "The Great Spirit loved that people. He tell us not to go there. They have a great man there. He great pray."[3]

Wow! God is faithful to those that honor Him. We see this played out throughout biblical history and American history; we will see it play out in the days ahead. The story continues:

> Even in New England's darkest hour, God's judgment could be seen to be tempered with mercy on behalf of His faithful...Throughout King Philip's war, as it came to be known, there were many recorded instances of God's mercy in the form of divine providence.[4]

This is Habakkuk 3:2 in action "In wrath remember mercy." Gods delights to show mercy when the opportunity is there.

Turning to God's Way = Life, Restoration and Refreshing

The story concludes:

> By April of 1676, there was scarcely a man or woman in all of New England who was not diligently searching his or her own soul for unconfessed and unrepented sin. In fact, it became unpatriotic not to do so—as if one were not doing one's part for the war effort.
>
> The tide of war had begun to turn...so many people had sincerely and publicly repented of their sinful ways, so many lives were truly reformed, so many broken relationships were restored and so many churches solemnly renewed their covenants that God relented and poured out His mercy. There was a sense of freshness in the colonies, a sense of cleanness and new hope. The colonies were united in a common cause.[5]

Please read those last two paragraphs again. Now, imagine that happening all across America today! You will see in God's Answer that this is the kind of repentance He is calling for from the pulpits, the pews, and the multitudes. This is the kind of refreshing restoration God wants to bring to His people and our nation. All God is asking is that His people cooperate with Him and respond to His answer for America.

Appendix C

DOES GOD STILL BRING JUDGMENT TODAY?

THE JUDGMENT OR wrath of God is not a popular subject today, to say the least. It is a subject with many misconceptions, questions, and objections. Many ask how a loving God can send judgment. Others say God doesn't bring judgment anymore since Jesus died on the cross. It is a subject filled with errors often caused by human reasoning and false teaching. And, like many subjects, there are extremes on both sides that need balance. We hope this will help shed light on this subject and provide some balance. Most of all we hope it reveals more of our glorious heavenly Father's heart.

We have provided two types of answers, the short version (here) and the expanded version (on our website www.shekinahtoday.org).

Judgment upon America

Many in the church are split on this subject. When people talk about possible judgment on America, the two main views that surface are:

> Statement 1: "If God doesn't judge America for all its sins, God has to apologize to Sodom and Gomorrah."[1]

> Statement 2: "If God judges America, He has to apologize to Jesus and what He has accomplished on the cross...God is not judging America (or any country in the world today)."[2]

Short Answer

Yes. God does still bring judgment today. As previously mentioned, we believe God's judgments are redemptive and motivated out of love. They are for the best, usually progressive, and often saved as a last resort. God is love (1 John 4:8) and everything He does is an extension of His divine love and nature. As we explain in the "expanded answer" on our website (shekinahtoday.org), one problem is many have a wrong view of what *real love* is.

Answering Objections to God's Judgment Today

Some of the main objections include:

> Objection 1: God's wrath was already poured out on Jesus on the cross, so God no longer brings judgment today. Therefore, God's wrath no longer comes upon sinful people or nations today.

> Objection 2: How can a loving God bring judgment that brings destruction and even death?

Objection 3: Cite Romans 2:4, interpreting that it is not the judgment of God but rather only the goodness of God that leads us repentance

Objection 4: God said He would have spared Sodom and Gomorrah if there were only ten righteous, and there are too many Christians in America for God to bring judgment upon our nation.

While we believe this book already answers many of these to an extent, we answer each of these specific objections and others on our website (www.sheki-nahtoday.org). We hope this will help bring greater clarity and provide understanding of God's amazing and unchanging character and His perfect ways.

DO TRUE PROPHETS STILL EXIST TODAY?

FIRST AND FOREMOST, God's written Word, the Holy Bible, is the standard by which every message (prophetic or not) is measured.

The Purpose of Prophecy

In Ephesians 4:11–13, the apostle Paul lists "prophet" as one of the five-fold ministry offices placed in the church to help equip, grow, and mature the body of Christ. We also see prophets, both male and female, in the Book of Acts. And the Book of Revelation speaks of the two witnesses prophesying during the end times.

The Book of Acts also tells how two prophets, Judas and Silas, greatly encouraged the church. "Judas and Silas, being prophets also themselves, exhorted the brethren with many words, and confirmed them" (Acts 15:32, KJV).

Test them

Paul exhorted the church not to despise prophecies, but test them (1 Thess. 5:21), because God will be speaking to His people. We encourage you to judge all prophecies in this book. Are they biblically sound? Have some of what has been said already begun to come to pass to confirm the word?

TYPES OF PROPHECY AND PROPHETS

Joel 2:28–32 says in the latter days God will pour out His Spirit, and His servants (both male and female) would prophecy. God's Word also says we are to pursue love and desire spiritual gifts, especially that we may prophesy (1 Cor 14:1).

Prophecy is for today; however, many tend to lump "prophecy" in to one bag. But when we look at God's Word we see there is a difference between prophecy and one operating in the office of the prophet. Besides speaking God's Word—a sure word of prophecy (2 Pet. 1:19), there are different levels and operations of prophecy, these include:

> Prophetic unction—God briefly speaking prophetically regarding something. It is possible for God to utter prophetically through anyone from time to time, like He did with Caiaphas the high priest when he said of Jesus that one had to die for the people (John 11:49–51).
>
> Prophetic gifts—most people in the "prophetic movement "seem to operate here. Most prophesy on personal level or general level with prophetic insight, dreams, visions, and words of wisdom

or knowledge, as Joel 2:28–32 describes. These are most often encouraging words.

Office of a prophet—called to speak to the church, to leaders, and nations. Most often prophets will be used to confront, speak correction, direction, warnings, exhortation, and a message of redemption with a strong call to turn back to God and His ways. As with the other five-fold ministry gifts, there is a level of authority for the office of a prophet. The office of a prophet is modeled by prophets such as Isaiah, Jeremiah, and Elijah.

False Prophets

Jesus warned of many false prophets in the last days (Matt. 24:11, 24). False prophets are deceptive. They often tickle the ears and warm the heart with words of comfort, yet rarely, if ever, call for repentance. When true prophets are warning of judgment because of great sin, the false prophets are usually saying everything is going to be OK, as they did in Jeremiah's day. They lead people astray from the true message God is speaking.

> Your prophets have said so many foolish things, false to the core. They did not save you from exile by pointing out your sins. Instead, they painted false pictures, filling you with false hope.
>
> —Lamentations 2:14, nlt

True Prophets

Typically, true prophets are those who devote much time to prayer, seeking the heart of God, then speak as He directs. We see throughout Scripture that the true prophets came on the scene in times of crisis or key times in history. They brought correction, direction, and many times warnings of judgment if the people did not turn from their sin. Many times God's prophets gave words and initial warnings years before their fulfillment, because God in His great mercy allows time for people to hear His voice clearly and repent. But there is a point when mercy must give way to God's holy justice. We believe America is at the very edge of this today.

True prophets do exist today, but there seem to be few who will speak even the hard and unpopular things and not compromise. As with most all the main prophets of old, they speak from the heart for God to His people and the nation. The prophet Jeremiah often wept for them. They speak God's Word, which even when hard and concerning judgment is often redemptive in message. They speak of what God sees and call for repentance to turn back to Him before judgment or destruction came. Really, they are not prophets of doom and gloom, but rather truth and hope.

In biblical times God's prophets often spoke in utterances, phrases, in poetic form, and sometimes even in prophetic song. We have found this to be true in the many of the prophecies we share with you. We present the message and all the prophetic words in this book for you to judge according to Holy Scripture.

Appendix E

AMERICA EMBRACING A LIE

Special Biblical Issue and Prophetic Perspective

P LEASE NOTE: SINCE the homosexual agenda has become highly divisive and prominent in our nation, we are going to take some extra time to address this serious moral and biblical issue and great deception. Please understand, it is out of a love (not hate) for our nation and for those bound by homosexual sin that we share these truths.

> Who *exchanged* the truth of God for a lie...
> —ROMANS 1:25, EMPHASIS ADDED

> You have *exchanged* My glory and My truth for a *lie*.
> —"AMERICA, AMERICA!" PROPHECY, 2007

AMERICA EMBRACING "A LIE"

There was a time when homosexual sin was viewed in mainstream society as an ungodly and shameful lifestyle, as Scripture teaches. However, over the decades Satan, in his cunning craftiness, has used certain agendas, mainstream media, and many politicians to repackage and rebrand homosexual sin as a "modern" lifestyle and "civil right" rather than the very unhealthy, destructive, and deceptive bondage that it is. Now, our youth are being indoctrinated to believe being "gay" is a brave and honorable thing.

Satan, as an "angel of light" (2 Cor. 11:14), has deceptively cloaked the homosexual lifestyle and agenda in a colorful façade so people will embrace it. Instead of shame, it's now called "pride." Instead of "queer" it's now called "gay" (which at one time meant "happy"). And now God's "rainbow" of promise has been hijacked and used in their branding, in an attempt to mask the debasement and bondage of this sin (rainbow colors have always been very endearing and appealing to children; this is also very troubling).

While many try to paint the homosexual lifestyle as "modern" and even "liberating," they seem to ignore or attempt to mask the destructive, dark, and most vile side, such as public acts of sodomy in our streets at homosexual festivals and "Pride" parades—men with boys and other acts too reprehensible to mention.

Another lie and deception Satan has spawned is the belief that people are born gay. The truth is we are all born into sin, and we all have a choice to give into the temptations and tendencies, or to resist them.

An All-Out Assault

In addition we are seeing an all-out assault on traditional marriage and family values. This "lie" in the name of "love," "tolerance" and "equality," is being aggressively promoted and pushed upon our children, schools, entertainment, businesses, in the sports arena, the culture, throughout our government, and even upon our military. Then, those who will not embrace and celebrate this destructive lifestyle are labeled "homophobic" or "bigot" (even threatened with lawsuits) as LGBT activists often spew the very hate they claim to condemn. At the same time activist judges are overturning the will of the people by striking down bans on "gay" marriage in state after state.

All of this is being forced upon the majority of America in an aggressive attempt to reshape our culture, even though reports show only about 2 percent in America identify themselves as "gay!"[1]

> The reality is that fewer than one in 50 Americans identify themselves as gay, out of which only a minority wants to be "married." How foolish, then, to redefine marriage, restrict freedoms of conscience, speech, and religion, and engage in a massive social experiment based on such a tiny percentage of the population.[2]
>
> —MICHAEL BROWN

Shocking Agenda: The LGBT Presidential Project

Sad but true is the fact our current president is helping to lead the way. (We must earnestly pray for our president according to 1 Timothy 2:1–4.)

As of 2014 the Obama Administration has appointed more than 250 openly LGBT professionals to full-time and advisory positions in the executive branch; more than all known LGBT appointments of other presidential administrations combined. Most of these are high-level positions affecting every major area of America, even though they represent about 2 percent of our nation. This should be very concerning! To learn about this go to the "victoryinstitute.org" website (while it is up) and review the list.[3]

PROPHETIC INSERT: A CALL TO FAST AND PRAY

During a time of prayer regarding the LGBT agenda and our nation, the Lord clearly warned that if this aggressive agenda did not stop that He would cause a plague to break out in the homosexual community, especially the leaders.[4]

This prophetic warning and word drove us to our knees and to begin twenty-one days of fasting and prayer that God in His mercy would move by His Spirit in the homosexual community. We prayed (and continue to pray) He would open their eyes, bring them to repentance and set them free from the deception and bondage. People across the nation and even other countries joined with us.

> Cindy: The intercession and weeping for those bound by this sin was greater than any I had experienced before. I knew this was close to

God's heart and that He wanted to put a stop to the deception and bondage.

During this extended time of fasting and prayer Cindy was also given a revealing vision.

The Cage Vision

> I had a heartbreaking vision repeatedly for almost 2 days. At first I kept seeing a very thin and sickly man, unclothed, and sitting in a cage, like a circus animal cage. He seemed close to death, with no strength left in him. He kept trying to grab the bars of the cage, trying to get free, but he didn't have the strength, so he just seemed to give up trying. Then I saw another cage, and another, and another. They were all linked together like you would see circus animal cages. It was heartbreaking. And as I saw this it was clear that their master was Satan (almost like the Joker in Batman), and he was pulling the cages and laughing, mocking the men, and God, as though to say, "They are mine!" Many wanted out, but they had chosen to give themselves up to the homosexual lifestyle, and had become slaves to it.

OUR PRAYER AND REQUEST

We know God wants to move powerfully across our nation and set captives free. Please join us as we continue to pray for them and all those bound by sexual sin. Christ alone can set them free and make them like new (2 Cor. 5:17).

Prophetic Vision Insert: A powerful news-making event seen by Destiny

In June 2014 our fifteen-year-old daughter, Destiny, had joined us in a time of fasting and prayer regarding the homosexual community for the breaking of deception and bondage. Then one evening during prayer, the Holy Spirit came strongly upon her in intercession on her knees, and she began to weep and cry out deeply for about twenty minutes. Later, when she was finally able to speak, she shared what she saw.

Destiny had a vision that was so real and alive to her. She saw homosexuals running out of the bars and into the streets crying out in repentance. In the vision they hated anything to do with their sin and began tearing up their rainbow colored flags and throwing them on the ground as if they hated them.

> I saw the gay community in the streets, they were on their knees, and it was all over the news. People were coming out of the gay bars, ripping off the gay flags; tearing them down and ripping apart the gay flags in shame. And they were repenting of their uncleanness.
>
> It was all over the news everywhere. They were set free from homosexual bondage and they wanted nothing to do with it. They wanted to leave it all behind and they wanted to turn to Jesus. And they were free.

This is the power of *God's Answer* in action!

I WILL NOT BE SILENT!

Cindy: During a time of prayer regarding the pressure many pastors and Christians are feeling to be silent regarding truth, the following bold declaration came forth, titled "I Will Not Be Silent!"

I AM A CHRISTIAN and I WILL NOT BE SILENT!

I am not a racist.

I am not a bigot.

I am not a homophobe.

I am not a hater.

I am a Christian who loves God and the sinner too much to be silent.

I will not be silent when I know multitudes are racing towards an eternal hell!

I will not be silent and allow Satan to deceive the whole world.

I will not be silent knowing that sin destroys lives, families, and nations.

I will not be silent knowing that the wages of sin is still death.

I will not be silent knowing that I can save even just one from the clutches of sin and hell!

TO BE SILENT…

To be silent would be the greatest demonstration of hatred and selfishness I know.

I will not be silent, but

I will speak the truth in love,

I will shout it out from the rooftops.

So, go ahead and call me names; but I will not change!

I will love you even more and I will pray for you,

But I will not be silent!

For Christ paid too high a price,

And He shall receive the reward of His sacrifice!

RELATED PROPHETIC WORDS

Y OU CAN ACCESS the below related prophetic words mentioned in this book and more at www.shekinahtoday.org.

TO AMERICA

Shifting Economies
Smoke and Mirrors
Deadly Storms and Greater Storms
Bin Laden, Enemies Arise, and Word to Leaders
To America: My Canopy of Protection
America—I Am Numbering Your Days
The Coming Cleansing and Revolution
Mayors and Governors Will Come
Going into the Dark Places

TO THE CHURCH

A Vision: "Are You With Me?"
A Great Sword of Separation
Judgment Is Coming to the Pulpits of America
My Fully Devoted Ones
Houses of Prayer Everywhere
Prayers of the Saints Like Rain
An Hourglass and Two Tidal Waves
Heaven and Earth Collide

END TIMES

Days of Wonder and Days of Dread…Ahead
Like Never Before—Prepare Yourself
Great Glory, Judgment, Draw Closer, and Watch Jerusalem

NOTES

Section 2—How Far We Have Fallen and Why

1. Larry Tomczak, "Obama's Former Bodyguard: 'It's Worse Than People Know," *Charisma News*, http://www.charismanews.com/opinion/heres-the-deal/41723-obama-s-former-bodyguard-it-s-worse-than-people-know (accessed February 2, 2014).
2. Ibid.
3. Ibid.
4. Ibid.

4—Where We Began: America's Godly Foundations

1. Church of the Holy Trinity v. United States, 143 U.S. 457 (1892).
2. Peter Marshall and David Manuel, *The Light and the Glory: 1492–1793* (Grand Rapids, MI: Revell, 2009), 109. Used by permission.
3. Caleb Johnson, "The Mayflower Compact," *Mayflower History.com*, http://mayflowerhistory.com/mayflower-compact/ (accessed January 2, 2015).
4. John Winslow, "A Model of Charity," (speech, 1630), found at Mass Moments, *The Massachusetts Foundation for the Humanities*, http://www.massmoments.org/teachers/primedoc.cfm?pid=12 (accessed January 2, 2015).
5. Ben Franklin, "Constitutional Convention Address on Prayer," *American Rhetoric*, http://www.americanrhetoric.com/speeches/benfranklin.htm (accessed January 2, 2015).
6. Ibid.
7. Jonathan Cahn, *The Harbinger* (Lake Mary, FL: FrontLine, 2011).
8. David Barton, "Endorsement," *National Council on Bible Curriculum in Public Schools*, http://bibleinschools.net/Endorsements/David-Barton.php (accessed January 2, 2015).
9. Peter G. Mode, *Sourcebook and Biographical Guide for American Church History* (Menasha, WI: George Banta Publishing, 1991), 75–75, found at http://www.bible-history.com/quotes/harvard_university_1.html (accessed January 2, 2015).
10. "History of Harvard," *AllAboutHistory.org*, http://www.allabouthistory.org/history-of-harvard.htm (accessed January 2, 2015).
11. "Regulations at Yale College (1745)," *consitution.org*, http://www.constitution.org/primarysources/yale.html (accessed January 2, 2015).
12. "Noah Webster," *Webster's Dictionary 1828—Online Edition*, http://webstersdictionary1828.com/NoahWebster (accessed January 2, 2015).
13. "Notable Quotations [Noah Webster]," *Webster's Dictionary 1828—Online Edition*, http://webstersdictionary1828.com/Quotes (accessed January 2, 2015).
14. In Vidal v. Girard's Executors, 43 U.S. 127 (1844), the U.S. Supreme Court ruled unanimously (9-0) that the Bible could not be extracted from the education of our youth.
15. Daniel Webster, *The Writings and Speeches of Daniel Webster* (Boston, MA: Little, Brown, & Company, 1903).

5—America—A Prodigal Nation

1. John Winthrop, "A Model of Christian Charity by Governor John Winthrop, 1630," *The Winthrop Society*, http://www.winthropsociety.com/doc_charity.php (accessed February 3, 2015).

2. Billy Graham, "My Heart Aches for America," ©2012 *Billy Graham Evangelistic Association*, Used with permission, All rights reserved, http://billygraham.org/story/billy-graham-my-heart-aches-for-america/ (accessed February 4, 2015). Used by permission.

3. "Message to America: Full Version: Jonathan Cahn Addresses the Presidential Inaugural Prayer Breakfast," YouTube video, 39:28, from the 2013 Inauguration Prayer Breakfast, posted by Beth Israel Jonathan Cahn, https://www.youtube.com/watch?v=S9xMxkNROto (accessed February 4, 2015).

4. School Prayer: Engel v. Vitale (No. 468) 370 U.S. 421 (1962), http://www.law.cornell.edu/supremecourt/text/370/421 (accessed February 4, 2015).

5. Paul Strand, "Anti-Christian Faith Sentiment Growing at Breakneck Speed," *Charisma News*, October 15, 2013, http://www.charismanews.com/us/41373-study-anti-christian-faith-sentiment-growing-at-breakneck-speed (accessed February 13, 2015).

6. Jerome Corsi, "Harvard Hosting Satanic 'Black Mass,'" May 9, 2014, *WND Education*, http://www.wnd.com/2014/05/harvard-hosting-satanic-black-mass/ (accessed February 13, 2015).

7. "Obama: 'Fundamentally Transforming the United States of America,' Long Version," *YouTube* video, 1:37, from his presidential candidacy campaign on October 30, 2008, posted by jbranstetter04, https://www.youtube.com/watch?v=KrefKCaV8m4 (accessed February 4, 2015).

8. "Lesbian mayor subpoenas sermon notes and communications from Houston pastors," October 16, 2014, *American Family Association*, http://www.afa.net/action-alerts/lesbian-mayor-subpoenas-sermon-notes-and-communications-from-houston-pastors/ (accessed February 13, 2015).

9. Todd Starnes, "Atlanta Fire Chief: I was fired because of my Christian faith," *Fox News*, January 7, 2015, http://www.foxnews.com/opinion/2015/01/07/atlanta-fire-chief-was-fired-because-my-christian-faith/ (accessed February 13, 2015).

10. Matt Bynum, "The Motion Picture Production Code of 1930 (Hays Code)" *ArtsReformation.com*, www.artsreformation.com/a001/hays-code.html (accessed February 13, 2015).

11. Ibid.

12. Ibid.

13. "Study Shows 'Gay Married' Lifespans Average 24 Years Shorter than Hetero Marrieds in Norway, Denmark," April 3, 2007, *Americans for Truth about Homosexuality*, http://americansfortruth.com/2007/04/05/study-shows-gay-married-lifespans-average-24-years-shorter-than-hetero-marrieds-in-norway-denmark/ (accessed February 13, 2015).

14. Frank Joseph, "Everyone Should Know These Statistics on Homosexuals," October 15, 2005, *Tradition in Action, Inc.*, http://www.traditioninaction.org/HotTopics/a02rStatistcs.html (accessed February 13, 2015).

15. Bryan Fischer, "SPLC's ten "myths" about homosexuality turn out to be ten truths," November 26, 2010, *Renew America*, http://www.renewamerica.com/columns/fischer/101126 (accessed February 13, 2015).

16. Marc Graser, "Sales are a record for the franchise and publisher Take-Two Interactive," September 18, 2013, *Variety Media, LLC*, variety.com/2013/digital/news/grand-theft-auto-v-earns-800-million-in-a-day-more-than-worldwide-haul-of-man-of-steel-1200616706/ (accessed February 13, 2015).

17. Hollie McKay, "New study says full-frontal nudity on prime-time TV up 6,300 percent over last year," *FoxNews.com*, August 23, 2012, www.foxnews.com/entertainment/2012/08/23/new-study-says-full-frontal-nudity-on-prime-time-tv-up-400-over-last-year/ (accessed February 13, 2015).

18. Randy O'Bannon, "56,662,169 Abortions in America Since Roe vs. Wade in 1973," *LifeNews.com*, January 12, 2014, www.lifenews.com/2014/01/12/56662169-abortions-in-america-since-roe-vs-wade-in-1973/ (accessed February 13, 2015).

19. "ECLIPSE OF REASON—Live Abortion Documentary/Prolife Anti-Abortion Video," YouTube video, 27:03, a 1987 documentary video directed, filmed, and narrated by Dr. Bernard Nathanson, published with permission by rosary films, https://www.youtube.com/watch?v=_nff8I2FVnI (accessed February 3, 2015).

20. Thomas Jefferson, "Quotations on the Jefferson Memorial," Panel Three, Notes on the State of Virginia, Query XVIII, http://www.monticello.org/site/jefferson/quotations-jefferson-memorial (accessed February 3, 2015).

21. Abraham Lincoln, "Abraham Lincoln's Second Inaugural Address," March 4, 1865, Primary Documents in American History, *Library of Congress*, http://www.loc.gov/rr/program/bib/ourdocs/Lincoln2nd.html (accessed February 3, 2015).

22. Dr. Bill Bright, in "The Power of the Pulpit" by Charles Crismier, Save America, http://saveus.org/renewing-america-the-church/for-pastors/the-power-of-the-pulpit/ (accessed February 11, 2015). Used by permission.

23. George Washington, "Farewell Address (1796)," "Washington's Farewell Address," *Wikisource*, last modified November 7, 2014, http://en.wikisource.org/wiki/Washington%27s_Farewell_Address#1.

6—THE STATE OF THE AMERICAN CHURCH

1. Tiana Wiles, "Why 68% of Christian Men Watch Porn," Conquer Series, Kingdom Works Studios, http://www.conquerseries.com/why-68-percent-of-christian-men-watch-porn/; Mike Genung, "How Many Porn Addicts are in Your Church; Revisited," October 31, 2013, *Crosswalk.com*, www.crosswalk.com/church/pastors-or-leadership/how-many-porn-addicts-are-in-your-church-revisited.html (accessed February 3, 2015).

2. Chris Woodward, "Barna: Many Pastors Wary of Raising 'Controversy,'" *OneNewsNow*, August 1, 2014, http://onenewsnow.com/church/2014/08/01/barna-many-pastors-wary-of-raising-controversy? (accessed February 3, 2015).

3. E.M. Bounds, *The Necessity of Prayer* (Grand Rapids, MI: Baker Book House, 1991).

4. Leonard Ravenhill, *Why Revival Tarries* (Minneapolis: Bethany House, 1959).

5. Woodward, "Barna."

6. David Kinnaman, *You Lost Me: Why Young Christians are Leaving Church and Rethinking Faith* (Grand Rapids, MI: Baker Books, 2011); Ken Ham, C. Britt Beemer, Todd Hillard, *Already Gone* (Hebron, KY: Answers in Genesis, 2009).

7. Quote by John Paul Jackson. Used by Permission.

8. "'Nones' on the Rise," *Pew Research Center*, October 9, 2013, http://www.pewforum.org/Unaffiliated/nones-on-the-rise.aspx (accessed February 3, 2015).

7—THE GATEKEEPERS

1. Part of "Opening the Door to War!" prophecy from June 7, 2010, through Cindy deVille. The prophecy is also in chapter 11 and on our website at Shekinahtoday.org.

2. Charles G. Finney, "The Decay of Conscience," *The Independent of New York*, December 4, 1873, http://www.gospeltruth.net/1868_75Independent/731204_conscience.htm (accessed February 3, 2015).

3. Ibid.

4. Martin Luther King Jr., "Martin Luther King Jr. Quotes," *123Holiday.net*, http://martin-luther-king-day.123holiday.net/king_quotes.html (accessed February 3, 2015).

9—THE BIBLICAL PATTERN: THREE WAYS

1. Barak Obama, "Remarks by the President in the State of the Union Address," February 12, 2013, The White House, Office of the Press Secretary, http://www.whitehouse.gov/the-press-office/2013/02/12/remarks-president-state-union-address (accessed February 16, 2015).

2. Henry Wadsworth Longfellow, "Henry Wadsworth Longfellow > Quotes Quotable > Quote," *Goodreads, Inc.*, http://www.goodreads.com/quotes/255749-though-the-mills-of-god-grind-slowly-yet-they-grind (accessed February 5, 2015).

3. Abraham Lincoln, "Proclamation Appointing a National Fast Day," *Abraham Lincoln Online*, http://www.abrahamlincolnonline.org/lincoln/speeches/fast.htm (accessed February 5, 2015).

4. Jonathan Edwards, "Sinners in the Hands of an Angry God," Spiritual Life in God, *The Christian Broadcasting Network*, http://www.cbn.com/spirituallife/churchandministry/churchhistory/Jonathan_Edwards_Sinners.aspx?option=print (accessed February 5, 2015).

10—A REVEALING PROPHETIC SEQUENCE

1. *Tara Clarke, "Stock Market Crash History: The Dow's 10 Biggest One-Day Plunges," MoneyMorning.com, February 13, 2013, moneymorning.com/2014/02/13/stock-market-crash-history-dows-10-biggest-one-day-plunges/ (accessed February 13, 2015).*

11—WHAT'S COMING NEXT, IF...?

1. Kimberly Amadeo, "Stock Market Crash of 2008," About News, July 19, 2014, usecKimberly Amadeo, "Stock Market Crash of 2008," *About News*, July 19, 2014, useconomy.about.com/od/Financial-Crisis/a/Stock-Market-Crash-2008.htm (accessed February 135, 2015).

2. Rex Nutting, "U.S. recession began in December 2007, NBER says," *MarketWatch*, December 1, 2008, http://www.marketwatch.com/story/us-recession-began-in-december-2007-nber-says (accessed February 13, 2015).

3. Anna Bernasek, "Typical Household, Now Worth a Third Less," *The New York Times*, July 26, 2014, www.nytimes.com/2014/07/27/business/the-typical-household-now-worth-a-third-less.html? (accessed February 13, 2015).

4. Ylan Mui, "Americans saw wealth plummet 40 percent from 2007 to 2010, Federal Reserve says," *The Washington Post*, June 11, 2012, http://www.washingtonpost.com/business/economy/fed-americans-wealth-dropped-40-percent/2012/06/11/gJQAlIsCVV_story.html (accessed February 13, 2015).

5. Rick Moran, "Record 20 Percent of Households on Food Stamps," *American Thinker*, January 22, 2014, www.americanthinker.com/blog/2014/01/record_20_of_homes_on_food_stamps_last_year.html (accessed February 13, 2015).

6. Peter Ferrara, "After Five Years of Obamanomics, A Record 100 Million Americans Not Working," *Forbes*, January 24, 2014, www.forbes.com/sites/peterferrara/2014/01/24/after-five-years-of-obamanomics-a-record-100-million-americans-not-working/ (accessed February 13, 2015).

7. Dave Boyer, "That's rich: Poverty level under Obama breaks 50-year record," January 7, 2014, *The Washington Times*, http://www.washingtontimes.com/news/2014/jan/7/obamas-rhetoric-on-fighting-poverty-doesnt-match-h/ (accessed February 13, 2015).

8. Brett Arends, "It's official: America is now No. 2," December 4, 2014, *MarketWatch, Inc*, http://www.marketwatch.com/story/its-official-america-is-now-no-2-2014-12-04 (accessed February 13, 2015).

9. "Natural Disasters Becoming More Frequent," *Worldwatch Institute*, http://www.worldwatch.org/node/5825 (accessed February 13, 2015).

10. "Tornadoes of 2008," modified January 8, 2015, *Wikipedia*, en.wikipedia.org/wiki/Tornadoes_of_2008 (accessed February 13, 2015).

11. "Our Extraordinary Tornado Year, Early 2008 Has Set an Unprecedented Pace for Twisters," www.thedailygreen.com/environmental-news/blogs/hurricanes-storms/tornado-trends-55030501 (website no longer available).

12. Doyle Rice, "2008 tornado season could blow away records," *USA Today*, October 31, 2008, usatoday30.usatoday.com/weather/storms/tornadoes/2008-10-12-Tornado_N.htm (accessed February 13, 2015).

13. "Flooding Hits Historic 500-Year Levels in Iowa," *Fox News*, June 12, 2008, www
.foxnews.com/story/2008/06/12/flooding-hits-historic-500-year-levels-in-iowa/ (accessed
February 13, 2015).

14. Bill Kaczor, "Fay's 4th Florida Landfall One for the Record Books," *The Huffington
Post*, September 23, 2008, www.huffingtonpost.com/2008/08/23/fays-4th-florida-landfall
_n_120803.html (accessed February 13, 2015).

15. Marcus Wohlsen, "Lightning sparks 800-plus fires in California," *USA Today*,
June 22, 2008, usatoday30.usatoday.com/news/nation/2008-06-22-4094219729_x.htm
(accessed February 13, 2015).

16. "Calif. facing worst drought in modern history," *USA Today*, January 30, 2009, usa
today30.usatoday.com/weather/drought/2009-01-30-california-drought_N.htm?loc
=interstitialskip (accessed February 13, 2015).

17. Susan Kelleher, "Washout: Unprecedented flooding forces evacuations, closes highways," *The Seattle Times*, January 7, 2009, http://seattletimes.com/html/localnews/2008
602613_flood08m0.html (accessed February 13, 2015).

18. Jim Skillington, "KY ice storm called worst in history," *Disaster News Network*, February 2, 2009, http://www.disasternews.net/news/article.php?articleid=3829 (accessed
February 13, 2015).

19. "2010 Tennessee floods," *Wikipedia*, modified December 2, 2014, http://en.wikipedia
.org/wiki/2010_Tennessee_floods (accessed February 13, 2015).

20. "April 25–28, 2011 tornado outbreak," *Wikipedia*, modified February 11, 2015,
http://en.wikipedia.org/wiki/April_25%E2%80%9328,_2011_tornado_outbreak (accessed
February 13, 2015).

21. "Magnitude 5.8 Earthquake Hits Virginia, Sends Shockwaves Throughout East
Coast," *Fox News*, August 23, 2011, http://www.foxnews.com/us/2011/08/23/magnitude
-58-earthquake-hits-virginia-sends-shockwaves-throughout-east-coast/ (accessed February
13, 2015).

22. Lee Coleman, "Irene: Official data confirm record flood," *The Daily Gazette*, September 2, 2011, http://www.dailygazette.com/news/2011/sep/02/0903_record/ (accessed
February 13, 2015).

23. Amy Bingham, "Obama Has Declared Record-Breaking 89 Disasters So Far in
2011," *ABC News*, October 28, 2011, http://abcnews.go.com/blogs/politics/2011/10/
obama-has-declared-record-breaking-89-disasters-so-far-in-2011/ (accessed February 13,
2015).

24. Jim Suhr, "U.S. Drought 2012: Half of Nation's Counties Now Considered Disaster
Areas," *Huffington Post*, August 2, 2012, http://www.huffingtonpost.com/2012/08/02/us
-drought-2012-disaster-areas_n_1731393.html (accessed February 13, 2015).

25. Alan Duke, "Superstorm Sandy breaks records," *CNN*, October 31, 2012, http://
www.cnn.com/2012/10/30/us/sandy-records/ (accessed February 13, 2015).

26. IWB, "100-year flood hits VT twice—in three years!" *InvestmentWatch*, May
25, 2013, http://investmentwatchblog.com/100-year-flood-hits-vt-twice-in-three-years/
(accessed February 13, 2015).

27. "Monster Oklahoma tornado was top-of-the-scale EF-5," *FloridaToday.com*, May 21,
2013, http://www.floridatoday.com/article/A9/20130521/NEWS01/305210025/Monster
-Oklahoma-tornado-top-scale-EF-5 (accessed February 13, 2015).

28. Tyler Durden, "'Historic', 'Catastrophic' Winter Storm Paralyzes Atlanta as Pax
Creeps Up east Coast," February 12, 2014, http://www.zerohedge.com/news/2014-02-12/
historic-catastrophic-winter-storm-paralyzes-atlanta-pax-creeps-east-coast (accessed February 13, 2015).

29. "'Storm of Historic Proportions' Dumps 13 Inches of Rain in Some Spots of
LI," *CBS New York*, August 13, 2014, http://newyork.cbslocal.com/2014/08/13/

flash-flood-watches-warnings-in-effect-as-heavy-rain-drenches-parts-of-tri-state/ (accessed February 13, 2015).

30. Andre Heath, "Arctic Blast," The Celestial Convergence, Andre Heath, http://www.thecelestialconvergence.com/ice-age-now-historic-biblical-think-uncharted-territory-coldest-temperatures-season-break-records-u-s-northeast-latest-blizzard-puts-boston-th/ (accessed February 17, 2015).

31. "Repeat Deadly Storms 'Unusual but Not Unknown,'" Fox News, May 24, 2011, www.foxnews.com/us/2011/05/24/repeat-deadly-storms-unusual-unknown/#ixzz1NH rdXKGk (accessed February 13, 2015).

32. Gene Cherry, "Massive Hurricane Sandy takes aim at East Coast," Reuters, October 27, 2012, www.reuters.com/article/2012/10/27/us-storm-sandy-hurricane-idUSBRE89N1 6J20121027 (accessed February 13, 2015).

33. "Tornado devastates Moore, Oklahoma," CNN, May 22, 2013, www.cnn.com/interactive/2013/05/us/moore-oklahoma-tornado/ (accessed February 13, 2015).

34. Andy Lines, "Boston Marathon bombings: City in total lockdown after worst terror attack in US since 9/11," Mirror, April 15, 2013, www.mirror.co.uk/news/world-news/boston-marathon-bombings-city-total-1834655 (accessed February 13, 2015).

35. Phil Cross, "Senator Inhofe warns of potential terrorist attacks on U.S. soil," Fox25, August 20, 2014, http://www.okcfox.com/story/26331734/senator-inhofe-warns-of-potential-terrorist-attacks-on-us-soil (accessed February 13, 2015).

36. Jamie Weinstein, "ISIS Threatens America Again: 'We Will Drown All of You in Blood,'" The Daily Caller, August 18, 2014, dailycaller.com/2014/08/18/isis-threatens-america-again-we-will-drown-all-of-you-in-blood (accessed February 13, 2015).

37. Missy Ryan, "Islamic State threat 'beyond anything we've seen': Pentagon," Reuters, August 21, 2014 http://www.reuters.com/article/2014/08/22/us-usa-islamicstate-idUSK BN0GL24V20140822 (accessed February 13, 2015).

38. "Prepare for War—3 Enemies Attack," YouTube video, 1:57, posted by Shekihah-Today1, http://www.youtube.com/watch?v=P56E_bD0Szk&noredirect=1 (accessed February 13, 2015).

39. David Wilkerson, Set the Trumpet to Thy Mouth (Lindale, TX: World Challenge, 1985), 15.

40. "Henry Gruver Russian Invasion of America," YouTube video, 6:46, from a 1986 vision Henry Gruver had of attacks upon America, posted by Carlos Sandovol, .https://www.youtube.com/watch?v=4oB4feKSFUA (accessed January 3, 2015).

41. Larry Stockstill, The Remnant (Lake Mary, FL: Charisma House, 2008), preface, xii. Used by permission

42. Ibid., xii-xiii.

43. Lee Grady, "Larry Stockstill's Urgent Plea: 'We Have a Window of Time for Repentance,'" 2007, Fire in My Bones, Charisma, www.charismamag.com/fireinmybones/Columns /022908.html (accessed February 11, 2015).

44. Ibid.

12—AMERICA HAS A DECISION TO MAKE!

1. Neville Johnson at Shekinah Worship Center's "Lancaster Prophetic Conference 2014 Session 1 Neville Johnson," YouTube video, 48:55, from the Lancaster Prophetic Conference on August 6, 2014, at Shekinah Worship Center, posted by ShekihahWorshipTV, youtube.com/watch?v=OekO8KZ1Lns.

15—GOD'S LETTER TO HIS PASTORS AND LEADERS

1. E.M. Bounds, the Complete Works of E.M. Bounds (Radford, VA: Wilder Publications, 2008).

17—The Pulpits Hold the Keys

1. Stockstill, *The Remnant*, xii.

18—Key 1: Opening the Door for Change

1. Chuck Colson, "A Nation That Has Forgotten God," *SBC Life*, April 1997, http://www.sbclife.net/articles/1997/04/sla11 (accessed February 13, 2015).
2. Lee Grady, "Larry Stockstill's Urgent Plea."

19—Key 2: The Power to Change Everything

1. Billy Graham, *Unto the Hills* © Billy Graham, used by permission, all rights reserved.
2. J. Sidlow Baxter, "J. Sidlow Baxter > Quotes > Quotable Quotes," *Goodreads Inc.*, http://www.goodreads.com/quotes/493178-men-may-spurn-our-appeals-reject-our-message-oppose-our (accessed February 11, 2015).
3. Sadhu Sundar Selvaraj, "Prophetic Message to the Church," June 2002, http://www.telusplanet.net/public/tsgibson/messageselvaraj.htm (accessed February 11, 2015).
4. Jonathan Edwards, *The Works of Jonathan Edwards*, Vol. III (New York: Robert Carter and Brothers, 1897), 417.
5. "Prayer and Intercession," Gateway Church, http://nfw.gatewaypeople.com/ministries/prayer-intercession (accessed February 11, 2014).

22—Step 3: The Pulpit Level

1. Woodward, "Barna."

24—Step 3: The National Level

1. "Declaration of Independence," The Charters of Freedom, http://www.archives.gov/exhibits/charters/declaration_transcript.html (accessed February 13, 2014).
2. Paul Dienstberger, *The American Republic* (Ashland, OH: P. Dienstberger, 2000), under "The Noonday Prayer Revival 1858–1865," http://www.prdienstberger.com/nation/Chap6ndp.htm (accessed February 13, 2015).

26—A Call to America's Leaders

1. "Declaration of Independence."
2. Lincoln, "Proclamation Appointing a National Fast Day."
3. Ibid.
4. George Washington, "Washington's Thanksgiving Proclamation," October 3, 1789, http://www.heritage.org/initiatives/first-principles/primary-sources/washingtons-thanksgiving-proclamation (accessed February 13, 2015).
5. George Washington, "Washington's Inaugural Address of 1789," American Originals, *National Archives and Records Administration*, http://www.archives.gov/exhibits/american_originals/inaugtxt.html (accessed March 6, 2015).
6. Webster, *The Writings and Speeches*.
7. Ronald Reagan, "Remarks at a White House Ceremony in Observance of National Day of Prayer," May 6, 1982, http://www.reagan.utexas.edu/archives/speeches/1982/50682c.htm (accessed February 13, 2015).
8. Ronald Reagan, "Remarks at an Ecumenical Prayer Breakfast in Dallas, Texas," August 23, 1984, http://www.reagan.utexas.edu/archives/speeches/1984/82384a.htm (accessed February 13, 2015).
9. Lincoln, "Proclamation Appointing a National Fast Day."
10. "Declaration of Independence."

11. Billy Graham, "Official AFJ Memorabilia," America for Jesus, http://www.afj2012.org/ (accessed February 13, 2015).

12. Lincoln, "Proclamation Appointing a National Fast Day."

13. "In God We Trust," National Legal Foundation, http://www.nlf.net/Activities/briefings/in_god_we_trust.htm (accessed February 13, 2015).

14. Ibid.

15. Ibid.

Appendix B—A Classic Example from Early America

1. Peter Marshall and David Manuel, The Light and the Glory: 1492–1793 (God's Plan for America), exp. ed. (Grand Rapids, MI: Revell, a division of Baker Publishing Group, June 15, 2009), Used by permission.

2. Ibid.

3. Ibid.

4. Ibid.

5. Ibid.

Appendix C—Does God Still Bring Judgment Today?

1. Joseph Prince, Destined to Reign (Tulsa, OK: Harrison House, 2007), 49.

2. Ibid.

Appendix E—America Embracing a Lie

1. Brian W. Ward et al., "Sexual Orientation and Health among U.S. Adults: National Health Interview Survey, 2013, National Health Statistics Reports no. 77 (July 15, 2014): http://www.cdc.gov/nchs/data/nhsr/nhsr077.pdf (accessed February 13, 2015).

2. Michael Brown, "Gays Are 1 in 50, Not 1 in 4," Charisma News, August 14, 2014, http://www.charismanews.com/opinion/in-the-line-of-fire/44885-gays-are-1-in-50-not-1-in-4 (accessed February 13, 2015).

3. "Presidential Appointments,' Gay and Lesbian Victory Institute, www.victoryinstitute.org/programs/presidential-appointments (accessed February 13, 2015).

4. "God's Warning and Promise to the Homosexual Community & Leaders: A Redemptive Cry," A Prophetic Message, March 3, 2014, Shekinah Today Ministries, http://shekinahtoday.org/PW14_ENEWS-Warning-Promise-to-Homosexuals.htm (accessed March 6, 2015).

ABOUT THE AUTHORS

DARREL AND CINDY deVille are founders of Shekinah Today Ministries, located in the North Dallas Metroplex. The call on their lives and hearts' cry is to help raise up the glorious church (Eph. 5:27) and turn America back to God. In 2010 with few resources and lots of faith, they launched the Pray, America! Pray! Campaign, which includes the 12 O'clock Prayer Challenge, now in over 350 cities across the nation.

With a prophetic voice and a passion for truth, they believe God has called them to the church, to America, and to the nations. Current plans also include the launch of Shekinah Today Worship and World Prayer Center, a local and global church with big vision to reach the city, the nation, and the world.

Darrel and Cindy reside in Frisco, Texas. They have been married for over twenty-nine years.

To learn more about their ministry visit www.shekinahtoday.org.

CONTACT THE AUTHORS

Website:
shekinahtoday.org

Mailing Address:
PO Box 98, Frisco, TX 75034